D1189652

Wittgenstein

and Political Philosophy

The University of Chicago Press *Chicago and London*

Wittgenstein
and Political Philosophy

A Reexamination of the Foundations of Social Science

John W. Danford

JOHN W. DANFORD, educated at Dartmouth College, the University of California at Berkeley, and Yale University, was for three years a Harper Post-doctoral Teaching Fellow at the University of Chicago. He is now assistant professor of political science at the University of Houston.

The University of Chicago Press, Chicago 60637
The University of Chicago Press, Ltd., London

Printed in the United States of America
82 81 80 79 78   5 4 3 2 1

Library of Congress Cataloging in Publication Data

Danford, John W
  Wittgenstein & political philosophy.

  Originally presented as the author's thesis.
  Bibliography: p.
  Includes index.
  1. Political science—Methodology.   2. Locke, John, 1632–1704—Political science.   3. Hobbes, Thomas, 1588–1679—Political science.   4. Aristoteles. Ethica.   5. Plato. Meno.   6. Languages—Philosophy. 7. Wittgenstein, Ludwig, 1889–1951.   I. Title.
JA73.D33   1978   320.5′092′2   78-6716
ISBN 0–226–13593–4

To my parents

Acknowledgments ix

Abbreviations of
Works Cited xi

Notes 207

Bibliography 243

Index 257

Contents

1.   Introduction   1

2.   Hobbes: The New Political Science and Its Dependence on Language   16

3.   Language, Signification, and Meaning in Hobbes and Locke   43

4.   Wittgenstein's *Philosophical Investigations*: A Critique of the Commonsense Notion of Language   73

5.   Wittgenstein's Account of Meaning   96

6.   Aristotle's *Ethics*: The Place of Classical Political Science   122

7.   Plato's *Meno*:
        The Method of Classical
        Political Science   155

8.   Wittgenstein and
        Political Philosophy   190

Contents

Acknowledgments

This study was originally written as a doctoral dissertation, and so its publication permits me to acknowledge my great debt to my teachers. I would like to thank Hanna Pitkin, who, because of the brief time I studied with her, cannot know how much she helped me but may recognize my debt in these pages. I am also grateful to Joseph Hamburger and Charles Fairbanks, who served on my dissertation committee and whose careful criticism caused me to reconsider and to reformulate parts of this study.

To Thomas Pangle, both teacher and friend, I owe a debt of a different kind. It is safe to say that without his persistent challenges to my understanding of things, this work would not only not have its present shape but would never have taken shape at all. Perhaps only those fortunate enough to have known such a teacher can appreciate what this meant to me.

I am grateful also to my wife, Laurie Fendrich Danford, whose exacting critical standards and unflagging moral support were indispensable in this project from beginning to end. She alone can know the extent of my debt to her. Finally, I wish to thank my parents, to whom this book is dedicated, for the unstinting love which helped to shape my goals and the patient sacrifice which helped me to reach some of them.

Abbreviations
of Works Cited

Thomas Hobbes

De Cive *De Cive*, ed. Sterling P. Lamprecht (New York: Appleton-Century-Crofts, 1949). Followed by page number.

De Corpore *The English Works of Thomas Hobbes of Malmsbury*, ed. Sir William Molesworth, 11 vols. Vol. 1, *De Corpore* (London: John Bohn, 1839–45). Followed by part, chapter, and section numbers.

Elements *The Elements of Law*, ed. Ferdinand Tönnies (London: Frank Cass & Co., 1969). Followed by part, chapter, and section numbers.

De Homine *Man and Citizen*, trans. C. T. Wood, T. S. K. Scott-Craig, and B. Gert, ed. B. Gert (Garden City, N.Y.: Doubleday & Co., 1972). Followed by chapter number.

Leviathan *Leviathan*, ed. C. B. MacPherson (Harmondsworth, England: Penguin Books, 1969). Followed by chapter and page number. Although it is more common to cite the Molesworth edition noted above, the edition cited here has a twofold advantage: it is both more readily available, and it is a facsimile reproduction of the original and more authentic *Head* edition. We have not altered the spelling except when it was necessary for a word to stand on its own.

John Locke

Essay

An Essay concerning Human Understanding, ed. A. C. Fraser (New York: Dover Publications, 1959). Followed by book, chapter, and section numbers.

Second Treatise

The Second Treatise of Government, ed. T. P. Peardon (New York: Bobbs-Merrill Co., 1952). Followed by section number.

Ludwig Wittgenstein

BB

The Blue and Brown Books (New York: Harper & Row, 1965). Followed by page number.

Notebooks

Notebooks 1914–1916, Bilingual edition with trans. by G. E. M. Anscombe, ed. G. H. von Wright and

Abbreviations of
Works Cited

G. E. M. Anscombe (New York: Harper & Row, 1969). Followed by page number.

PI   *Philosophical Investigations*, Bilingual edition with trans. by G. E. M. Anscombe (Oxford: Basil Blackwell, 1968). Pt. 1, followed by paragraph number; pt. 2, followed by page number.

Tractatus   *Tractatus Logico-Philosophicus*, Bilingual edition with trans. by D. F. Pears and B. F. McGuiness (London: Routledge & Kegan Paul, 1971). Followed by sentence number.

Aristotle

Ethics

Nicomachean Ethics. The edition cited is *Nichomachean Ethics*, trans. Martin Ostwald (New York: Bobbs-Merrill Co., 1962) unless otherwise noted. Except where indicated, references to Aristotle in chapter 6 are to the *Ethics* and are cited by Bekker number.

Post. An.   *Posterior Analytics*, trans. G. R. G. Mure, in *The Basic Works of Aristotle*, ed. Richard McKeon (New

Abbreviations of
Works Cited

York: Random House, 1941). Followed by Bekker number.

Topics   *Topics*, trans. W. A. Pickard-Cambridge, in *The Basic Works of Aristotle*, ed. Richard McKeon (New York: Random House, 1941). Followed by Bekker number. My own translations, where necessary, are noted.

Plato

Meno   Unless specifically marked otherwise, all references to Plato are to the *Meno*. Translations are my own except where indicated, and are based on the Oxford text edited by Burnet. Cited by Stephanus number.

Abbreviations of
Works Cited

1 Introduction

This study begins with the claim that our science of politics, as it is now constituted, is radically defective. This claim arises from two considerations. The first is a familiar complaint about contemporary political science, namely its alleged inability to deal with the questions which are most important in politics. But this is in fact only a special case of the second and more fundamental consideration, which is the serious doubts which have been raised in philosophical circles about the very foundations of science. To expose the reason for these doubts, it is wise to begin by examining the more familiar complaint.

According to what may be described as the predominant view among social scientists today, the sciences of man and society have an overall goal which is easily stated, if difficult to achieve: to supply us with complete explanations of politics, of economics, indeed of social behavior in general. Such explanations must order our factual information into coherent theories, which in turn account for what we can observe of human social activity, both present and past. Social science, then, is concerned with empirical questions rather than with normative questions. Nevertheless, it would be a mistake to deny the normative *importance* of social science. There is no obstacle to its being, as Herbert Simon puts it, "concerned with how things *ought* to be—ought to be, that is, in order to attain goals, and to function."[1] That is, a social science has normative implications because it can indicate to us the proper course of action to achieve the ends we seek.

As for the ends themselves, however, it is generally agreed that social science has little to tell us. We cannot discover, empirically, how men ought to live, because empirical science is concerned with facts and not values. No actual or possible state of affairs can tell us anything about what state of affairs *ought* to exist. Genuine scientific knowledge concerning the proper ends of human activity is regarded as impossible. At most, social science can provide us with knowledge about the goals which are in fact sought; it is not qualified to judge these or to supply us with the goals themselves.

This might be taken to indicate that only one political system can claim to be just, namely, one based on the principle that no one has legitimate authority for telling any individual what his goals should be, and which recognizes an individual's right to seek any goals he pleases so long as he does not interfere with the like right of any other individual. Within the scope of such a principle, there is considerable room for debate as to the degree of government activity necessary to supply the conditions under which each individual can seek his own goals.[2] What is important here is the fact that the most widely accepted view regarding the scope of social science seems to lead us to the conclusion that only one form of political constitution—a liberal democracy—is legitimate or rational.

But if we are ruthlessly philosophic, we are compelled to admit that there is no more rational justification for liberalism than for any other political constitution. This may be seen simply by a consideration of what has already been stated: there is no rational or scientific validity to claims about the proper values or goals, according to the predominant view. A society based on the principle of tolerance of a variety of goals is nevertheless a particular kind of society, namely, a tolerant one, and there is no legitimate ground for preferring the value of tolerance over any

Introduction

other value. Hence we are forced to the conclusion, on this understanding of social science, that the foundation of a liberal society is not more justifiable than the foundation of an intolerant society, whether it be Rousseau's Geneva or Hitler's Germany.

However much we may dislike this state of affairs, our distaste for it does not mean that it is wrong. The fact that political science is unable to direct itself to the most important political questions[3] may be simply a fact—an unpleasant fact to be sure, but one to which we must accustom ourselves. This conclusion is rendered questionable, however, by philosophic inquiry into the roots of scientific knowledge. In light of such an inquiry, the problem of the status of normative judgments is revealed to be only one aspect of a more fundamental problem, namely, the relationship between scientific knowledge, on the one hand, and the actual and concrete world in which human beings live and act, on the other. Questions about this relationship have no doubt occurred to every student of the social sciences. When we move from the vivid and concrete world of real political activity into the realm of political science, with its constructs, models, and abstract conceptual schemes, we cannot help but wonder whether the knowledge we achieve does full justice to the phenomena we seek to understand.[4] The real world of politics, the world we find in newspapers or in the memoirs of great political figures, is colorful and alive, full of normative judgments and choices among goals. Political science gives us a new perspective; it makes us sophisticated; it imposes a new cognitive framework on that political reality. But what is the foundation of political science's claim to be in touch with the reality which precedes it and which it seeks to comprehend? This may be recognized as a problem not unique to political science or any other social science. For nearly a century it has been a major concern for philosophers of science in all fields. The fundamental problem of the foundations of scientific knowledge has been raised with unrivaled clarity in the twentieth century by Edmund Husserl, the most famous as well as the most intransigent critic of the philosophical presuppositions of modern science. This is evident above all in his last great work, *The Crisis of European Sciences and Transcendental Phenomenology*.

Science claims to produce knowledge and to be the *only* source of genuine knowledge, as distinct from belief or opinion. Scientific knowledge is genuine because science is "objective"; opinion or belief is subjective. Science refines and clarifies the vague views of common sense and immediate perception by subjecting them to testing, and discovers laws which underlie all natural processes.[5] We know that this is what truth or genuine knowledge is, science tells us, because of the way the human mind works (see below, chap. 2).

But what grounds do we have for accepting this epistemology or account of scientific knowledge? After all, it is an epistemology supplied by the very enterprise which it claims to underlie. According to Husserl, science has been permitted to produce its own foundations by giving an account of logic which is based on scientific psychology. Why should science supply, by its own procedure, a standard which is then used to examine *prescientific* knowledge and judge it inadequate? Science itself is grounded in our prescientific awareness of the world, and begins as a search for truth about that prescientific world and all the things in it. It threatens to lose its connection with that world, according to Husserl, by denying that truths other than its own can exist; the reality which science presents is said to be the only reality. But for science to lose its connection with our prescientific world is precisely to lose its meaning for us. The most glaring symptom of this loss of meaning is our very inability to speak objectively about meaning, or, what comes to the same thing, our incapacity to make objective value judgments. This, on Husserl's view, is our great problem.

But the problem is yet worse. The deepest thinkers about science had already realized by the end of the nineteenth century that there is no reason to claim that science supplies us with truth. The concept of truth is "a relic of metaphysical prejudices";[6] it may be replaced by the concept of acceptability, because the claim that a proposition is true is only the claim that it has been found to be acceptable or reliable when we act on it. According to the theoretical physicist Pierre Maurice Duhem, writing in 1906, when we speak of the laws of physics, "the words 'truth' and 'error' no longer have any meaning; so, the logician who is concerned about the strict meaning of words will have to answer anyone who asks whether physics is true or false, 'I do not understand your question.' "[7] He goes on to say, "Every physical law is an approximate law. Consequently, it cannot be ... either true or false; any other law representing the same experiments with the same approximation may lay as just a claim as the first to the title of a true law or, *to speak more precisely, of an acceptable law*."[8] If we accept, then, the epistemology of modern science, we must abandon altogether what was the goal of philosophy for more than two millenia. That goal, according to Husserl, was unconditional truth about everything that exists.[9] The goal must be abandoned if we give up the belief that reason can supply us with genuine truth as opposed to mere formulations found to be acceptable.[10]

This is, however, more than a philosophical issue. What is important here is not that science is wrong in its claim to be sole producer of genuine knowledge: we do not know that. Nor can we refute the claim that truth should be abandoned as a goal in favor of experience, or "whatever works." We must, however, be clear that these issues have not been decisively resolved, and we must confront what is entailed *should* the claims of these philosophers of science prove to be correct. If we abandon, along with Mach, Duhem, Carnap, and others, all pretension to genuine truth and settle for acceptability, we are in fact admitting that our science is simply *our* culture's response to age-old questions about the universe, and is not in principle different from the myths which, in other times, purported to account for the phenomena human beings observed.[11] If this is correct, we must concede that reason offers no guidance and no standard for our actions, that our scientific theories are actually *creations* of the human will, more or less reliable, and with no other support than our acceptance of them. It is but a short step from this to radical nihilism, which teaches that there are no values or that all values are equally worthless, and which opens the door to undreamed of brutality and destruction. In the words of Husserl himself:

> Scientific, objective truth is exclusively a matter of establishing what the world, the physical as well as the spiritual world, is in fact. But can the world, and human existence in it, truthfully have a meaning if the sciences recognize as true only what is objectively established in this fashion, and if history has nothing

more to teach us than that all the shapes of the spiritual world, all the conditions of life, ideals, norms upon which man relies, form and dissolve themselves like fleeting waves, that it always was and ever will be so, that again and again reason must turn into nonsense, and well-being into misery? Can we console ourselves with that?[12]

Husserl's life work may be said to have been conceiving a project intended to supply the deficiency in the foundations of science, to establish the connection between our prescientific awareness of phenomena and the sciences which were originally intended to produce truth about that world. He called this project transcendental phenomenology. Transcendental phenomenology can supply the foundations for all the particular sciences by providing an account of all the objects of prescientific consciousness from which the sciences take their bearings. Husserl claims that this account constitutes the only possible basis, or starting point, for our science; no deeper or lower foundation exists. Transcendental phenomenology is itself philosophy, but it is philosophy directed to arrive at truth about the whole, and not just about the "objective" part of the whole with which science deals.[13] Hence it recovers the goal which motivated all western philosophy from the time it was developed by the Greeks, up to the time it was "decapitated" by the invention of modern science. Husserl's project thus raises our hopes for eventually arriving at a philosophic understanding of the whole, of everything that is.

This universal philosophy, or transcendental phenomenology, essentially restores to science its wholeness or unity by supplying the connection between the objective knowledge provided by particular sciences and the foundation of that knowledge in what Husserl calls the "life-world," or the "attitude of original natural life."[14] In Husserl's words,

[n]atural life can be characterized as a life naïvely, straightforwardly directed at the world, the world being always in a certain sense consciously present.... Waking life is always a directedness toward this or that, being directed toward it as an end or as means, as relevant or irrelevant, toward the interesting or the indifferent, toward the private or public, toward what is daily required or intrusively new.[15]

Supplying this connection between the phenomena as we first are conscious of them and scientific knowledge gives back to the project of science its bearings, its ground for knowing what is important and what is not. When we begin to reflect back on the origins of science, to discover its presuppositions, we see, according to Husserl, that science and its method are "like a machine, reliable in accomplishing obviously very useful things, a machine everyone can learn to operate correctly without in the least understanding the inner possibility and necessity of this sort of accomplishment."[16]

Husserl's project, however, was neither attractive to scientists nor considered necessary by them. The reason for this has been exposed with great clarity by Leszek Kolakowski, whose words are worth quoting at some length. Kolakowski presents the argument between Husserl and his opponents as a dispute over the foundations of scientific logic, between Husserl's claim that science cannot supply its own foundations but must be grounded in the pre-scientific life-world, and his opponents' claims that scientific psychology is the only basis we can have because only science itself can give us knowledge.

> The controversy between the psychological and Husserlian interpretations of logic is the controversy between empiricism and the belief in transcendental Reason. . . .
> It is arguable that the controversy cannot be decided with appeal to premises which the antagonists—an empiricist and a transcendentalist—would both agree to be valid. The empiricist will argue that transcendental arguments imply the existence of the realm of ideal meanings, and that we have no empirical grounds to believe in it. The transcendentalist will argue that this very argument, just advanced by the empiricist, implies the monopoly of experience as the highest tribunal of our thought, that this privileged position is precisely under question, and that it is arbitrary to establish such a monopoly. The transcendentalist compels the empiricist to renounce—for the sake of consistency—the concept of truth; the empiricist compels the transcendentalist to confess that in order to save the belief in Reason, he is in duty bound to admit a kingdom of beings (or quasi-beings) he cannot justify. This was Husserl's great merit: to lead this discussion to the extreme point.[17]

Are we forced to consider this extreme point the last word that can be said, the terminus of genuine discussion?

If the seriousness of this issue for all social scientists is not evident, we should be alerted to it by the fact that Kolakowski, a political thinker in a tradition markedly different from Anglo-American social science, considered it worth long and profound reflection. The very possibility of a political science that can deal with the questions most important in political life depends on our ability to resolve the problem posed for us as the "extreme point" in the discussion we have sketched.[18] But to recognize the significance of the problem is not to solve it. Such recognition is an indispensable step, however, which puts us in a position to investigate the issue.

How can we begin? When we think through the implications of either Husserl's view or the view he criticizes, we are likely to find both unsatisfactory. We have on one side a mysterious project which raises hopes for transcendental knowledge, but which raises these hopes in none but the most sanguine students of philosophy. We face on the other side the abyss of a fundamental nihilism, to which we have been led by the claim of modern science that the only genuine knowledge is scientific knowledge, which cannot tell us anything about the questions which matter most. In a predicament of this sort, common sense suggests that we try to understand how we came to be in this predicament. We must make an attempt to retrace our intellectual path, to see if we can find decisive steps which directed us to this point. In this case, we need to inquire into the nature of scientific knowledge. When we look for the roots of our understanding, we discover that the monopolistic attitude toward knowledge which characterizes modern scientific method (what Kolakowski called empiricism) emerged in the great intellectual revolution of the seventeenth century. Where now we speak of the scientific method, the method of science, men in earlier ages spoke of not one method but many, each for a different science. Political science, for example, did noi simply apply to politics a method appropriate also to the science of mechanics or the science of geometry.[19] Even among the theoretical sciences there was not a unity of method. Each method led to a kind of knowledge, but these were not all understood to be reducible to or variants of one sort of knowledge. In the seventeenth century, however, when what we call scientific method began to emerge, there were thinkers who felt themselves compelled to *argue* for the new method of science by claiming that it was the one way which is superior to all other approaches. It may be said that our current assumptions are testimony to the power of their arguments.

What were the issues in that argument about knowledge, the argument as a result of which the founders of modern scientific method succeeded in replacing the multiplicity of methods by one method? What possible argument of merit could be made on the other side? It should be evident that, in order to fully come to grips with these issues, we must be willing to move away from our customary viewpoint, because from the perspective of our current assumptions the argument has been resolved. We must try to think ourselves back in time, to recover the perspective in which these issues are genuinely issues, however strange and different things might look to us. Fortunately, we have the testimony of great thinkers to guide us here, but in order to see what the issues are it is necessary to try to reconstruct the losing arguments in this debate because they are much less evident to us than those which were successful.

It should be clear that we are interested primarily in political science, the sole original member of the heterogeneous collection which today we call social sciences. When we try to transport ourselves back to unfamiliar terrain, in trying to see the path along which we have come, we are directed again and again by signs of all sorts to the "century of greatness," the century of Bacon and Descartes, of Galileo, Hobbes, Spinoza, Newton, and Leibniz, to say nothing of lesser figures. And when we scrutinize the history of political philosophy in particular, with questions about the status of knowledge, one thinker stands out from all the rest: Thomas Hobbes. Hobbes raised with surprising directness the most searching questions about knowledge of politics. Some of his answers to those questions may be said to have dominated in one way or another the philosophy of the last three centuries.

Hobbes proclaimed himself the founder of political science qua science, the first man to truly understand the foundations of the knowledge called political science. If Hobbes's assessment of his achievement is correct, he must be accorded the honor of being the founder of modern social science altogether. What did Hobbes do? Political science began, long before Hobbes, as the search for knowledge about what is good for human beings. It began by asking simple questions such as, What is justice? What is courage? What is a good citizen? How can good citizens be educated? These questions were asked by the earliest political thinkers in a certain spirit of directness which we find troublesome. The classical thinkers appear to have been genuinely concerned with knowledge about the political world, but to have been insufficiently concerned about how this knowledge was to be discovered or secured. In a word, they appear not to have worried enough about methodology. This makes them seem somehow naive, not to say unphilosophic. And this is precisely the charge brought against them by Hobbes. Hobbes claims that what is required to make knowledge scientific is nothing more than attention to method.

The idea that Hobbes is the founder of modern political science is likely to meet with some objections. Our political science, as well as our natural science, it is said, does not resemble Hobbes's deductive model of science, and thus no critical examination of his thought is capable of teaching us anything about the assumptions we wish to examine. It is wise to indicate at the outset why this view is incorrect. Hobbes, according to this view, copied the method of his science from geometry, which is deductive. But natural science is not deductive. Hence we can be sure Hobbes was wrong. One might make this view even stronger by adding the following considerations: Hobbes began by distinguishing science from "prudence." Prudence is "much knowledge of antecedents and consequents," and is never certain or universal, and so on. It is Hobbes's prudence, then, which is more like what we call observational natural science, whose most thoughtful practitioners have believed it to be never certain or final because it is susceptible of infinite progress, and which is based on observation of antecedents and consequents with the aim of discovering relational laws.

But this is not the sort of "knowledge from experience" Hobbes means by prudence. The key to science, for Hobbes as for us, is to explain something by *resolving it into parts*. We don't understand something, be it the weather, a kidney, combustion processes, or stellar evolution, unless we take it apart conceptually and see why it does what it does or has the properties it has. What Hobbes means by prudence is more like what we mean by the term "conditioning": the direct experiential "knowledge" that Y follows X (in a psychological study, for example, that an electric shock follows a flashing light). This sort of knowledge from experience, which all animals share, according to Hobbes, may allow us to operate in the world, but it is in no sense science. Science—both Hobbes's and ours—always involves language, even if only mathematical language.

This is not to say that Hobbes's science is identical with ours. But the idea that his was strictly deductive and a priori—a view so often attributed to Hobbes—and therefore like geometry but not like science, is mistaken. Hobbes insisted that his knowledge began from his observations of men and manners and thus was, in principle, accessible to anyone able to look at the world and follow, with Hobbes, the steps of his analysis. Analysis or resolution is the first step of a two-step method. Analysis reveals to us the simple elements or universals out of which, in the second step, we construct a system which accounts for reality and of whose truth we can be absolutely certain. His first attempts to construct a science necessarily involved only hypotheses which tested the explanatory elements, until the true elements or "simples" were discovered. It is Hobbes's procedure, with its hypothesis, testing, and resulting model, for which Hobbes is important, and not his conclusions.[20] We will examine this in the pages to come.

The purpose of this study, then, is to reconstruct for ourselves the terms of a debate which, more than three centuries ago, decided both the foundation and the direction of our modern social sciences. It may be of some help to the reader to explain precisely why the thinkers considered below were selected from among the many contributors to that original controversy.

The initial impetus for this study was the discovery of what seemed to be a broad affinity between the philosophy of Ludwig Wittgenstein and the general approach of Aristotle. Modern political science finds it difficult or impossible to take Aristotle seriously (as anything but a very early precursor of the observational method), because he was, by our standards, unscientific. He was continually mixing up value judgments and factual observations. But it is difficult to reconcile the power and richness of Aristotle's understanding with his lack of scientific foundations, and this interested me especially because of my concern—as a result of my own training as a natural scientist—with the status of the social sciences as sciences. The discovery that Aristotle's political science seemed to accord to a striking degree with the epistemology presented in the later work of Wittgenstein aroused my curiosity. For we *do* take Wittgenstein's epistemological claims very seriously, partly because of his concern with many of the questions mentioned earlier, in connection with Husserl.[21]

The link which for the purposes of this study connects Aristotle with Wittgenstein is the thought of Thomas Hobbes. The unique importance of Hobbes may be seen from the following considerations. It is well known in the history of political thought that Hobbes was highly critical of Aristotle and intended his new teaching to replace Aristotle's, even to the extent of replacing the latter in the university curriculum. It is in chapter 46 of *Leviathan* that Hobbes makes explicit his judgment of the philosophy of his illustrious predecessor: "And I beleeve that scarce any thing can be more absurdly said in naturall Philosophy, than that which now is called *Aristotles Metaphysiques*; nor more repugnant to Government, than much of that hee hath said in his *Politiques*; nor more ignorantly, than a great part of his *Ethiques*." This, together with Hobbes's claim to be the first to make the study of politics a science, was a strong indication that the problem of knowledge in political science might profitably be examined here.

What connects this issue with Wittgenstein is that Hobbes's objections to Aristotle, and classical political science generally, are based in large part, as we will see, on Hobbes's understanding of the way language works. Hobbes's striking and unusual concern with language as the key to scientific method leads us directly to the so-called language philosophy of Wittgenstein, whose understanding of language does not accord with Hobbes's, and whose account of knowledge we wished to compare with Aristotle's. Hence we can say that the basis for Hobbes's rejection of Aristotle is the very portion of Hobbes's thought about which Wittgenstein's philosophy raises serious questions.

The steps by which I proceeded have been rearranged for this study in what I hope is a sequence more logical than either a strict chronological order or the more haphazard sequence of actual intellectual discovery. The general plan of this work is this: we begin, in chapter 2, with an attempt to grasp in detail Hobbes's own understanding of his method and of what it promised. We find that this method is connected to a particular picture of language which Hobbes himself took to be the foundation of his procedure. In fact, Hobbes claims, it was lack of attention to language and thus to method which was responsible for the futility of all earlier political science. But the understanding of language Hobbes offers is incomplete; it fails to answer our questions satisfactorily. We find that Hobbes's philosophical successor Locke also devotes a great deal of attention to language. Not only does he share Hobbes's conception of language, as we will see, but in the *Essay concerning Human Understanding* he presents that conception in great detail.[22] We will explore this conception in chapter 3. By the end of chapter 3 we will be partially able to see how what Hobbes and Locke accomplished has led to some of the questions about political science or knowledge with which we began.

We then turn to a consideration of Wittgenstein's understanding of language. We show in chapter 4 why, according to Wittgenstein's account, we must conclude that Hobbes and Locke were mistaken in their understanding of language. This chapter is essentially critical. In chapter 5 we explore the possibility of a replacement for the understanding criticized in chapter 4, by asking how, on Wittgenstein's understanding, we can inquire into the meanings of our terms.

The possibility that Hobbes and Locke were wrong about language forces us to wonder if they were right in their account of the proper method for political science. We have already noted that Hobbes began in self-conscious opposition to a long tradition of philosophy whose claim to the status of political science he denied. He established, or helped to establish, in its place, a particular scientific method. Since Hobbes's position has come under suspicion, the policy of examining the merits of his opponents' views recommends itself to us. This we undertake to do in chapters 6 and 7, which consider, respectively, the status of political science as it is presented in Aristotle's *Nicomachean Ethics*, and the method of investigation exemplified in Plato's *Meno*. At the same time we need to consider whether Hobbes's accusations against the political science of his predecessors were not perhaps well founded. If they were justified, and if Hobbes's position is equally unsatisfactory, we must inquire into the possibility of a third alternative. We consider this issue in the eighth and final chapter.

The reasons for the selection of Aristotle's *Nicomachean Ethics* will become clear in chapter 6. It suffices here to say that Aristotle is most concerned there with the place which the study of virtues ("a kind of political science") should occupy in the framework of the intellect. The selection of Plato's *Meno* is less easy to explain. There are, for one thing, other dialogues which deal more directly with knowledge. But the *Meno* presents a confrontation between two perspectives which, as we shall see by chapter 7, seem to be the permanent alternatives in the debate over how to ground our knowledge of politics and political goals.

A final word of clarification is necessary. Although the study which follows is partly about scientific knowledge, it is not directly about such matters as verifiability, explanation, or prediction. The portion of literature on the philosophy of science which deals with these matters does not seem to help us in understanding what distinguishes modern science from earlier rationalism. For that end, the reconstruction of the terms of the original debate has proven more fruitful. And although much of this investigation concerns various understandings of the nature of language, the great debate which is its underlying theme was *not* about language. That debate was about method, and the question of language only entered because Hobbes claimed his predecessors had ignored language, not that they had misunderstood it. Both Hobbes and his predecessors might be said to agree on what the main issue is, at least. We are not investigating Plato's or Aristotle's conceptions of language (although that might be worthwhile), except indirectly, by asking what sort of understanding they must have had in order to have proceeded as they did.

Both Plato and Aristotle will be seen to have wrestled with the same questions about knowledge and science which were the source of this study. They answered them, in general, differently from the way we answer them in modern political science. In addition, and connected with this, they do not present their understandings as does Hobbes, in the form of statements which are easily accessible to a reader; we are compelled to uncover their complicated answers by our own efforts. Whether the answers which we manage to uncover can stand up to Hobbes's accusations must for now remain open to question.

2

Hobbes

The New Political Science and Its Dependence on Language

In 1655, in the Epistle Dedicatory to *De Corpore*, Thomas Hobbes boasted that while "astronomy and natural philosophy in general" were but young, "Civil Philosophy" was "yet much younger, as being no older ... than my own book *De Cive*" (p. ix). We must try to understand the transformation Hobbes accomplished in the foundation of political philosophy, which enabled him to proclaim himself the founder of the first political science worthy of the name.

Hobbes's Claim and His Evidence for the Claim

Hobbes draws a comparison between the progress of the natural sciences and the stage of development in civil philosophy. "I know," he writes, "that the hypothesis of the earth's diurnal motion was the invention of the ancients; but that both it, and astronomy, that is, celestial physics, springing up together with it, were by succeeding philosophers strangled with snares of words" (*De Corpore*, Epistle Dedicatory, p. viii). But Hobbes goes on to claim that the true beginning of astronomy, "except observations," is "not to be derived from farther time than from Nicolaus Copernicus." Hobbes credits Copernicus with the achievement of founding astronomy even while he admits that Copernicus only "revived the opinion" of Pythagoras, Aristarchus, and Philolaus. That is, what qualifies Copernicus as founder is not the hypothesis itself, which he did not invent, but something else which has to do with the changed character of that hypothesis: it was no longer merely an "opinion" susceptible of being "strangled with snares of words."[1]

A similar progress is traced in physics and in biological science, the honor of founder being accorded to Galileo and Harvey, respectively. "Before these, there was nothing certain in natural philosophy but every man's experiments to himself, and the natural histories, if they may be called certain, that are no certainer than civil histories" (De Corpore, Epistle Dedicatory, p. ix). What Copernicus, Galileo, and Harvey had each accomplished, according to Hobbes, was to achieve certainty for something more than simply "every man's experiment to himself." The old natural philosophy, or, properly speaking, the precursor of natural philosophy, was "rather a Dream than Science," as Hobbes puts it in Leviathan (chap. 46, p. 686).

Immediately after his shocking claim to have founded civil philosophy with his De Cive, Hobbes poses for himself this question: "But what? were there no philosophers natural nor civil among the ancient Greeks?" He answers: "There were men so called; witness Lucien, by whom they are derided; witness divers cities, from which they have been often by public edicts banned. But it follows not that there was philosophy." The implication is that men were mistaken in thinking that what they said or heard was "philosophy," although, as Hobbes says, it was "a little like philosophy." Now, whatever this mislabeled phenomenon was, it was enough like philosophy that "unwary men," thinking it to be philosophy, "adhered to the professors of it, some to one, some to another, though they disagreed among themselves ..." (De Corpore, Epistle Dedicatory, pp. ix–x). Those who are taught by these professors of so-called philosophy learn "instead of wisdom, nothing but to dispute, and neglecting the laws, to determine every question according to their own fancies" (ibid., p. x). That is, the political philosophy of Hobbes's predecessors was not only un-

Hobbes: The New Political Science

certain but also subversive. It was subversive precisely because it was uncertain, because it taught men to disagree, to "neglect the law," to decide each for himself what was right or just. If political philosophy is to be justified, it must show itself to be useful rather than subversive. Classical political philosophy failed on two counts, then, according to Hobbes: it was not philosophy truly because it was not scientific and certain; and it was subversive and thus could not be justified in a community, even on grounds of utility. It was both theoretically and practically unsatisfactory.

Hobbes does not doubt that philosophy is the quest for wisdom. In this respect he is in agreement with his predecessors. But clearly, whatever the ancients thought they had, it wasn't true philosophy, and hence not wisdom. "Wisdom properly so called is nothing else but this, the perfect knowledge of the truth in all matters whatsoever" (*De Cive*, Epistle Dedicatory, p. 2). But if the ancients were wrong in thinking they possessed some knowledge of the truth, what makes Hobbes so certain that he isn't equally mistaken in thinking they failed? He offers, by way of evidence, some "signs," or "manifest arguments," that "what hath hitherto been written by moral philosophers, hath not made any progress in the knowledge of the truth." These signs consist in the following: "that there should still be such siding with the several factions of philosophers, that the very same action should be decried by some, and as much elevated by others; that the very same man should at several times embrace his several opinions, and esteem his own actions far otherwise in himself than he does in others" (*De Cive*, Epistle Dedicatory, p. 4). Controversy, according to Hobbes, is a sure sign of the absence of wisdom.

If we turn to the *Elements of Law*, Hobbes's earliest work on civil or moral philosophy, we find Hobbes at his most self-conscious with respect to this question of controversy and knowledge. Already in the first paragraph in chapter 1, in introducing his subject matter, he writes, "And seeing that true knowledge begetteth not doubt nor controversy, but knowledge; it is manifest from the present controversies, that they which have heretofore written thereof, have not well understood their own subject" (*Elements*, 1.1.1). In chapter 13 he makes this claim stronger yet: "The infallible sign of teaching exactly, and without error, is this:

18

Hobbes: The New Political
Science

that no man hath ever taught the contrary; not that few, how few soever, if any" (*Elements*, 1.13.3). Indeed, he says, "When in opinions and questions considered and discussed by many, it happeneth that not any one of the men that so discuss them differ from another, then it may be justly inferred, they know what they teach, and that otherwise they do not" (ibid.). We may ask where Hobbes could have expected to find such pure knowledge. Knowing that his statement will be hard to credit, he claims that "this appeareth most manifestly to them that have considered the divers subjects wherein men have exercised their pens, and the divers ways in which they have proceeded; together with the diversity of the success thereof" (ibid.). Hobbes invites his reader to follow the train of thought by which he himself had arrived at the surprising conclusion. It turns out that the "divers subjects" he compares number exactly two, as do the "divers ways" of proceeding, and, as we might expect, the "diversity of the success thereof." What Hobbes does is to compare directly the approach and results in geometry with the approach and results of classical political philosophy. As to geometry, he writes, "To this day was it never heard of, that there was any controversy concerning any conclusion in this subject; the science whereof hath nevertheless been continually amplified and enriched with conclusions of most difficult and profound speculation" (*Elements*, 1.13.3). When he compares this with the tradition of classical political philosophy, the contrast is sharp indeed:

> On the other side, those men who have written concerning the faculties, passions, and manners of men, that is to say, of moral philosophy, or of policy, government, and laws, whereof there be infinite volumes, have been so far from removing doubt and controversy in the questions they have handled, that they have very much multiplied the same; nor doth any man at this day so much as pretend to know more than hath been delivered two thousand years ago by Aristotle. [*Elements*, 1.13.3]

What, Hobbes asks, has prevented civil or political philosophers from achieving as much as the geometers who have "been the authors of all those excellences, wherein we differ from such savage people as are now the inhabitants of divers places in America?"

Hobbes: The New Political
                                            Science

What is the reason for the immense progress in their science? The reason, he says, "is apparent to every man that looketh into their writings; for they proceed from most low and humble principles, evident even to the meanest capacity; going on slowly, and with most scrupulous ratiocination [viz.] from the imposition of names they infer the truth of their first propositions; and from two of the first, a third; and from any two of the three a fourth; and so on . . ." (Elements, 1.13.3). He expressed this somewhat differently in De Cive where he warns, "We may not, as in a circle, begin the handling of a science from what point we please" (Epistle Dedicatory, p. 4). Hobbes is aware, as he indicated in De Corpore, that "the first grounds of all science are not only not beautiful, but poor, arid, and, in appearance, deformed" (De Corpore, Introduction). It is characteristic of a science to start from "humble principles" with which no one can disagree, and to proceed from them by syllogism. But science is justified, indeed recognized, according to Hobbes, not by its beauty but by its utility.[2] And this includes civil and moral philosophy, no less than natural philosophy or physics. Hobbes's great ambition was to make civil philosophy as useful as the natural philosophy being developed by his contemporaries, and to accomplish this by the same method, namely, the method of geometry. In his later treatise on the first principles of philosophy, De Corpore, Hobbes even defines philosophy itself as "such knowledge of effects or appearances, as we acquire by true ratiocination from the knowledge we have first of their causes or generation: And again, of such causes or generations as may be from knowing first their effects" (1.1.2).

The Difference between Prudence and Science

Why did Hobbes think the enterprise of which he claimed to be the founder could only succeed on the terms of the geometer? Could not the political world, or the human world, be "known" in a way different from the way the geometer knows geometry? We must look again and more deeply at Hobbes's conception of knowledge, in an effort to see why he boldly attempted something which the classics either did not think of, or did not think possible.

Except for chapter 9 of Leviathan ("Of the Severall Subjects of

Hobbes: The New Political
Science

Knowledge"), the only systematic treatment of the meaning of "knowledge" in Hobbes's major works is to be found, as we might expect, in his first and most self-conscious work, the *Elements of Law*. And even here it must be pieced together from remarks in three different chapters. The most important of these is chapter 6, which, although the chapters themselves are not titled, is labeled, in the "Order" which precedes the Epistle Dedicatory, "Of knowledge, opinion, and belief." Thus we may suppose it contains Hobbes's most direct as well as earliest treatment of "knowledge." (Indeed, the relevant chapter in the much later *Leviathan* is a distillation of this earlier discussion.)

The first sort of knowledge consists in "experience of fact." This is, according to Hobbes, not peculiar to man but something in which "brute beasts also participate" (*Elements*, 1.6.4). His formulation in the *Elements of Law* is consistent with the later one in *Leviathan*. In the former he describes this kind of knowledge as "nothing else but sense, or knowledge original ... and remembrance of the same" (*Elements*, 1.6.1). In *Leviathan* it is "nothing else, but Sense and Memory, and is *Absolute Knowledge*; as when we see a Fact doing, or remember it done" (chap. 9, p. 147). Hobbes equates this sort of knowledge, "if it be great," with prudence (*Elements*, 1.6.4). And prudence, which he discusses at much greater length elsewhere, is "nothing else but conjecture from experience" (*Elements*, 1.4.10), which is itself the result of many times observing antecedents and consequents, until one has a fair picture of what goes on in the world. Prudence is "to conclude from experience, what is likely to come to pass, or to have passed already" (*Elements*, 1.6.11). But Hobbes warns that prudence is never certain, because "experience concludeth nothing universally" (*Elements*, 1.4.20). The "taking of signs from experience," that is, prudence, offers no access to truth; this knowledge is never certain because "these signs are but conjectural; and according as they have often or seldom failed, so their assurance is more or less [*sic*]; but never full and evident; for though man hath always seen the day and night to follow one another hitherto; yet can he not thence conclude they shall do so, or that they have done so eternally" (*Elements*, 1.4.10).[3]

There would seem to be a certain resemblance between what

Hobbes: The New Political
Science

Hobbes calls prudence and our natural science. He seems to be speaking of predictive power which comes from much observation of sequences of events—from experiments, we might say. But the possibility that he means something like physics here is precluded by the fact that prudence is inarticulate: it is shared by "brutes" and resembles more the "knowledge" of a dog who expects food to appear after observing his master perform certain motions. We call this kind of knowledge from experience "conditioning." Science, as we will see below, may observe the same sequences of events observed by prudence (such as weather patterns). It differs not because of its subject matter, but because of its *method*.

Hobbes's discussions of experience and prudence immediately follow those of sense and imagination (which begin the work in each case), but precede all discussions of knowledge.[4] The order of chapters is an important clue here. Chapter 4 of the *Elements of Law*, from which the above discussion of prudence is taken, is entitled in the "Order," "Of the several kinds of discursion of the mind." Yet Hobbes does not present the discussion as a treatment of knowledge. We are led to see it in this way only by his later equation, in chapter 6, of one sort of knowledge with prudence. The chapter which comes between these two is, it turns out, logically prior (as far as Hobbes is concerned) to any treatment of knowledge in the precise sense (as distinguished from prudence): chapter 5 is entitled "Of names, reasoning, and discourse of the tongue." The same sequence appears in *Leviathan*: chapter 5, "Of Reason, and Science," comes only after the chapter "Of Speech." The reason for this order is most clearly expressed, however, in the *Elements of Law*. What is this reason?

The opening paragraph of chapter 6 is something of an anomaly for Hobbes, for it is an anecdote:

There is a story somewhere, of one that pretended to have been miraculously cured of blindness, wherewith he was born, by St. Alban or other St., at the town of St. Alban's; and that the Duke of Gloucester being there, to be satisfied of the truth of the miracle, asked the man, What colour is this? who, by answering, It is green, discovered himself, and was punished for a counterfeit: for though by his sight newly received he might distinguish between green, and red, and all other colours, as well as any that should interrogate him, yet he could not possibly

Hobbes: The New Political
Science

know at first sight, which of them was called green, or red, or by other name. By this we may understand, there be two sorts of knowledge, whereof the one is nothing else but sense, or knowledge original (as I have said at the beginning of the second chapter), and remembrance of the same; the other is called science or knowledge of the truth of propositions, and how things are called, and is derived from understanding. Both of these sorts are but experience; the former being the experience of the effects of things that work upon us from without; and the latter the experience men have of the proper use of names in language. [*Elements*, 1.6.1]

The second sort of knowledge, then, is science. It can be introduced to the reader only after Hobbes has introduced speech, or language, or, as he says, "names and appellations." And not only to the reader, but to men simply, for "the invention of names hath been necessary for the drawing of men out of ignorance" (*Elements*, 1.5.13). Before men have language, or naming, they can indeed "know" in a sense, a direct phenomenal sense, just as the man of St. Alban's "knew" how to distinguish colors by sight, one from the other. But until the colors were named, he could not know "which of them was called green, or red, or by other name." In this prelinguistic condition men's knowledge does not differ from that of "brute beasts" which can know the world phenomenally in the same way. But, writes Hobbes, "by the advantage of names it is that we are capable of science, which beasts, for want of them, are not; nor man, without the use of them: for as a beast misseth not one or two out of her many young ones, for want of those names of order, one, two, three, &c., which we call number; so neither would a man, without repeating orally, or mentally, the words of number, know how many pieces of money or other things lie before him" (*Elements*, 1.5.4). It is language, or naming, which makes possible the second sort of knowledge, the sort peculiar to man, the "registers" of which "are called the sciences" (*Elements*, 1.6.1).[5]

The De Facto Reduction of Knowledge to Science and the New Meaning of "Truth" and "Evidence"

To find our way to the core of Hobbes's conception of language, we need to begin with a closer inspection of how he defines knowledge.

Hobbes: The New Political Science

There is at least a tension, if not a contradiction, in Hobbes's conception of knowledge. The tension arises from the fact that, while Hobbes explicitly states that there are "two sorts of knowledge" (*Elements*, 1.6.1), for the most part he seems to consider only one of these real knowledge, and in one place even defines knowledge so as to exclude implicitly the sort he for the most part ignores anyway. The closest he ever comes to a definition of knowledge simply is in chapter 6 of the *Elements of Law*. It is this "definition," or rather the resemblance between it and the more explicit definitions of science which occur in the *Elements of Law* and *Leviathan*, which betrays the inclination of Hobbes to identify all real knowledge with one and only one of the two sorts whose existence he explicitly declares.

> There are two things necessarily implied in this word knowledge; the one is truth, the other evidence; for what is not true can never be known. For let a man say he knoweth a thing never so well, if the same shall afterwards appear to be false, he is driven to a confession, that it was not knowledge, but opinion. Likewise, if the truth be not evident, though a man holdeth it, yet is his knowledge of it no more than theirs that hold the contrary. For if truth were enough to make it knowledge, all truths were known: which is not so. [*Elements*, 1.6.2]

Two characteristics, then, identify this second sort of knowledge: truth and evidence. Let us see first what Hobbes means by the former. Truth, as he immediately points out, "hath been defined in the precedent chapter," that is, in the chapter on names and "discourse of the tongue." Turning back, we find the following: "In every proposition, be it affirmative or negative, the latter appellation [i.e., the predicate] either comprehendeth the former [i.e., the subject], as in this proposition, charity is virtue, the name of virtue comprehendeth the name of charity (and many other virtues besides), and then is the proposition said to be TRUE or TRUTH: for, truth, and a true proposition, is all one. Or else the latter appellation comprehendeth not the former ... and then the proposition is said to be FALSE, or falsity" (*Elements*, 1.5.10). Clearly, since propositions are essential to this account, language is required. We are thus forced to conclude that he speaks here of the peculiarly human way of knowing, the second sort, as distinct from prudence shared with beasts.[6]

Hobbes: The New Political
Science

Evidence, the second characteristic, is more complicated. Evidence "is the concomitance of a man's conception with the words that signify such conception in the act of ratiocination" (*Elements*, 1.6.3). It is not enough that a man pronounce the words of a true proposition. Something else must accompany his pronouncing; he must have the right conceptions in his head while he says the words. To take the man from St. Alban's again, we might say that even if he answered the duke correctly, he could not be said to "know" the color if his answer had been only accidentally correct, as, for example, if he had simply guessed. "For the truth of a proposition is never evident, until we conceive the meaning of the words or terms whereof it consisteth, which are always conceptions of the mind" (*Elements*, 1.6.4). By "conceptions" Hobbes means "images" or "representations of the qualities of things without us" (*Elements*, 1.1.8). Although this is not especially technical, he makes a point of distinguishing the *conceptions* which we have of things from the *actual* things, the nature of which is inaccessible to us.[7]

Hobbes's explanation of evidence is also curious: "For when a man reasoneth with his lips only, to which the mind suggesteth only the beginning, and followeth not the words of his mouth with the conceptions of his mind, out of a custom of so speaking; though he begin his ratiocination with true propositions, and proceed with perfect syllogisms, and thereby make always true conclusions; yet are not his conclusions evident to him, for want of the concomitance of conception with his words" (*Elements*, 1.6.3). (We will see in chapter 4 Wittgenstein's criticism of this kind of separation of words from the mental processes they are supposed to represent.) Hobbes himself notes, "If the words alone were sufficient, a parrot might be taught as well to know a truth, as to speak it" (ibid.). Now what Hobbes is explaining here is undoubtedly correct: the man who claims knowledge must understand his words; they cannot be an empty formula repeated after the manner of a parrot. Evidence, for Hobbes, always involves language, because it has something to do with one's having in mind the proper meanings for words, or understanding the words in the correct sense.[8]

Hobbes does not, we believe, give a sufficient account of evidence. We may understand why evidence is a problem, why he is compelled to deal with this subject, if we reflect on the picture of

Hobbes: The New Political Science

language which seems to guide his thought here. It is a picture which is curious in several respects. He seems to suggest that if we are careless we may find ourselves speaking, or using language, like parrots, which suggests that meaning and speaking are distinct. What troubles Hobbes is that words or names are arbitrary marks or signs, which "stand for" our thoughts. Hence he must admit the possibility that one could say a word while an inappropriate thought—that is, a thought different from the one which the word *really* signifies—is actually in one's mind. This leaves unresolved a further difficulty, namely, how we can ever be sure the thought which *we* use a word to signify is the same as someone else's. If truth is not merely private or subjective—and it must not be if science can exist—then there must be some way to guarantee that words have meanings which are objective, that is, that we agree on the conceptions which words signify. Hobbes never, to our knowledge, satisfactorily resolves this problem.[9] That task remains for Locke to deal with (by insisting that we are passive in receiving ideas), as we shall see in chapter 3.

Once he has discussed truth and evidence, the "two things necessarily implied in this word knowledge," Hobbes proceeds to define the second of the two sorts of knowledge he has already mentioned. "Knowledge, therefore, which we call SCIENCE, I define to be evidence of truth, from some beginning or principle of sense" (*Elements*, 1.6.4). This seems scarcely different from the earlier discussion of the word "knowledge" (*Elements*, 1.6.2; see above); it would appear that the most important knowledge, if not all knowledge, is "science." Without any restriction to one or the other sort of knowledge (the inferior sort, which is knowledge from sense, i.e., experience, and the proper sense of knowledge, i.e., science), Hobbes now goes on:

> The first principle of knowledge therefore is, that we have such and such conceptions; the second, that we have thus and thus named the things whereof they are conceptions; the third is, that we have joined those names in such manner, as to make true propositions; the fourth and last is, that we have joined those propositions in such manner as they be concluding. [*Elements*, 1.6.4]

Hobbes thus says that there are two sorts of knowledge, yet when

Hobbes: The New Political Science

he discusses knowledge simply, that is, without qualification, the discussion excludes one of the two sorts of knowledge previously identified. Perhaps this is Hobbes's attempt to explain what the model of true knowledge is, the knowledge whose four "principles" he lists, and at the same time account for the fact that we so often call "knowledge" something which does not satisfy his "principles."

The Epistemological Failing of Classical Thought: Starting Points and Definitions

Now we are in a better position to see precisely what the failing of classical political philosophy is, which is the source of the endless controversy. The so-called knowledge of Hobbes's predecessors in political philosophy was knowledge only in the first sense, prudential knowledge, and therefore lacking the certainty characteristic of the knowledge called "science." How could this have escaped the notice of earlier thinkers? "The reason whereof is no other, than that in their writings and discourse they take for principles those opinions which are vulgarly received, whether true or false; being for the most part false" (*Elements*, 1.13.3). The objection Hobbes raises is an objection to the starting point of the old political philosophy. "There be two sorts of men that be commonly called learned," he writes in *Elements of Law*; "one is that sort that proceedeth evidently from humble principles ... the other are they that take up maxims from their education, and from the authority of men, or of custom, and take the habitual discourse of the tongue for ratiocination ..." (1.13.4). There is no doubt as to which category is meant to include Aristotle and the tradition of classical political thought. Even in the Epistle Dedicatory to this early work, Hobbes writes, "They that have written of justice and policy in general, do all invade each other, and themselves, with contradiction." If moral science or philosophy is to be reduced "to the rules and infallibility of reason, there is no way, but first to put such principles down for a foundation, as passion not mistrusting, may not seek to displace; and afterward to build thereon the truth of cases in the law of nature (which hitherto have been built in the air) by degrees, till the whole be inexpugnable" (*Elements*, Epistle Dedicatory, p. xv).

In Hobbes's most purely philosophical work, *De Corpore*, his complaint about starting points in science is stated most clearly. For the ancients, with the exception of geometry, "there was no ratiocination certain, and ending in science, their doctrines concerning all other things being nothing but controversy and clamour; which, nevertheless, happened, not because the truth to which they pretended could not be made evident without figures, but because they wanted true principles, from which they might derive their ratiocination" (De Corpore, 1.6.16). What are the "true principles" which they lacked? Hobbes answers in a word: definitions. "There is no reason," he writes, "but that if true definitions were premised in all sorts of doctrines, the demonstrations also would be true" (ibid.).[10]

The exact status of definitions in Hobbes's philosophy is difficult to determine, but it is also of the greatest importance.[11] If definitions are to serve as the first principles in science, as the starting point of any reasoning capable of leading to true and certain knowledge, their fundamental significance is obvious. How does Hobbes think we arrive at definitions when we philosophize? That it is necessary to begin from correct definitions may be seen, according to Hobbes, from the fact that "the errours of Definitions multiply themselves, according as the reckoning proceeds; and lead men into absurdities, which at last they see, but cannot avoyd, without reckoning anew from the beginning; in which lyes the foundation of their errours" (Leviathan, chap. 4, p. 105). How then do we define something, and how (by what standard) do we tell when we have gotten it right?

Hobbes's practice of discussing definitions in the same breath with geometry suggests a preliminary answer. In geometry, which, as he says, "is the onely Science that it hath pleased God hitherto to bestow on mankind, men begin at settling the significations of their words; which settling of significations, they call Definitions; and place them in the beginning of their reckoning" (Leviathan, chap. 4, p. 105). From this it would appear that Hobbes is suggesting that a definition is something on which we "settle" before beginning, something arbitrary, perhaps. Definitions, he seems to say, are strictly a matter of convention, to be specified for purposes of clarity as the case requires.[12] What is important is only that they be clear, and "settled." This is reinforced by a passage in De Corpore, to which we will return later: "Whatsoever the common use of words be, yet philosophers, who were to teach their knowledge to others, had always the liberty and sometimes they both had and will have a necessity, of taking to themselves such names as they please for the signifying of their meaning, if they would have it understood" (1.2.4). Euclid's *Elements* begins by setting down that "a point is that which has no part," and "a line is breadthless length." Is it in this fashion that Hobbes intends philosophers to begin, by "settling the significations" of the terms they will use?[13] Without, for the moment, our reflecting on the peculiarity of this approach when applied to political matters, we may cite further support for this interpretation from Hobbes's even later writing, *De Homine*, where, in the chapter "On Speech and Sciences," we find the following:

> Science is allowed to men through the former kind [involving truth of propositions, not fact] of *a priori* demonstration only of those things whose generation depends on the will of men themselves. . . .
> Since the causes of the properties that individual figures have belong to them because we ourselves draw the lines; and since the generation of the figures depends on our will; nothing more is required to know the phenomenon peculiar to any figure whatsoever, than that we consider everything that follows from the construction that we ourselves make in the figure to be described. Therefore, because of this fact (that is, that we ourselves create the figures), it happens that geometry hath been and is demonstrable. . . .
> Finally, politics and ethics (that is, the sciences of *just* and *unjust*, of *equity* and *inequity*) can be demonstrated *a priori*; because we ourselves make the principles—that is, the causes of justice (namely laws and covenants)—whereby it is known what *justice* and *equity*, and their opposites *injustice* and *inequity*, are. [*De Homine*, chap. 10]

In this passage Hobbes reveals clearly the extent to which he wants to use the science of geometry as the model for political science.[14] There is a difficulty here, however, on the resolution of which depends Hobbes's ultimate success or failure in founding a new political science. The difficulty is that there does not seem to be an

Hobbes: The New Political Science

exact parallel between the sort of definition used in a geometric demonstration and the definition of something like "justice" which is appropriate to political science. This is not a simple difficulty, nor was it for Hobbes.[15] But in the end his understanding of this difficulty is controlled by something deeper, namely, his understanding of the way language works, of what language is.

The Place of Definitions in Hobbes's Conception of Science

We must begin by ascertaining the position occupied by definitions in the overall system of philosophy as conceived by Hobbes. Philosophy is the knowledge of causes, or of the manner of generation of a thing (see *De Corpore*, 1.6.1). It is, as Hobbes says, "common to all sorts of method, to proceed from known things to unknown" (*De Corpore*, 1.6.2). What we know primarily—that is, before we begin to use any "method"—is that a thing exists. (Hobbes calls this knowledge the *hoti*, the "that" of anything.) We know this by means of sense. But in order to know anything scientifically, we need to know its causes, or the manner of its "generation" (or, as Hobbes puts it, the *dioti*). In the knowledge that a thing exists, we know it as a "whole" first; we do not know its parts.[16] As to knowledge of *causes*, however, we know more about the causes of the parts (they are more accessible to us) than of the whole thing: "For the cause of the whole is compounded of the causes of the parts; but it is necessary that we know the things that are to be compounded, before we can know the whole compound" (ibid.). Hobbes adds, to forestall confusion: "Now, by parts, I do not here mean parts of the thing itself, but parts of its nature; as, by the parts of man, I do not understand his head, his shoulders, his arms, &c. but his figure, quantity, motion, sense, reason, and the like; which accidents being compounded or put together, constitute the whole nature of man, but not the man himself" (ibid.).

What Hobbes means by this statement can be understood more clearly if we compare it with the method used by Euclid in the thirteen books of his *Elements*. Euclid's geometry is based on the principle that we can know the truth of geometric propositions only because we construct, step by step, every proposition with which geometry is concerned, using for proof nothing but agreed-upon definitions and first principles. We thus understand the "wholes" of geometry (squares, triangles, pentagons), because we see how they are constructed from, or can be reduced to, simple "parts." By parts we do not mean only the three sides of a triangle, but "universals" such as angles and lines. In the case of Hobbes, too, the "parts" of a science are understood to be "universal things," such as figure, motion, visibility, etc. (*De Corpore*, 1.2.9).

The certainty of geometry in no way conflicts with the fact that, as Euclid following Aristotle knew, any science rests on a foundation which is assumed or unprovable. There are three types of "first principles" at the foundation of Euclid's system: definitions, postulates, and axioms (or "common notions," *koinai ennoiai*). Geometry (or any science, for that matter) assumes its subject matter only in the sense that the definitions are not proven: *what* we mean by "square" is explained by a definition, but *that* squares exist and what the properties of squares are, are what geometry demonstrates.[17] The definitions require only to be understood; the propositions must be demonstrated or proven. Thus the definitions with which Euclid begins are supplemented by two kinds of first principles without which nothing could be demonstrated. These are (1) postulates, the status of which is in Euclid not perfectly clear but which may be said to be assumptions necessary to the practice of geometry but in themselves unprovable (such as, that all right angles are equal); and (2) common notions or axioms, which for our purpose in understanding Hobbes may be said to be simply the rules of logic (in Euclid, e.g., that equals subtracted from equals are equal). Within its own subject matter, geometry is absolutely certain because we construct, in full view and from principles accepted by all (who practice geometry), the propositions concerning the nature of triangles, circles, rectangles, and so on.

Even in geometry, the making or construction begins from observing.[18] The idea of a line, breadthless and infinitely extended, is understood only by abstraction from the lines we see, which have breadth and are never perfectly straight nor infinite. The key to the method is not to deny the validity of observation, but to take nothing on faith, to expose even the apparently obvious facts to doubt, and to require proof. What one constructs is the necessary and incontrovertible framework which underlies everyday triangles or everyday politics. But the science is not constructed out of thin air, or on the basis of merely arbitrary principles.[19] The conceptions which lie at its base are the result of careful analysis of the sensible, observable world. It is emphatically *empirical*.[20] What makes it abstract is not the fact that it has no relation to observation, but that the observation begins from what evidently is and abstracts the universal out of the particular and unnecessary. Hobbes's political science is intended to be analogous to Euclid's geometry, but the project itself is not without difficulties. What is questionable about applying this method to political phenomena is the requisite assumption that they are reducible to, or can be understood as, constructions out of simpler elements.[21] To put this another way: although political institutions are creations of men, we must wonder if they are creations in the same sense as geometric figures. Can we understand political principles and institutions as constructions from simpler elements, as a square is constructed out of lines and angles? If Hobbes seeks to understand what "justice" is by resolving it into its component parts, we must ask whether, or how, it can be understood to *have* component parts.

We proceed in philosophy from known things to unknown, and we must begin from our prephilosophic (or prescientific) knowledge that a thing exists. We know the existence of the singular things, the wholes, by our senses. We must find some way to get from our beginning point to knowledge of the causes of parts if we hope to be able to compound this knowledge into scientific knowledge of a whole, that is, knowledge of the causes or "manner of generation" of a whole. For example, in seeking to understand the nature of political communities, Hobbes begins from the known fact that they exist, and that they are composed of individual men. Individual men, in turn, are understood by resolving them—their actions and beliefs—into the psychological components which in combination explain behavior. These components turn out to be, when analyzed, the basic "impulses" Hobbes calls appetite and aversion, the two kinds of motion which lie at the root of all human psychology. These motions—and specifically the two fundamental types (motion toward, motion away from)—are universals. Knowl-

Hobbes: The New Political Science

edge of universal things "is to be acquired by reason, that is, by resolution" (*De Corpore*, 1.6.4). That is, the discovery of the component parts is the end of the first half of the famous resolutive-compositive method.²² The transition from our prescientific knowledge of wholes to knowledge of parts is accomplished by what Hobbes calls "resolution," or the analytical method (ibid.).

The parts or simplest things are discovered by analysis. But how do we know the causes of these parts? By what bridge do we cross to the compositive side of the scientific method? The bridge is supplied by the fact that "the causes of universal things (of those, at least, that have any cause) are manifest of themselves, or (as they say commonly) known to nature" (*De Corpore*, 1.6.5). In other words, the last step in the analytical process leaves the philosopher with the most universal conceptions, the lowest common denominators, as it were, which resolve his original sense knowledge. And for knowledge of these universals, "and of their causes (which are the first principles by which we know the *dioti* of things)," says Hobbes, "we have in the first place their definitions, (which are nothing but the explication of our simple conceptions)" (*De Corpore*, 1.6.6). Definitions, then, the "first principles" of demonstration, occupy in the overall philosophical system an absolutely central position. They are the keystone of Hobbes's epistemological archway.²³ Between the two processes of resolution (from sense to first principles) and composition (from first principles to true scientific knowledge of the thing sensed) lie definitions, "the explication of our simple conceptions." What Hobbes means by our simple conceptions is also made clear.²⁴ "For example, he that has a true conception of *place*, cannot be ignorant of this definition, *place is that space which is possessed or filled adequately by some body*; and so, he that conceives *motion* aright, cannot but know that *motion is the privation of one place, and the acquisition of another*" (*De Corpore*, 1.6.6). From these simple conceptions may be generated, by the compositive or synthetical method, all the principles of geometry: "*A line is made by the motion of a point, superficies by the motion of a line*," and so on. From these considerations of motion, we "pass to the consideration of what effects one body moved worketh upon another," which leads us eventually to physics (ibid.). From physics we can

Hobbes: The New Political Science

eventually construct psychology (or moral philosophy) and in turn, political science (or civil philosophy). It should now be clear why definitions are of such importance in Hobbes's account of science. The resolutive-compositive method itself is closely connected with an understanding of language according to which unambiguous definitions are in principle possible and which permit us to give a clear account of the nature of anything. The view of language must teach that words "stand for" concepts which can be defined—in principle—in some unambiguous way.[25] It is this view which will be scrutinized in chapters 4 and 5.

Hobbes's Political Science and the Scientific Method

In Hobbes's overall view, psychology and political science follow, in order, after physics; they are, in fact, generated from it. In his words, "the reason why these are to be considered after physics is, that they have their causes in sense and imagination, which are the subject of *physical* contemplation" (*De Corpore*, 1.6.6). But civil philosophy may be learned, and even constructed, independently of physics. We do not need to begin from the ground up every time. This is true because we may be content to interrupt the resolution when we have reached simples which are sufficient to explain politics. This requires, of course, the assumption that *these* simples can be adequately defined so that we have "explication" of the simple conceptions to which political terms (such as laws, justice, etc.) are reducible.[26] Just as we arrive at first principles by successive resolutions in philosophy generally, the principles of civil philosophy are reached by resolution of political wholes, or the terms which stand for political concepts. And when one has attained the principles proper to this part of science, by means of a resolution of its conceptions, "from hence he may proceed, by compounding, to the determination of the justice or injustice of any propounded action" (*De Corpore*, 1.6.7). The greatest example of the application of this method, of course, is in Hobbes's own early work *De Cive*, which was written prior to, and independently of, the sections of his philosophical system which in principle should have preceded it.

Forthright and unidealistic observation of the political world, according to Hobbes, quickly teaches one that the central fact of politics is competition and the struggle of each individual to further his own interests. This much had been claimed many times before, from the time of the earliest political thinking.[27] But what Hobbes adds, or believes he adds, is a method whereby that opinion is transformed into knowledge. Societies are simply aggregations of individual, atomic men, each motivated by his own passions. To understand politics, then, one must begin by resolving the commonwealth into its parts, and these, further, into their elements. Hobbes's own example is that we may resolve "unjust" into "fact against law," and "law" into "command of him or them that have coercive power," and so on (*De Corpore*, 1.6.7).

Political science wishes to discover what a commonwealth or what justice really is, in order to secure peace, according to Hobbes. Since all men use the term "justice" carelessly and ambiguously in vulgar discourse, each advancing his own claims as just, we must penetrate beneath vulgar discourse and ignore these claims. How then can we discover the conception for which "justice" really stands, that is, the necessary or original meaning of justice before men learned they could further selfish interests by cheating, so to speak, in the use of the word? We do this, according to Hobbes's political science, by analyzing or breaking down the commonwealth into parts, thinking our way back to men's primary or basic motivations, and then inventing in our minds the circumstances in which justice would be constructed for the first time in fact. By clear-sighted observations of political reality, we try to discover what makes men do what they do—obey laws or break them, fight wars, study medicine, lock their doors, or whatever. At first one might despair, in this analysis, because it appears that men act from a variety of motives, seeking many different goals. But, Hobbes tells us, we soon see that, despite an almost perfect relativism of goals,[28] the great variety of motivations can be reduced to a few simple passions, including desires (e.g., for honor or for commodious living) and fears. Even the reduction to a relatively small number of ends is not sufficient, however. It turns out, according to Hobbes, that despite the variety of ends men may pursue, they are all alike in one respect: they each require the same means, namely, power, which is necessary to attain *any* end. From this we may conclude that there will be universal competition, and war, which in turn will force each man to the realization of his one truly fundamental need, his *sine qua non*, which is to stay alive. The basic motivation, then, once men realize their situation, emerges as a desire for self-preservation. Once we have penetrated, by means of this analysis, beneath the apparent variety of political communities and their beliefs to the fundamental truth about human beings and what moves them, we bring these elements together again and compose or construct a commonwealth. The necessary features of this commonwealth must be the core of every political community, however much these features are covered over in the world of vulgar speech.

We perform the construction in a manner precisely analogous to the way Euclid determines the properties of a triangle: by constructing it from the simplest elements (lines), in a self-evident manner, using only postulates and axioms (rules of logic, we may loosely say), and propositions previously proven. The simplest elements of the political universe considered by itself are the two fundamental passions, that is, appetites and aversions. From these may be constructed by combination (using also the undefined terms "motion," "opinion," "overcoming," etc.) a complete human psychology which clearly defines everything from laughter to courage. (Courage, for example, is constructed by combining fear [which equals aversion, with opinion of hurt from the object] with hope [which equals appetite with opinion of attaining] of overcoming that hurt by resistance.)

The resolution of man into his passions or motivations leads Hobbes to articulate a terrible state of nature, and from that he is led to the need for a sovereign to guarantee peace and hence civil society. The geometric analogy is present at every stage of his argument because it consists of a series of clear propositions, linked by logic. Hobbes's conclusion about the meaning of justice (which is "whatsoever is not Unjust"; injustice in turn is *"the not Performance of Covenant"* [*Leviathan*, chap. 15, p. 202]) is based on the propositions previously proven, just as Euclid bases the proof of proposition 1 of book 2, concerning rectangles, on the earlier proofs and constructions of book 1.

Hobbes: The New Political Science

The necessary features of a political community which emerge from Hobbes's political science include, among others, the fact that politics is a permanent struggle for power (channeled, in Hobbes's commonwealth, into the peaceful struggle for power in the form of wealth), and the fact that at the very core of politics is the desire for peace, which in turn comes from man's fear of violent death. The raison d'être of any political community, no matter what illusions it may have about itself, is *always* peace and security, no more and no less, according to Hobbes. It is important to note, however, that the content of Hobbes's political philosophy and his substantive claims about politics are less important to us here than his method, his understanding of how political science must proceed.

Nevertheless, Hobbes claims his theory "fits" the world. That he considers this absolutely crucial is shown by his attempt to adduce empirical evidence of the state of nature, immediately following the description of that state. Some reader, Hobbes is aware, may not trust the inference of the state of nature, an inference "made from the Passions," and consequently may

> desire . . . to have the same confirmed by Experience. Let him therefore consider with himselfe, when taking a journey, he armes himselfe, and seeks to go well accompanied; when going to sleep, he locks his dores; when even in his house he locks his chests; and this when he knows there bee Lawes and publike Officers, armed, to revenge all injuries shall be done him; what opinion he has of his fellow subjects, when he rides armed; of his fellow Citizens, when he locks his dores; and of his children, and servants, when he locks his chests. Does he not there as much accuse mankind by his actions, as I do by my words? [*Leviathan*, chap. 13, pp. 186–87]

Hobbes is concerned lest one take this theory to be an arbitrary construction, bearing no relation to the world we know from common sense. He makes clear that it is an attempt to explain that world by penetrating beneath the surface of our everyday experience. The resolutive-compositive method must be seen to be concerned with the world we live in, despite the fact that it attempts to explain by means of a break with common sense.[29]

Hobbes did not, of course, intend his scientific "reconstruction" of the political reality as a description of what actually happened in fact, in history. In this sense one might say that he is attempting to "reform" language by showing what political terms can legitimately mean, what they necessarily mean. The fact that most philosophers before Hobbes had not understood this he would attribute to their delusions about language and science. In the actual historical circumstances everything was confused, every meaning rendered ambiguous, by certain "phantasms of the mind" which men invented to cover over their anxiety, to explain what they did not understand. Thus justice was understood by primitive man to be dispensed by gods. It was religion which prevented the rational development of language, but it does not prevent Hobbes from figuring out how political terms would have been invented, that is, what they should have meant, if men had had no delusions or had understood themselves scientifically.

Science and the World: Theory and Practice

The difficulty we alluded to earlier in the matter of definitions is now apparent. The clarity and power of a demonstration, it appears, depend directly on definitions which are derived by the analytic procedure. Unfortunately, definitions, "because they are principles, cannot be demonstrated" (*De Corpore*, 1.6.12). Although they cannot be demonstrated, Hobbes quickly adds that "they need no demonstration, though they need explication" (ibid.). This, however, raises a difficulty. If definitions are impossible to prove, but acceptance of them is necessary in order, quite simply, to do science, how are we to understand the relation of science to the world? Does Hobbes understand his political science to be provisionally correct, an abstract framework which underlies political practice?

What is involved here is a question about the status of geometry as a science. The classical thinkers considered it theoretical, as opposed to political science which was practical. The clarity of the eternal and absolute truths of geometry was due in part to the fact that geometry is abstract. It abstracted from a world in which, for example, points do have breadth and lines are not infinitely extended. Hobbes apparently hoped that a true political science could be constructed which would be theoretical and certain just

Hobbes: The New Political Science

as is geometry. One must wonder, however, whether there is not something problematic about the idea of a theoretical science of a practical matter like politics.

In classical thought this problematic relationship was of very serious consequence; for us, on the other hand, the problematic aspect is somewhat elusive, precisely because of the success of Hobbes's attempt to reforge the connection between theory and practice. Why it was a problem may be seen from the following considerations. One component of the theoretical rigor of geometry, of its excellence as a "pure science," is its abstractness. That is, geometry is theoretical because it "abstracts" from the complexity of the empirical world—it abstracts from, among other things, color, which is always part of the figures we can see. For the classical thinkers, the purity and rigor of geometry were purchased at a price. What geometry tells us about the universe was recognized to be only one side of things, to require supplementation from the world of common experience, in order to be practical, or useful.[30] For Hobbes, on the contrary, the natural or commonsense understanding is itself useless precisely *because* of its complexity, heterogeneity, and diversity. And theoretical science is useful precisely because it is abstract, since the only way the human mind can deal with a chaotic world of nothing but sense impressions is to impose order, to simplify.[31] Consequently, for Hobbes the abstract, the theoretical, is the *only* access to truth about the world. It is more "real" than common sense because naming, the process which precedes any science, is a matter of imposing a framework on the natural chaos. The abstraction from the world of sense which characterizes geometry is a necessary component, on Hobbes's understanding, of any theoretical science which hopes to be practical or useful. What was for the classics a defect, in one sense, of theoretical science—its abstractness—is for Hobbes the *sine qua non* of its utility. Theoretical science can be practical only because it orders, simplifies, abstracts, and so makes the world manageable.

This approach was attractive to Hobbes, even aside from the reasons we have attempted to elucidate above, because he had in front of him the model of the new natural science, which was based on a new understanding of that relationship between theoretical

Hobbes: The New Political Science

purity and practical utility.[32] Classical physics had been, to say the least, unproductive. But in Hobbes's time the abstract truths of mathematics, applied to the physical world, were producing a new practical science which was true because it worked, and which worked with wonderful success. On Hobbes's understanding of language, it is difficult to see why this should not be equally if not more effective when applied to human constructs such as political institutions: no one, after all, denies that men make these. In fact, it is precisely this which permits Hobbes to claim that political science can achieve greater certainty than natural science.[33] It is important that we grasp the implication of this assertion. Hobbes is not attempting to model his political science on the pattern of natural sciences. Rather, his claim is that his new civil philosophy will be the first to meet the requirements of science—that is, of scientific knowledge—simply. It is the invention of language which permits man access to knowledge properly speaking.

Knowledge, according to Hobbes, is expressed in statements which are constructed syllogistically. It is this fact which makes the terms of politics knowable. We know only what we construct. We name things, we agree on names by "operationalizing" their definitions, but we recognize that, as regards nature, this is an imposition of our own construction on a world which already exists. But the political phenomena, the "conceptions" which political terms refer to, are artificial: we can know them more fully because we make them. This is to say, political science is capable of more certainty not because we make political science, but because we make the political phenomena, the things to which our terms of political discourse refer—laws, states, monarchs, etc. Of course, as Hobbes realizes, we ourselves don't make them; they have been in existence for great stretches of time. But we can know them fully nevertheless because we can recover the circumstances in which the concepts were created. By carefully observing human nature and history, and reducing it to the essential elements which must always have been present, we can reconstruct the situation in which the first terms of political discourse were needed and thus invented.[34] And we can use the new understanding to establish a secure basis for the truly necessary political institutions (by weeding out myths such as divine right of kings and showing the real basis of legitimacy).

Hobbes: The New Political
Science

The question whether moral science is different in principle (more knowable) from physical is not, we believe, satisfactorily resolved by Hobbes. On the one hand, he seems to say that all knowledge is hypothetical (of names), moral science or geometry no less than physics. Both require testing against the facts, the real world (see note 28). On the other hand, the formulation that "we know only what we make" seems to suggest that geometry is knowable in some way more completely than physics. If that is not the case, Hobbes is forced into the position of assuming some underlying harmony between the geometry we construct with human logic and the working of the physical universe—a harmony which he nowhere proclaims and which seems to contradict the spirit of his philosophy. Although Hobbes in his later works seems more clearly to differentiate physics from moral science (*De Corpore*, 3.25.1), his position is far from clear in *Leviathan*, most notably in the famous diagram in chapter 9. In any event, we will, in what follows, make use of Locke's more systematic attempt to deal with this issue, since Hobbes leaves us unsatisfied. That there is an ambiguity in Hobbes's teaching is sufficiently demonstrated by the fact that numerous attempts to resolve the issue have led to two main schools of thought on the question of the connection between his political thought and his physical science.[35]

Hobbes's claim that the meanings of the political terms are the result of human construction, together with the fact of the existence of diverse, not to say radically different, languages, cannot help but raise the question of whether political terms such as justice are not merely conventional, with different meanings at different times. It thus opens up the possibility that political science may be of only limited validity because of its being time- or place-bound. That is to say, it forces us to recognize the possibility that political science may be historical. That Hobbes is aware of this possibility seems very likely from the second paragraph of chapter 4 of *Leviathan*, where he mentions "the diversity of Tongues" in the "severall parts of the world." Hobbes rejects the historicist conclusion, because he believes that meanings necessarily emerge in the same way everywhere because of man's permanent nature. Nevertheless it was possible to argue, after Hobbes, that what he thought was a necessary historical sequence (emerging from the state of nature) was in fact only the result of accident.[36] And clearly, if

Hobbes: The New Political Science

meanings are understood to be dependent on accidental historical circumstances, concepts might very well be different in different times. This implication of his understanding was later decisive in the abandonment of the task which he believed to be the core of political science: the understanding of justice.

Historicism did not entirely succeed in devitalizing Hobbes's approach, however. At least one version of Hobbes's method responded to the claim that justice and other political terms are historical by simply retrenching: it abandoned the attempt to study scientifically those things which began to be called value terms, and instead simply tried to describe political systems or organizations. It attempted this by reducing the variety of political organizations[37] to a set of fundamental elements—what Hobbes would have called "universals"—and describing the relationship among them.

Hobbes, in any case, thinks that clear definitions actually uncover what justice *is*, because they remove the ambiguity which grows onto a word in vulgar usage and restore to it its proper or necessary meaning. It should be clear from this that Hobbes's understanding of the possibility of a political science, including the resolutive-compositive method and the understanding of propositions, is connected with a particular attitude toward common speech. Behind that, in turn, lies a certain understanding of the nature of language. In the next chapter we will explore that conception of language and try to bring out some of the problems into which Hobbes's successors were led by his new method. Once the connection between his method and his view of language is clear, it will be possible to raise some serious questions about both.

3

Language, Signification, and Meaning in Hobbes and Locke

We may well be sympathetic to Hobbes's palpable impatience with the approach of his predecessors in political science. It is understandable that he would feel, as do we, frustration at the circularity, ambiguity, and even contradictions to be found in works which purported to be knowledge (see chaps. 6 and 7, below). We have now examined the grounds for Hobbes's claim that he is the true founder, the first to see clearly the relation between language or words on the one hand and knowledge or science on the other. If his claim seems immodest, it can only be because what he took to be so striking and powerful about science is now so commonplace: in other words, it can only be because of the success of Hobbes himself.

We wish now to inquire into the particular understanding of language which permitted Hobbes to claim so much.[1] His understanding is one we are not given to questioning, because it accords with common sense. At the same time, it is characteristic of natural science,[2] and natural science normally claims to question and probe beneath common sense. That in this case natural science and common sense agree makes our questioning doubly unlikely. What is this understanding of language upon which Hobbes builds his philosophy? Only after we come to see it in its complete form can we begin to understand the true foundation of Hobbes's political science. We will supplement Hobbes's statements about language with those of John Locke, who treats of words and language much more systematically and at greater length than Hobbes. (Book 3 of Locke's *Essay concerning Human Understanding* is devoted exclusively to language.)[3] It is not difficult to show that Hobbes and Locke share the conceptions of knowledge and language we are exploring, although, of course, they differ in other respects.[4] The conception of language that we are interested in, it should be noted, is so fundamental that it remains untouched by other changes Locke made in Hobbes's political philosophy.

Hobbes's Understanding of Language

Language, on Hobbes's view, is a kind of communications code, a code set up by men to transmit messages to each other. The creation of this code was a technical problem, an inventor's problem. Indeed, Hobbes compares it to other inventions: "The invention of *Printing*, though ingenious, compared with the invention of *Letters*, is no great matter. . . . But the most noble and profitable invention of all other, was that of SPEECH . . ." (*Leviathan*, chap. 4, p. 100). One may say that the invention of language is not different in principle from, although of course of vastly greater significance than, the invention of the telephone, which solves another problem in communications, namely, communicating instantly over long distances.[5] According to Hobbes, language itself is a tool, created by men.

Language consists of words, which are used to communicate our thoughts or conceptions to one another.[6] But words had a prior use, namely, to serve an individual as reminders of what his thoughts or conceptions were in the past. The first use of words was as marks. "A MARK therefore is a sensible object which a man erecteth voluntarily to himself, to the end to remember thereby somewhat past, when the same is objected to his sense again. As men that have passed by a rock at sea, set up some mark, whereby to

Language, Signification, and Meaning

remember their former danger, and avoid it" (*Elements*, 1.5.1). Moreover, words are only a type of mark, a subset of the class of all imaginable marks. "In the number of these marks, are those human voices (which we call the names or appellations of things) sensible to the ear, by which we recall into our mind some conceptions of the things to which we give those names or appellations" (*Elements*, 1.5.2).

Such marks, however, are only a preliminary to genuine language. As long as words serve only as marks, men cannot communicate with each other. And "though some one man, of how excellent a wit soever, should spend all his time partly in reasoning, and partly in inventing marks for the help of his memory, and advancing himself in learning; who sees not that the benefit he reaps to himself will not be much, and to others none at all?" It is necessary, then, for words to take on another function, because "unless he communicate his notes with others, his science will perish with him" (*De Corpore*, 1.2.2). This second function of names Hobbes calls "signs." Words function as "signs," says Hobbes, "when many use the same words, to signifie (by their connexion and order,) one to another, what they conceive, or think of each matter; and also what they desire, feare, or have any other passion for" (*Leviathan*, chap. 4, p. 101).[7] Generally or philosophically speaking, signs exist wherever we find correlations between phenomena; Hobbes offers an example from nature. "A thick cloud is a sign of rain to follow, and rain a sign that a cloud has gone before, for this reason only, that we seldom see clouds without the consequence of rain, nor rain at any time but when a cloud has gone before" (*De Corpore*, 1.2.2). Words are merely a human counterpart of this more general phenomenon. And this means, as Hobbes notes, that we can distinguish between natural signs, and those which "are *arbitrary*, namely, those we make choice of at our own pleasure, as a bush hung up, signifies that wine is to be sold there; a stone set in the ground signifies the bound of a field; and words so and so connected, signify the cogitations and motions of our mind" (ibid.). Words, whether as marks or as signs, are strictly arbitrary, created by men for a specific purpose: to stand for a conception. Marks and signs differ only in that, as Hobbes says, "we make those for our own use, but these for the use

Language, Signification,
and Meaning

of others" (ibid.). The arbitrary symbols which we call words, when connected as signs of our thoughts, "are called SPEECH, of which every part is a name" (*De Corpore*, 1.2.3). Hobbes defines the term "name" in *De Corpore* as follows: "*A NAME is a word taken at pleasure to serve for a mark, which may raise in our mind a thought like to some thought we had before, and which being pronounced to others, may be to them a sign of what thought the speaker had, or had not before in his mind*" (*De Corpore*, 1.2.4). Language, we may say, is in Hobbes's understanding what we call a symbolic system, remarkably like a code. Each symbol in the code is a name, which stands for a conception, with which in turn we have learned to identify it. This accords with our commonsense view of words.

Complications because of Universal Names

How do we understand someone who uses a word like "rational," or a general term which has no obvious referent, like "man"? Hobbes carefully points out that names are never signs for things, but only for conceptions of things: "that the sound of this word *stone* should be the sign of a stone, cannot be understood in any sense but this, that he that pronounces it thinks of a stone" (*De Corpore*, 1.2.5). Thus "man" proves to be no difficulty even though it has no clear referent. "Man" is what Hobbes calls a "universal name," or a name "common to many things." A name of this type "is imposed on many things, for their similitude in some quality, or other accident: And whereas a Proper Name bringeth to mind one thing onely; Universals recall any one of those many." Universal names stand for a class of things, or for what is common to our conception of each. Such classes may be broad and general, or narrow; the former may encompass the latter entirely. "And of Names Universall, some are of more, and some of lesse extent; the larger comprehending the lesse large: and some again of equall extent, comprehending each other reciprocally." The picture Hobbes draws is one of words or names as so many labels, each attached to our conceptions in such a way as to stand for either a class of conceptions, or an individual conception, or some "quality or other accident" common to various conceptions. He offers an

Language, Signification, and Meaning

example: "The Name *Body* is of larger signification than the word *Man*, and comprehendeth it; and the names *Man* and *Rationall*, are of equall extent, comprehending mutually one another" (*Leviathan*, chap. 4, p. 103).

Once we begin to see that words are names for conceptions, we might wonder why there is ever any problem understanding what someone says. The explanation, according to Hobbes, is that universal names are problematic. "The appellations that be universal, and common to many things, are not always given to all the particulars, (as they ought to be) for like conceptions and considerations in them all; which is the cause that many of them are not of constant signification, but bring into our minds other thoughts than those for which they were ordained" (*Elements*, 1.5.7). Such words, Hobbes adds, "are called EQUIVOCAL." That is, by the very fact that universal names are universal, they are often not as clear as particular and proper names. They have what Hobbes considers a defect in their use if not in their nature; we cannot always know exactly what they mean, because everyday usage does not stick to one meaning.

> This equivocation of names maketh it difficult to recover those conceptions for which the name was ordained; and that not only in the language of other men, wherein we are to consider the drift, and occasion, and contexture of the speech, as well as the words themselves; but also in our own discourse, which being derived from the custom and common use of speech, representeth not unto us our own conceptions. It is therefore a great ability in a man, out of the words, contexture, and other circumstances of language, to deliver himself from equivocation, and to find out the true meaning of what is said: and this is it we call UNDERSTANDING. [*Elements*, 1.5.8]

We understand what is said, according to Hobbes, when the conception for which a name is the sign actually occurs to us. How do we know it is the right conception, the conception which really goes with the name? This, apparently, is decided by discovering "those conceptions for which the name was ordained." Presumably, this means the conceptions to which the name was assigned or ordained by its first user or its inventor, or perhaps (since the first user might have been confused) simply ordained by nature, by

Language, Signification,
and Meaning

the order of things.[8] Where do we get these conceptions, in the absence of some sort of ancient dictionary? Hobbes is less clear about this than we might hope.

The Problem of Common Speech

Now if "naming" a conception, that is, the act referred to just above, is the origin of all our words, understanding consists in having in our minds the right conceptions for names, or in "figuring out" the true meanings of names, the conceptions of which they are the "signs." But common speech is ambiguous, not to say inaccurate and misleading.[9] It is necessary to penetrate beneath the ambiguity of vulgar and ordinary language, to cut away its vagueness and sloppiness and get at the conceptions themselves. The fact that names are entirely a matter of convention, according to Hobbes, points to the fact that a large number of philosophical disputes are nothing but disputes about words whose significations are not settled. And the conventionality of language is what permits Hobbes to seek to end disputes by penetrating beneath the names and dealing with the conceptions, or phenomena, which are really in question.[10]

It is easy to see why this approach appeared to promise so much, especially three and a half centuries ago, when schools were still dominated by that phenomenon Hobbes so bitterly hated, Scholastic philosophy, the "canting of Schoolemen" (*Leviathan*, chap. 5, p. 115; cf. chap. 46). In contrast to the abundant use of "names that signifie nothing; but are taken up, and learned by rote from the Schooles, as *hypostatical, transubstantiate, consubstantiate, eternal-Now*, and the like . . ." (*Leviathan*, chap. 5, p. 115), Hobbes's hard-headed insistence on clear and consistent use of terms could only be a breath of fresh air. But Hobbes's approach is not without problems.

If words or names stand for conceptions, how can we be sure we agree in those conceptions? Names, after all, are defined by other words, and how will we be sure we share the conceptions for which they stand? The invention of names, Hobbes says, drew men out of ignorance "by calling to their remembrance the necessary coherence of one conception to another" (*Elements*, 1.5.13). But what is the

Language, Signification, and Meaning

source of this "necessary coherence"? In *De Homine*, Hobbes proves that names are conventional by citing the fact that "languages are diverse," while "the nature of things is everywhere the same" (10.2). But what authority can he cite in support of that claim? If language is radically conventional, men must all see the world in the same way or there would be no possibility of communication. We must all share conceptions, or at least some fundamental few conceptions, out of which others can be constructed. The "necessary coherence" of our conceptions is not adequately explained by Hobbes in the limited space he devotes to his understanding of language.[11]

Locke's Understanding of Language

In the hope of discovering something more about this understanding of language, we must turn to John Locke's *Essay concerning Human Understanding*. In doing so, we will try to make explicit the features of a more general understanding of language—that is, the understanding tacitly accepted in much of modern thought—which considers language as a symbol system or tool for human communication.[12]

We wish to inquire into the claim that there exists a "necessary coherence of one conception to another" and the accompanying implication that men share the conceptions for which their words stand as labels. That Locke is in agreement with Hobbes on this matter may be seen from the following passage, in which he concludes his elucidation of a philosophical dispute:

> The knowing precisely what our words stand for, would, I imagine, in this as well as a great many other cases, quickly end the dispute. For I am apt to think that men, when they come to examine them, find their simple ideas all generally to agree, though in discourse with one another they perhaps confound one another with different names. I imagine that men who abstract their thoughts, and do well examine the ideas of their own minds, cannot much differ in thinking; however they may perplex themselves with words ... though amongst unthinking men, who examine not scrupulously and carefully their own ideas, and strip them not from the marks men use for them, but confound

Language, Signification, and Meaning

them with words, there must be endless dispute, wrangling, and jargon. . . . But if it should happen that any two thinking men should really have different ideas, I do not see how they could discourse or argue with one another. [*Essay*, 2.13.28]

Locke shares with Hobbes the view that words are signs of something else, that language is a set of symbols, like a code, for communicating messages to one another.[13] Words are "made use of by men as signs of their ideas; not by any natural connexion that there is between particular articulate sounds and certain ideas, for then there would be but one language amongst all men; but by a voluntary imposition, whereby such a word is made arbitrarily the mark of such an idea" (*Essay*, 3.2.1). This would appear to lead to some difficulties. If a man's words stand only for "the ideas he has, and which he would express by them," it would seem that meaning is determined exclusively by the user of a word, which makes it hard to see how one could ever be said to use a word improperly, or how a word could be said to have a "meaning" at all. But the reason for Locke's insistence on this point is not difficult to find: "Words being voluntary signs, they cannot be voluntary signs imposed by him on things he knows not. That would be to make them signs of nothing, sounds without signification" (*Essay*, 3.2.2). A man cannot use words to stand for ideas he doesn't have. This recalls Hobbes's discussion of "evidence" (see above, pp. 25–26). Moreover, says Locke, despite the fact that words can "properly and immediately" stand for nothing but ideas "in the mind of the speaker," men are constantly tempted to "give them a secret reference" to something else. "*They suppose their words to be marks of the ideas in the minds also of other men, with whom they communicate*: for else they should talk in vain, and could not be understood, if the sounds they applied to one idea were such as by the hearer were applied to another, which is to speak two languages" (*Essay*, 3.2.4). Locke appears to be in a difficult position here. On the one hand he maintains that "it is a perverting the use of words, and brings unavoidable obscurity and confusion into their signification, whenever we make them stand for anything but those ideas we have in our own minds" (*Essay*, 3.2.5). On the other hand, unless a man applies a word to the idea which the word truly signifies, "he does not speak properly: and . . . unless a man's

Language, Signification, and Meaning

words excite the same ideas in the hearer which he makes them stand for in speaking, he does not speak intelligibly" (*Essay*, 3.2.8). If our words can stand only for our own ideas, as it would seem from Locke's account they must, and if we are nevertheless to be understood or to "speak intelligibly," then the ideas themselves must be the same in each of us.[14]

Now, ideas are not innate, as book 1 of the *Essay* is intended to prove. How then do we learn the proper association between words and the ideas for which they stand, and which we share with those to whom we speak? Locke admits that "men stand not usually to examine, whether the idea they, and those they discourse with have in their minds be the same: but think it enough that they use the word, as they imagine, in the common acceptance of that language; in which they suppose that the idea they make it a sign of is precisely the same to which the understanding men of that country apply the name" (*Essay*, 3.2.4). How do we come to learn these "significations," the meanings of words "in the common acceptance" of our language? Before we can deal with Locke's account of language learning, there is a prior question, namely, How do we acquire the ideas themselves? After a brief discussion of ideas, we can ask how we learn to associate them with the words which signify them.

Locke's Account of the Origin of Ideas

Ideas precede language in the human understanding. The ideas themselves, starting from the very beginning of the life of a human being, come, as Locke says, "in one word, from EXPERIENCE" (*Essay*, 2.1.2). This experience he divides into two parts, sensation and reflection. Our senses "convey into the mind several distinct perceptions of things, according to those various ways wherein those objects do affect them. And thus we come by those *ideas* we have of *yellow, white, heat, cold, soft, hard, bitter, sweet,* and all those which we call sensible qualities" (*Essay*, 2.1.3).[15] The other source of ideas is our own mental operations which, "when the soul comes to reflect on and consider" them, "do furnish the understanding with another set of ideas, which could not be had from things without. And such are *perception, thinking, doubting,*

believing, reasoning, knowing, willing, and all the different actings
of our own minds . . ." (*Essay,* 2.1.4). These two taken together,
"when we have taken a full survey of them, and their several
modes, combinations, and relations, we shall find to contain all our
whole stock of ideas; and that we have nothing in our minds which
did not come in one of these two ways" (*Essay,* 2.1.5).[16]

Immediately after his discussion of "ideas in general, and their
origin" in the first chapter of book 2, Locke introduces a crucial
distinction. Chapter 2 opens with this sentence: "The better to
understand the nature, manner, and extent of our knowledge, one
thing is carefully to be observed concerning the ideas we have; and
that is, that some of them are *simple* and some *complex*" (*Essay,*
2.2.1). We have already been given some examples of what Locke
means by simple ideas, in the discussion of experience as the source
of all our ideas. But now he elaborates further.

> Though the qualities that affect our senses are, in the things
> themselves, so united and blended, that there is no separation,
> no distance between them; yet it is plain, the ideas they produce
> in the mind enter by the senses simple and unmixed. For, though
> the sight and touch often take in from the same object, at the
> same time, different ideas;—as a man sees at once motion and
> color; the hand feels softness and warmth in the same piece of
> wax: yet the simple ideas thus united in the same subject, are
> as perfectly distinct as those that come in by different senses.
> The coldness and hardness which a man feels in a piece of ice
> being as distinct ideas in the mind as the smell and whiteness of
> a lily; or as the taste of sugar, and smell of a rose. And there is
> nothing can be plainer to a man than the clear and distinct per-
> ception he has of those simple ideas; which, being each in itself
> uncompounded, contains in it nothing but *one uniform appear-
> ance, or conception in the mind,* and is not distinguishable into
> different ideas. [*Essay,* 2.2.1]

The most important fact about simple ideas is that, in dealing
with them, the understanding "is merely passive; and whether or
no it will have these beginnings, and as it were materials of
knowledge, is not in its own power" (*Essay,* 2.1.25).[17] These, then,
are the bedrock of our mental processes, the raw materials which
are "given," and with which we can operate. They are "furnished to

Language, Signification,
                                                              and Meaning

the mind" by experience only, and "it is not in the power of the most exalted wit, or enlarged understanding, by any quickness or variety of thought, to *invent* or *frame* one new simple idea in the mind, not taken in by the ways before mentioned: nor can any force of the understanding *destroy* those that are there" (*Essay*, 2.2.2). We can now see that the foundation for Locke's claim that men share the same ideas is his understanding that, at the most basic level, where the mind gets the first ideas with which it can operate, the human understanding is entirely passive.

We must distinguish between the ordering of ideas in the understanding and the order in which these ideas come to us in our experience as human beings. Locke's simple ideas, in other words, though they constitute the building blocks out of which all our complex ideas are made, do not appear to us as "simple ideas" in first experience. Yellow or white, warm or soft, appear to us in combination with other ideas. We experience, in sensation, particular things as mixtures or combinations of sensory qualities. The nineteenth-century editor of the *Essay*, Alexander Campbell Fraser, comments in a note that "in distinguishing *simple* from *complex* ideas Locke does not assert that the former are, or can be, received, or represented, *in their simplicity*; nor does he deny that a 'simple' idea of sense, *as such*, is an abstraction from our actual experience." The simple ideas, in Fraser's words, "are 'simple' in the sense of being incapable of analysis, while all complex ideas can be analysed."[18] The distinction Locke draws between simple and complex ideas is an analytical distinction.

Our ideas, then, can all be traced to the simple ideas which we receive passively and which, in a multitude of combinations, account for the complex ideas they comprise. It remains to be seen how we learn to attach words, or "names," to ideas. We experience the world first in a series of sensations of particular things. "All things that exist being particulars, it may perhaps be thought reasonable that words, which ought to conform to things, should be so too,—I mean in their signification: but yet we find quite the contrary. The far greatest part of words that make all languages are general terms: which has not been the effect of neglect or chance, but of reason and necessity" (*Essay*, 3.3.1). Languages are not made up primarily of proper nouns, in other words. This fact, which

Language, Signification, and Meaning

seems to strike Locke initially as peculiar, is explained by several reasons. According to Locke's account in the previous book, "The use of words then being to stand as outward marks of our internal ideas, and those ideas being taken from particular things, if every particular idea that we take in should have a distinct name, names must be endless" (*Essay*, 2.11.9). Aside from this "practical" difficulty, however, there is a problem which is more serious philosophically. If only particular things had names, Locke points out, language would be useless, or there would be no language (see below, pp. 109–10). The reason is this. The end of language is that men may "communicate their thoughts." This can only happen when, "by use or consent, the sound I make by the organs of speech, excites in another man's mind who hears it, the idea I apply it to in mine, when I speak it. This cannot be done by names applied to particular things; whereof I alone having the ideas in my mind, the names of them could not be significant or intelligible to another, who was not acquainted with all those very particular things which had fallen under my notice" (*Essay*, 3.3.3). If a language consisted only of proper names, apparently, men could not know whether they shared the same ideas. But what about simple ideas, which, according to the above account, *are* shared by all men? The difficulty is resolved by Locke's explanation of the process by which we arrive at general terms.

Abstraction and Naming

"Words become general," Locke explains, "by being made the signs of general ideas: and ideas become general by separating from them the circumstances of time and place, and any other ideas that may determine them to this or that particular existence" (*Essay*, 3.3.6). An almost identical account of this process can be found in book 2:

> This is called ABSTRACTION, whereby ideas taken from particular beings become general representatives of all of the same kind; and their names general names, applicable to whatever exists conformable to such abstract ideas. Such precise, naked appearances in the mind, without considering how, whence, or with what others they came there, the understanding lays up (with names commonly annexed to them) as the standards to

Language, Signification, and Meaning

rank real existences into sorts, as they agree with these patterns, and to denominate them accordingly. Thus the same color being observed to-day in chalk or snow, which the mind yesterday received from milk, it considers that appearance alone, makes it a representative of all of that kind; and having given it the name *whiteness*, it by that sound signifies the same quality wheresoever to be imagined or met with; and thus universals, whether ideas or terms, are made. [*Essay*, 2.11.9]

Since language itself rests on the creation of general terms by abstraction, it is clear that nothing at all can be communicated until we have performed that process. Yet it also appears that "whiteness"—which is a simple idea—cannot become an idea for us until we have abstracted it from other sensible qualities.[19] The recognition of simple ideas, or better, self-consciousness about our simple ideas, rests on the mental process called abstraction. Before we abstract, our ideas cannot be simple ideas but only particular ideas. Language is impossible without abstraction. Thus Locke can claim that simple ideas are the same for everyone, even though in order to speak or even think about them we need abstraction. When he says (as above) that without general terms our ideas "could not be significant or intelligible to another," he is not claiming that we need language in order to have ideas. He claims only that without general terms we cannot be understood at all, could not communicate even though we share the simple ideas, simply because we would not be able to establish *which* ideas names stand for.

This leads directly to the question of how we learn to abstract. Locke explains what abstraction is in book 2; in book 3 he undertakes "to trace our notions and names from their beginning, and observe by what degrees we proceed, and by what steps we enlarge our ideas from first infancy" (*Essay*, 3.3.7). But he never really tells us how we learn abstraction. He explains only how children begin to do it, but apparently we are to assume that the "faculty" of abstraction is natural or inherent. We do not learn to abstract, we simply abstract:

There is nothing more evident, than that the ideas of the persons children converse with (to instance in them alone) are, like the persons themselves, only particular. The ideas of the nurse and mother are well framed in their minds; and, like pictures of them there, represent only those individuals. The names they first gave to them are confined to these individuals; and the names of *nurse* and *mamma*, the child uses, determine themselves to those persons. Afterwards, when time and a larger acquaintance have made them observe that there are a great many other things in the world, that in some common agreements of shape, and several other qualities, resemble their father and mother, and those persons they have been used to, they frame an idea, which they find those many particulars do partake in; and to that they give, with others, the name *man*, for example. And thus they come to have a general name, and a general idea. Wherein they make nothing new; but only leave out of the complex idea they had of Peter and James, Mary and Jane, that which is peculiar to each, and retain only what is common to them all. [*Essay*, 3.3.7]

Although Locke notes that this process is characteristic of both language learning and what he calls "mental discourse" generally, he does not claim that language and thought are necessarily connected.[20] Because of his understanding of words as signs which "stand for" ideas, Locke can imagine someone abstracting general ideas without ever having a language or communicating his ideas to others.[21]

Not only do humans share the faculty of abstraction, but, as Locke is at pains to show, it is the possession of this faculty of abstraction which distinguishes human beings from brutes. "Whatever rudimentary mental faculties beasts have," writes Locke, "this, I think, I may be positive in,—that the power of abstracting is not at all in them; and that the having of general ideas is that which puts a perfect distinction betwixt man and brutes, and is an excellency which the faculties of brutes do by no means attain to" (*Essay*, 2.11.10). Brutes, we may say, have ideas in the primitive sense: their senses allow them to distinguish odors or colors, or a master from others, just as a growing child "begins to know the objects which, being most familiar with it, have made lasting impressions" and thus "comes by degrees to know the persons it daily converses with, and distinguishes them from strangers; which are instances and effects of its coming to retain and distinguish the ideas the senses convey to it" (*Essay*, 2.1.22). Considered in this light, brutes and children alike can be said to have ideas, but only

Language, Signification,
and Meaning

experientially, that is, from particulars and not by abstraction. It is the faculty of abstraction which distinguishes the human understanding. Just as the passivity of the mind in experience is the guarantee that all men have the same simple ideas, it is the faculty of abstraction, also shared, which permits men to think and speak.

Complex Ideas and Definitions

Let us return to the question in light of which we embarked on this inquiry into Locke's thought. We wished to discover how we learn "significations," or the meanings of words "in the common acceptance" of our language (see above, p. 51). Words stand for ideas. Ideas have been distinguished in two ways. First, Locke distinguishes ideas into particular and general. This is necessary in order to square his account of our experience with our capacity for language, since language is mostly general, whereas experience is all "of particular things." The latter fact, namely, that we experience only particulars, makes necessary Locke's second distinction. By this distinction, we have simple ideas and complex ideas. Only the fact that the mind is passive in receiving simple ideas guarantees that men share the same ideas simply.

Simple ideas are received in combinations or groups. Although the simple ideas which make up something like gold, that is, "yellowness, great weight, ductility, fusibility, and solubility in *aqua regia*, &c." (*Essay*, 2.23.37), are experienced by our senses separately, the understanding is accustomed to experiencing them together, and consequently combines them into one complex idea.[22] The mind, as Locke says, "has a power to consider several [simple ideas] united together as one idea; and that not only as they are united in external objects, but as itself has joined them together" (*Essay*, 2.12.1). That is, the mind makes the complex idea, either from simple ideas which appear together, as when they come from an external object, or in some combination which is arbitrary. "Ideas thus made up of several simple ones put together, I call *complex*;—such as are beauty, gratitude, a man, an army, the universe; which, though complicated of various simple ideas, or complex ideas made up of simple ones, yet are, *when the mind pleases*, considered each by itself, as one entire thing, and signified by one name" (*Essay*, 2.12.1; emphasis added). Locke notes that all our ideas are founded on simple ideas in this way: "All those sublime thoughts which tower above the clouds, and reach as high as heaven itself, take their use and footing here ..." (*Essay*, 2.1.24). The mind, despite its "great power in varying and multiplying the objects of its thoughts," must always start from simple ideas because "the mind *can* have no more, nor other than what are suggested to it" (*Essay*, 2.12.2). "But when it has once got these simple ideas, it is not confined barely to observation, and what offers itself from without; it can, by its own power, put together those ideas it has, and make new complex ones, which it never received so united" (*Essay*, 2.12.2). The mind can form, on its own, complex ideas, in addition to the complex ideas which come to it naturally. The latter, which are ideas of particular things in the world which always present the same combination of simple ideas, Locke calls complex ideas of *substances*. The former sort of complex ideas are called *mixed modes*.

We are now in a position to see the basis of Locke's claim that words stand for ideas, and his certainty that if we used words properly, they would stand for the same "clear and distinct" ideas for each of us. As he puts it, "definition being nothing but making another understand by words what idea the term defined stands for, a definition is best made by enumerating those simple ideas that are combined in the signification of the term defined ..." (*Essay*, 3.3.10). This understanding is presented by Locke in direct opposition to the classical Aristotelian understanding of a definition, and will be examined by us again when we turn to Aristotle. As far as Locke is concerned, enumerating the simple ideas which make up a complex one is the best definition, "and if, instead of such a definition, men have accustomed themselves to use the next general term, it has not been out of necessity, or for greater clearness, but for quickness and dispatch sake" (*Essay*, 3.3.10).

On Locke's view of language, the simplest and most primitive language is the key to understanding all language, just as the simple ideas are the key to "all those sublime thoughts which tower above the clouds." We understand the higher in terms of the lower, the sublime thought in terms of the building blocks of which it is comprised. It is easy to see why, on this view, most arguments and difficulties ought to be capable of resolution by careful definitions, "the greatest part of the questions and controversies that perplex mankind depending on the doubtful and uncertain use of words, or (which is the same) indetermined ideas, which they are made to stand for" (*Essay*, Epistle to the Reader).

It remains for us to examine in more detail Locke's division of complex ideas into *mixed modes* and *substances*.[23] The names which signify these types of complex ideas, Locke says, "have each of them something peculiar and different from the other" (*Essay*, 3.4.1). Mixed modes, according to Locke's account, are complex ideas which "contain not in them the supposition of subsisting by themselves" (*Essay*, 2.12.4). "Such are the complex ideas we mark by the names *obligation, drunkenness*, a *lie*, &c.; which consisting of several combinations of simple ideas of *different* kinds, I have called mixed modes.... These mixed modes, being also such combinations of simple ideas as are not looked upon to be characteristical marks of any real beings that have a steady existence, but scattered and independent ideas put together by the mind, are thereby distinguished from the complex ideas of sub-stances" (*Essay*, 2.22.1). We might put this in other words thus: the ideas for those things which exist independently of men—trees, bears, rocks, water, gold—are substances; the ideas of those things whose existence depends in some sense upon men, such as com-monwealth, justice, or philosophy, are "mixed modes." (There is some ambiguity here still: tables are made by men, but have substance because they are made from wood. The status of such ideas is not perfectly clear.)

Substances, by contrast, are complex ideas of those "things" which "exist."[24] Locke explains as follows:

> If any one should be asked, what is the subject wherein colour or weight inheres, he would have nothing to say, but the solid extended parts; and if he were demanded, what is it that solidity and extension adhere in, he would not be in a much better case than the Indian ... who, saying that the world was supported by a great elephant, was asked what the elephant rested on; to which his answer was—a great tortoise: but being again pressed to know what gave support to the broad-backed tortoise, re-plied—*something, he knew not what*.... The idea then we have,

Language, Signification, and Meaning

to which we give the *general* name substance, being nothing but the supposed, but unknown, support of those qualities we find existing. [*Essay*, 2.23.2]

The complex ideas called substances can never be perfectly known, because they are collections of simple ideas which we must discover; we have no control over the combination of sensible qualities "which we [are] used to find united in the thing called horse or stone" (*Essay*, 2.23.4), for example. The sensible qualities which belong to a particular substance like gold are not all known, because we may always discover new qualities by subjecting the substance to a new test. We do not decide the qualities of a substance, but instead we attempt to discover what they are.

The Conventionality of Mixed Modes

Locke distinguishes the "real essence" of ideas from their "nominal essence." Nominal essences are constituted by the abstract idea we *make* of something; if we know the idea of a man, as Locke says, we know the nominal essence of man. But the "real essence" is the "real internal, but generally (in substances) unknown constitution of things" (*Essay*, 3.3.15), that is, what a thing really is. The importance of this distinction may be seen by considering the fact that in complex ideas which we make, that is, in mixed modes, the nominal essence and the real essence "are always the same; but in substances always quite different" (*Essay*, 3.3.18). We can know the essence, both real and nominal, of the idea of a mixed mode, simply because it is a construction of the mind.[25] In this Locke follows Hobbes. "Thus, a figure including a space between three lines, is the real as well as nominal essence of a triangle; it being not only the abstract idea to which the general name is annexed, but the very *essentia* or being of the thing itself" (*Essay*, 3.3.18). "But it is far otherwise," notes Locke, "concerning that parcel of matter which makes the ring on my finger; wherein these two essences are apparently different" (ibid.). Since we cannot know the real essence of substances, we cannot achieve the same sort of clarity in our knowledge of substances; we must settle for a sort of progressive approximation of complete knowledge. Our knowledge of the physical or natural world will necessarily be less perfect than our knowledge of the human world simply because the real essence of that natural world is inaccessible to us. In the final book of his *Essay*, in a chapter devoted to an exploration of "the extent of human knowledge," Locke notes, "We shall do no injury to our knowledge, when we modestly think with ourselves, that we are so far from being able to comprehend the whole nature of the universe, and all the things contained in it, that *we are not capable of a philosophical knowledge of the bodies that are about us, and make a part of us*: concerning their secondary qualities,[26] powers, and operations, we can have no universal certainty" (*Essay*, 4.3.29; emphasis added).

We create by construction the ideas of mixed modes. Consequently, the standard by which to measure the knowledge of a mixed mode is within us; whereas simple ideas, as Locke says, "are perfectly taken from the existence of things, and are not arbitrary at all" (*Essay*, 3.4.17). The names of mixed modes, by contrast, "stand for ideas perfectly arbitrary; those of substances are not perfectly so, but refer to a pattern, though with some latitude" (ibid.). Ideas of substances, that is, must conform to some degree with what exists in nature; there is a natural standard. "The mind, in making its complex ideas of substances, only follows nature; and puts none together which are not supposed to have a union in nature" (*Essay*, 3.4.28). To violate or ignore the standard nature offers here would be not only foolish but disastrous.

> Men observing certain qualities always joined and existing together, therein copied nature; and of ideas so united made their complex ones of substances. For, though men make what complex ideas they please, and give what names to them they will; yet, if they will be understood *when they speak of things really existing*, they must in some degree conform their ideas to the things they would speak of; or else men's language will be like that of Babel. [*Essay*, 3.6.28]

We seek to discover more about the nature of plants or rocks, and by this means to improve the accuracy of our ideas about the substances we investigate. Our idea of gold must conform to what nature presents as gold: thus we test to see at what temperature

Language, Signification,
and Meaning

gold melts; we do not decide on our own. We seek continually to make our idea of a substance a more faithful copy of the natural arrangement of qualities.

Now, if the complex ideas of substances are only partly conventional because of the existence of standards in nature, the ideas called mixed modes are radically conventional. They are "not only made by the mind, but *made very arbitrarily, made without patterns, or reference to* any real existence." The mind does not, with regard to ideas of mixed modes, "verify them by patterns containing such peculiar compositions in nature. To know whether his idea of *adultery* or *incest* be right, will a man seek it anywhere amongst things existing? Or is it true because any one has been witness to such an action? No: but it suffices here, that men have put together such a collection into one complex idea, that makes the archetype and specific idea; whether ever any such action were committed *in rerum natura* or no" (*Essay*, 3.5.3). We know whether we have the right idea of incest, or parricide, or justice (to use some of Locke's most common examples), not by checking our idea against any standard in nature, but by asking someone else to list the simple ideas which together are signified by that name. The fact that they are arbitrary, says Locke, may be established by the fact that such ideas may be "made, abstracted, and have names given them" before any example of the idea actually existed or occurred (*Essay*, 3.5.5). The ideas are constructed by the mind for convenience only, in the sense that we may wish to communicate a set of simple ideas together many times, and so we tag them as a group, a complex idea. Thus we single out one type of murder, the murder of a father, and call it parricide, while leaving many other equally particular sorts of murder unnamed. It is "perfectly evident," Locke writes, that "the mind searches not its patterns in nature . . . but puts such together as may best serve its own purposes" (*Essay*, 3.5.6). Further proof of the conventionality of mixed modes is supplied by the fact that such complex ideas are different from one society to another, from one language to another, "which plainly shows that those of one country, by their customs and manner of life, have found occasion to make several complex ideas, and given names to them, which others never collected into specific ideas." The cultural relativism implied in this view is made much stronger by Locke a few sentences later. "Nay," he writes, "if we look a little more nearly into this matter, and exactly compare different languages, we shall find that, though they have words which in translations and dictionaries are supposed to answer to one another, yet there is scarce one of ten amongst the names of complex ideas, especially of mixed modes, that stands for the same precise idea which the word does that in dictionaries it is rendered by" (*Essay*, 3.5.8). Moreover, after using the example of the most conventional of conventions, namely, weights and measures, Locke goes so far as to claim that, although weights and measures differ indeed, "we shall find this much more so in the names of more abstract and compounded ideas, *such as are the greatest part of those which make up moral discourses*" (*Essay*, 3.5.8; emphasis added). How is it, then, that Locke is also the most famous and influential theorist of natural law?

Now, the first man who framed any given complex idea, and gave it a name, did so for convenience in repeating the set of simple ideas of which it consists, or communicating it to another (*Essay*, 3.5.15). The combination of ideas or the complex idea preceded the name. But it is common for us, since we inherit a language, so to speak, to learn names before or at least at the same time as the ideas. This fact, together with the often very great complexity of these mixed modes, makes for confusion and obscurity in the mind of someone learning a new idea of this sort. Learning the meaning of a "name," as Locke notes, "is the hardest to be done where, First, The ideas they stand for are very complex, and made up of a great number of ideas put together. Secondly, Where the ideas they stand for have no certain connexion in nature; and so no settled standard anywhere in nature existing, to rectify and adjust them by" (*Essay*, 3.9.5). Since names of mixed modes signify ideas which exist only in the understanding, the signification of such words will "be often various in the minds of different men" (*Essay*, 3.9.7). A child learning the language is told the meanings of the names he is taught. This is simple enough, according to Locke, when the names stand for things and ideas like white, sweet, milk, sugar, cat, or dog. "But as for mixed modes, especially the most material of them, *moral words*, the sounds are usually learned first; and then, to know what complex ideas they stand for, they are either beholden

Language, Signification,
and Meaning

to the explication of others, or (which happens for the most part) are left to their own observation and industry; which being little laid out in the search of the true and precise meaning of names, these moral words are in most men's mouths little more than bare sounds; or when they have any, it is for the most part but a very loose and indetermined, and, consequently, obscure and confused signification" (*Essay*, 3.9.9). Although we might hope that common usage would regulate the meanings of such words, and indeed to some extent "the rule of propriety" does accomplish this, its power is not sufficient for any more than restricting meanings to the rough degree needed in common conversation. Unfortunately, "nobody having an authority to establish the precise signification of words, nor determine to what ideas any one shall annex them," there is no regulation adequate to "Philosophical Discourses." Mixed modes are, then, constitutionally "liable to this imperfection, to be of doubtful and uncertain signification" (*Essay*, 3.9.8).

As if this natural defect in moral words were not sufficient in itself to make true understanding very difficult, such words are susceptible, in addition, to intentional misuse. They are subject to "willful faults and neglect," by means of which men "render these signs less clear and distinct in their signification than naturally they need to be" (*Essay*, 3.10.1). It is not necessary for us here to catalog the problems Locke raises in this respect, except to say that he points to what he considers a particularly vicious abuse in the "inconstancy" of use. "Words being intended for signs of my ideas, to make them known to others, not by any natural signification, but by voluntary imposition, it is plain cheat and abuse, when I make them stand sometimes for one thing and sometimes for another" (*Essay*, 3.10.5). The abuse may be intentional or simply the result of human laziness or vanity, as when men take words they have heard, and, "that they may not seem ignorant what they stand for, use them confidently, without much troubling their heads about a certain fixed meaning" (*Essay*, 3.10.4). Nevertheless, it is important to note that mixed modes are not entirely arbitrary for the individual person. One may not mean simply whatever he wants to by them; rather, the fact that Locke can speak of "abuse" and "neglect" implies that, while men are often sloppy in using

Language, Signification,
and Meaning

mixed modes, mixed modes do properly signify ideas which can be made clear.

The Possibility of a Political Science

It is the radical conventionality of mixed modes which leads to the obscurity and uncertainty which such ideas are prone to, because conventionality deprives us of any obvious standard for the right use of words. But the realization that moral words stand for strictly conventional complex ideas also opens us to a possibility of vast human importance. It leads us to realize that we are capable of a true moral science, of complete and perfect knowledge of moral matters and moral principles. This possibility reminds us of the claim advanced by Hobbes, that he was the founder of a truly scientific political science, the first true political philosophy. Locke and Hobbes agree on this point: it is possible, using the proper method, to construct a demonstrative science of justice and morality. This possibility exists because men make justice and all the ideas which we call moral ideas. For Locke as well as for Hobbes, the method of this science has at its foundations the procedure of definition. Since moral ideas are "combinations of several ideas that the mind of man has arbitrarily put together without reference to any archetypes, men may, if they please, know exactly the ideas that go to each composition, and so both use these words in a certain and undoubted signification, and perfectly declare, when there is occasion, what they stand for" (*Essay*, 3.11.15). Because moral words can be defined, says Locke, "I am bold to think that morality is capable of demonstration, as well as mathematics: since the precise real essence of the things moral words stand for may be perfectly known, and so the congruity and incongruity of the things themselves be certainly discovered; in which consists perfect knowledge" (*Essay*, 3.11.16). Discourses in morality can be "much more clear than those in natural philosophy" (*Essay*, 3.11.17). Morality itself, if properly grounded, might be placed "amongst the *sciences capable of demonstration*" (*Essay*, 4.3.18). "For certainty being but the perception of the agreement or disagreement of our ideas, and demonstration nothing but the perception of such

Language, Signification, and Meaning

agreement, by the intervention of other ideas or mediums; our moral ideas, as well as mathematical, being archetypes themselves, and so adequate and complete ideas; all the agreement or disagreement which we shall find in them will produce real knowledge, as well as in mathematical figures" (*Essay*, 4.4.7). Like Hobbes, Locke holds that the moral or political world is knowable to a greater degree than the natural world. We can understand the constituents of the political world perfectly because they are constructed by us, they are conventional and not natural.

It is far easier for men to frame in their minds an idea, which shall be the standard to which they will give the name justice; with which pattern so made, all actions that agree shall pass under that denomination, than, having seen Aristides, to frame an idea that shall in all things be exactly like him. For the one, they need but know the combination of ideas that are put together in their own minds; for the other, they must inquire into the whole nature, and abstruse hidden constitution, and various qualities of a thing existing without them. [*Essay*, 3.11.17]

Aristides the Just, according to Locke, is less knowable than the justice he dispensed, because he was part of the natural world, properly speaking, while his justice was conventional. The conventional character of moral and political terms does not, however, mean that they are arbitrary, according to Locke.

It is reasonable to suspect that Locke could not have failed to grasp the relativist implications of this view of language. Nevertheless he, like Hobbes, rejected them. This is most clearly seen, of course, in Locke's *Second Treatise of Government*, where Locke proceeds to derive principles of natural right from the facts of the state of nature. He understands the political principles he presents to be valid for men in all times and places, because they follow from that condition "all men are naturally in," that is, the state which is *natural* to all human beings (*Second Treatise*, 2.4). However corrupt and confused the meanings of moral and political terms in common usage, it is possible, according to Locke, to discover in human nature a standard which tells us what the minimum content of moral and political terms should be. Locke joins Hobbes in the claim that the starting point for this enterprise cannot be what men say in common speech. The scientific determination of the meaning of political terms must proceed by penetrating beneath common speech, by looking directly at the nature of human beings uncomplicated by their beliefs and opinions about why they do what they do.[27]

The question we must begin from, according to Locke, is why men construct the ideas called mixed modes. As he has shown,[28] men construct them for *convenience*. What is useful is connected with what one needs. Now, if we can determine what the real or natural human needs are, as distinguished from spurious needs which men may think or say they have, we can decide what conventional concepts they should have constructed. That is, in order to determine with accuracy the "natural" meanings of conventional mixed modes such as justice or sovereignty, we need to analyze human needs—empirically—down to their foundations. We will then be in a position to construct a science which gives us the meanings of the "conventional" terms of politics and morality. This means that our first requirement is an empirical study of human psychology, a study which analyzes human nature. An uncompromising focus on this human nature, as Locke holds in the *Second Treatise*, will show that human beings stripped of social conventions are radically individual seekers of property. This (together with nature's niggardliness) is all that is required to derive the fundamental principles of justice and social organization.

Although Locke departs from Hobbes in the content of his political philosophy, his method—the approach of imagining the construction of society from the elements themselves, and ignoring what men say—is identical with Hobbes's resolutive-compositive method. It thus attempts to supply a standard from nature for the admittedly conventional meanings of political terms, or mixed modes.

We are compelled to admit, on Locke's view, that clarity about political phenomena depends on our recovering or discovering the true meanings of the terms, the meanings thought of by the first namers or else ordained by nature.[29] This is only possible for us by means of a reconstruction in speech of the original situation in which such terms were first needed—that is, the state of nature. In order to discover the meanings of the political terms as they must originally have come into being, it was necessary to strip from man

Language, Signification, and Meaning

the merely conventional attributes which had been covering over his fundamental nature. According to Hobbes, at least, the state of nature reveals the basic drive of man to be self-preservation, which follows from the absolutely primary fact, which is the fear of violent death. Self-preservation is thus understood by Hobbes to be the one Right of Nature, "which Writers commonly call *Jus Naturale*" (*Leviathan*, chap. 14, p. 189). Once this is understood, it is possible to derive all the moral commands, or "natural laws," from that fundamental drive. Although Locke's state of nature is different from that envisioned by Hobbes, the two have at least one thing in common, namely, the method of deriving all moral and political principles from one primary natural law. In Locke's case this law is stated as follows: "Every one . . . when his own preservation comes not in competition, ought . . . as much as he can, to preserve the rest of mankind, and may not, unless it be to do justice to an offender, take away or impair the life, or what tends to the preservation of the life, the liberty, health, limb, or goods of another" (*Second Treatise*, 2.6).

Another question arises here. Why is it, if men have these natural needs, that they have not before now determined what the needs are? If the terms for mixed modes were invented for convenience, and based on natural needs, why haven't men managed to invent them properly? Have the ambiguity and confusion now so rife crept into their concepts, or were the concepts wrong from the start? Locke, like Hobbes, seems to think that the concepts were not corrupted so much as misconceived from the beginning—because men did not understand themselves or their true needs. Their vision was obscured above all by their pride, which caused them to miss seeing that they were in need, that nature did not provide bountifully, that their true condition was severe if not desperate. Out of pride, men told themselves that "God has given us all things richly" (1 Tim. 6:17), as Locke points out (*Second Treatise*, 5.31). But in the next section, Locke continues: "God, when he gave the world in common to all mankind, commanded man also to labor, and the penury of his condition required it of him." That is, had men understood the scriptures properly (or not been misled), their true neediness would have been apparent to them. Knowing their true needs, which Locke now shows them,

Language, Signification,
and Meaning

men can accurately determine the mixed modes (what justice means, for example) which will serve them properly.

There is a problem with this understanding, however. Not everyone agreed either with Hobbes or with Locke as to what constitutes the fundamental drive: Rousseau is the most famous thinker, but not the only one, to claim that Hobbes did not go far enough back to reveal the true state of nature, and thus was mistaken in thinking he had uncovered the fundamental drive. Where Hobbes and Locke were certain that the bedrock for a true science of politics had been exposed, those who came after were less sanguine. The certain and compelling political science of such terms as justice, obligation, virtue, or courage no longer seemed imminent: the meanings of such terms stubbornly resisted scientific clarification.

Conclusion

We have seen how the understanding of language in question here leads to a separation of knowledge into two realms: knowledge of what men construct themselves (mixed modes) and hence can know perfectly, and knowledge of those things in nature (substances) of which men can have only approximate knowledge. That this separation, accomplished philosophically by Hobbes and Locke, has had a profound impact on the modern world is obvious enough. Indeed, we should note that Hobbes and Locke did not "accomplish" the split by themselves; they participated along with many others in the process we now describe as the "emergence of modern science." But it is important for us to examine the philosophical roots of the split we are here speaking of, for the following reason. Hobbes and Locke did not succeed in creating— nor has anyone else—a successful moral science of the sort for which they thought they had laid the foundations. The reasons for this fact are important. But if Hobbes and Locke were unsuccessful in their hope, they nevertheless took the decisive step of establishing the split between the natural world and the world of human constructs on an epistemological footing. This footing is inextricably linked with a certain understanding of the way language works.

Language, Signification,
and Meaning

Although the classics of course recognized the distinction between the natural and the conventional, they did not claim what Hobbes and Locke asserted, namely, that we can truly know only the conventional, because we make it. This split was accomplished in the hope that a true and certain science of moral terms was a possibility. This hope has today all but disappeared. But the split itself, once it was a *fait accompli*, left whatever knowledge of the human world we did possess exposed to the erosion of subjectivism. Once men discovered that they could not define, with "clear and distinct ideas," the moral and political terms, the vision of language elaborated by Hobbes and Locke held them trapped: cut off from the possibility of partial, or approximate, or uncertain knowledge of justice, they could see only that justice must be defined by each user, or at most by each culture or historical epoch. Eventually this led to the conclusion that use of the word "justice" is subjective, and not subject to correction according to any standard either natural or conventional. Staking everything on the possibility of a clear and distinct definition meant that, with the gradual realization that no such definitions are possible in moral speech, because they can never be agreed upon, we have been left with nothing but "value words." If we know only what we ourselves construct, we now realize that we cannot know moral terms because we never really "make" them the way Locke explained. And attempts to "remake" them have not been successful. This does not, of course, prove that Locke was mistaken. It may be, rather, that the task of analyzing human nature is so difficult that we have barely begun. In that case Locke is guilty only of being too optimistic. It appears in any case that if Hobbes and Locke are correct in their understanding of knowledge, the imperatives of the resolutive-compositive method, and the necessity of reconstructing common speech, are unavoidable. Nevertheless, we must wonder whether the whole project is properly understood.

Is there any philosophically respectable alternative to this conclusion? There is of course the alternative Hobbes rejected, when his effort to think through the problem of what knowledge is led him to believe that the classical thinkers had taken too much for granted. But it would appear that to consider seriously the classical approach to the political universe, we would in turn have to break

Language, Signification,
and Meaning

with Hobbes's understanding of science and of knowledge, and the account of language which that understanding entails. Is it possible to do this?

The classical thinkers appeared to Hobbes to have sought a definition of justice, but to have begun incorrectly because they started from common opinions about what justice is, from what men say about justice, instead of rejecting ambiguous ordinary speech and penetrating beneath it. There is no denying that they did not reach satisfactory definitions. We may, however, entertain the possibility that their search for the meaning of justice was not a search for a definition in Hobbes's sense. That would mean that they did not agree with Hobbes as to what knowledge is, that is, about the relationship between naming (language) and knowledge. An alternative understanding of knowledge is indicated.

In seeking to know what justice is, one might say provisionally that the classics sought not a definition in Hobbes's sense, but rather an understanding of the place of justice in the human world, of the relation between justice and the family, the relation of justice to survival, to education, to punishment, and so on. Perhaps the classical thinkers inquired into the nature of justice in a way different from Hobbes's because they understood there to be more kinds of knowledge than Hobbes accepts. The goal of understanding the place of justice in human life would permit or even require that we begin, not by denying common speech or what men say, but by considering various ordinary opinions about it, opinions reflecting a variety of situations in which justice is relevant. Of course, the understanding which results—what classical thinkers might have called knowledge—would not be characterized by geometric certainty, and would not fulfill Hobbes's criteria of science or knowledge. Thus to reject Hobbes's and Locke's understanding of political science requires, at least, a different view of knowledge. On the other hand, if words do stand for certain ideas or conceptions in the way Hobbes and Locke said, we cannot deny their conclusion about what knowledge is. To avoid their conclusions we would need a different understanding of language, of how words have meanings and how we use them.

Now, perhaps we need to consider what Hobbes rejected. But neither Plato nor Aristotle gives anywhere a systematic account of

Language, Signification,
and Meaning

language.[30] It was perhaps this fact which led Hobbes to believe that they had failed to probe to the core of human knowledge or science and, as a result, had been overly careless in their standards for knowledge. The failure of the classics to supply a systematic account of language would thus seem to foredoom any serious attempt to recall their approach to understanding the political world. To do so would be to take a step backwards, to become *less* sophisticated in our thinking.

However, there is another alternative which poses a challenge to Hobbes's understanding of language and the account of human knowledge and political science based on it. It is that of Ludwig Wittgenstein, which we will explore in the next two chapters. It remains to be seen whether Wittgenstein's understanding leads us to a political science which resembles that of the classics, or to some third alternative, distinct from those of both Hobbes and his predecessors.

Language, Signification,
and Meaning

4

Wittgenstein's "Philosophical Investigations" A Critique of the Commonsense Notion of Language

Locke's picture of language was not original with him. Perhaps because of its powerful appeal to common sense, it has been a starting point for philosophical inquiries for centuries. It was not unknown to the classical thinkers.[1] And, in different form, it can be seen as the basis of Wittgenstein's *Tractatus Logico-Philosophicus* in this century. Wittgenstein is of particular interest to us here. Rare among philosophers, he profoundly changed his thought about language, though not his approach to philosophy, when he returned to philosophy after a break of more than a decade.[2] Wittgenstein became profoundly dissatisfied with the philosophy to which his early understanding of language had led him as a young man. Although we will not deal in detail with the understanding of language as presented in the *Tractatus*, it is necessary to consider it briefly. In the *Tractatus* Wittgenstein asserts that the propositions of which language consists are actually pictures of reality, of states of affairs in the world.[3] The truth or falsity of a proposition consists in agreement or disagreement between the state of affairs it pictures and the actual state of affairs. According to Wittgenstein, "in a proposition a name is the representative of an object," that is, words or names "stand for" things.[4] It is necessary to add that Wittgenstein asserted that all meaningful language consists of propositions. (He writes, "My *whole* task consists in explaining the nature of the proposition" [*Notebooks*, p. 39].) Thus, "Most of the propositions and questions to be found in philosophical works are not false but nonsensical" (*Tractatus*, 4.003). Despite numerous differences between this and Hobbes's picture of language, the two understandings have in common the idea that words or names "stand for" something (conceptions or objects), and the notion that much if not most of everyday language is obscure and confused. For Wittgenstein the truth of a proposition consisted in its accurate representation of reality, which required that we fix exactly *what* each sign or name "stands for"; for Hobbes or Locke, the truth of a proposition results from its expressing in symbols true relationships among the conceptions which, we have stipulated, the symbols represent.

We will focus here on Wittgenstein's later work, the *Philosophical Investigations*. This work contains, as he says in the Preface, "the precipitate of philosophical investigations which have occupied me for the last sixteen years." The *Investigations* present Wittgenstein's mature understanding of language.[5] It begins by considering one form of the commonsense picture of language, with a view to exposing its defectiveness. The first paragraph presents a passage from Augustine's *Confessions*, in which Augustine describes his learning of language. As we will see, that understanding is virtually identical with the understanding of language in Locke's *Essay concerning Human Understanding*. The first sixty-five paragraphs of Wittgenstein's *Investigations* are a development and treatment of precisely the problem of language that we are trying to unravel.

The Inadequacy of the Commonsense Picture

The *Investigations* opens, without any preparation, with a paragraph from Augustine in Latin. It is translated into English as follows:

When they (my elders) named some object, and accordingly moved towards something, I saw this and I grasped that the thing was called by the sound they uttered when they meant to point it out. Their intention was shewn by their bodily movements, as it were the natural language of all peoples: the expression of the face, the play of the eyes, the movement of other parts of the body, and the tone of voice which expresses our state of mind in seeking, having, rejecting, or avoiding something. Thus, as I heard words repeatedly used in their proper places in various sentences, I gradually learnt to understand what objects they signified; and after I had trained my mouth to form these signs, I used them to express my own desires. [From Augustine, *Confessions*, 1.8, quoted in *PI*, 1, 1]

"These words, it seems to me, give us a particular picture of the essence of human language" (*PI*, 1, 1). Wittgenstein characterizes Augustine's picture of language this way: "The individual words in language name objects—sentences are combinations of such names. ——In this picture of language we find the roots of the following idea: Every word has a meaning. This meaning is correlated with the word. It is the object for which the word stands" (*PI*, 1, 1). This picture of language had been worked into a sophisticated form by Wittgenstein in his earlier philosophical work, as we noted above, but here he subjects it to a critical scrutiny. "If you describe the learning of language in this way you are, I believe, thinking primarily of nouns like 'table', 'chair', 'bread', and of people's names, and only secondarily of the names of certain actions and properties; and of the remaining kinds of word as something that will take care of itself" (*PI*, 1, 1). Later he describes this as having a "one-sided diet of examples," to which he attributes many philosophical perplexities. His is an open, tentative method, raising questions by posing examples and counterexamples in a kind of argument with himself, and examining these examples to see what they teach without trying to fit them into a preconceived picture.

Does language really work the way Augustine pictures it? Wittgenstein begins his investigations by thinking up a fairly simple and commonplace use of language where the picture does not seem to fit. Let us follow Wittgenstein's investigation step by step, examining his examples and thinking along with him. He begins with the following:

Now think of the following use of language: I send someone shopping. I give him a slip marked "five red apples". He takes the slip to the shopkeeper, who opens the drawer marked "apples"; then he looks up the word "red" in a table and finds a color sample opposite it; then he says the series of cardinal numbers— I assume that he knows them by heart—up to the word "five" and for each number he takes an apple of the same color as the sample out of the drawer.——It is in this and similar ways that one operates with words.——'But how does he know where and how he is to look up the word 'red' and what he is to do with the word 'five'?"——Well, I assume that he *acts* as I have described. Explanations come to an end somewhere.—But what is the meaning of the word "five"?—No such thing was in question here, only how the word "five" is used. [*PI*, 1, 1]

Even so simple an example reveals a defect in the Augustinian or Lockean understanding of language. It reveals a problem in their claim that the meaning of each word is the object or mental conception or idea it stands for.[6] We don't see any object or idea which corresponds to or is signified by the word "five" in the example.[7] Rather, it seems to be related to an *action* of the shopkeeper, to something he *does*. But then how can the meaning of the word "five" be something it stands for? "That philosophical concept of meaning has its place in a primitive idea of the way language functions. But one can also say that it is the idea of a language more primitive than ours" (*PI*, 1, 2). Wittgenstein explores this by constructing an imaginary primitive language, one "for which the description given by Augustine is right." This imaginary language, he writes,

is meant to serve for communication between a builder A and an assistant B. A is building with building-stones: there are blocks, pillars, slabs, and beams. B has to pass the stones, and that in the order in which A needs them. For this purpose they use a language consisting of the words "block", "pillar", "slab", "beam". A calls them out,—B brings the stone which he has learnt to bring at such-and-such a call.——Conceive this as a complete primitive language. [*PI*, 1, 2]

Augustine's description of language, Wittgenstein goes on, is correct in part. Augustine does indeed "describe a system of communication: but not everything that we call language is this system" (*PI*, 1, 3). Augustine's examination of language is too restricted. "It is as if someone were to say: 'A game consists in moving objects about on a surface according to certain rules . . .'— and we replied: You seem to be thinking of board games, but there are others. You can make your definition correct by expressly restricting it to those games" (*PI*, 1, 3).

   Having satisfied himself that the Augustinian picture of language is misleading, Wittgenstein looks more closely at the primitive language he has constructed in imagination. How do its users get so they can speak it, or use it? We could imagine, he says, that this language "was the *whole* language of A and B; even the whole language of a tribe. The children are brought up to perform *these* actions, to use *these* words as they do so, and to react in *this* way to the words of others" (*PI*, 1, 6). We learn language in the context of human activities, and in particular in the activities where the language is used. The teaching of language, in this sense, "is not explanation, but training" (*PI*, 1, 5). This challenges our usual picture of a child being taught the meanings of words simply, independent of any but the teaching context itself. Wittgenstein realizes that such teaching does play some role in our language-learning. But he cannot accept learning the association of word and mental image as the *purpose* of even this sort of teaching. Part of the child's language training, as he says, "will consist in the teacher's pointing to the objects, directing the child's attention to them, and at the same time uttering a word; for instance, the word 'slab' as he points to that shape." Such "ostensive teaching" will produce some association "between the word and the thing." This may make us think that a picture of the object comes before the child's mind when it hears the word. And in fact this may occur. But in the language we have imagined, "it is *not* the purpose of the words to evoke images. (It may, of course, be discovered that that helps to attain the actual purpose.)" What Wittgenstein is seeking here is the meaning of "understanding," of what we mean when we say that the child understands the word "slab," for example. "Don't you understand the call 'Slab!' if you act upon it in such-and-such a way?—Doubtless the ostensive teaching helped to bring this about; but only together with a particular training. With different training the same ostensive teaching of these words would have effected a quite different understanding" (*PI*, 1, 6).

Our commonsense picture of words and meanings, the Lockean or Augustinian picture, looks only at the surface of things and assumes or ignores everything else. It is Wittgenstein's insight that that "everything else" is absolutely crucial in really understanding human language.[8] In the middle of these opening paragraphs of the *Investigations*, without preamble or explanation, we find Wittgenstein's distillation of this insight: " 'I set the brake up by connecting up rod and lever.'—Yes, given the whole of the rest of the mechanism. Only in connection with that is it a brake-lever, and separated from its support it is not even a lever; it may be anything, or nothing" (*PI*, 1, 6). What we do when we ignore the context of activities in which words are embedded is to take for granted "the whole of the rest of the mechanism." And the price we pay for this is to radically misconceive human language.

The Expanded Builder's Language and the Temptation to Reductionism

Wittgenstein next considers an expansion of the language of the builders, which makes it more complex. (He calls such a combination of activity and language a "language game," and we will explore this concept below.) In addition to the words "slab," "block," "pillar," and "beam," the expanded language is to include a series of words, the letters of the alphabet, to function as did the numerals of the shopkeeper in the first example. Besides numeral functions, he adds two words, "which may as well be 'there' and 'this' (because this roughly indicates their purpose), that are to be used in connexion with a pointing gesture" (*PI*, 1, 8). Finally, Wittgenstein adds to the language a set of color samples. The language comes to life in his description:

A gives an order like: "d—slab—there". At the same time he shews the assistant a colour sample, and when he says "there" he points to a place on the building site. From the stock of slabs B takes one for each letter of the alphabet up to "d", of the same colour as the sample, and brings them to the place indicated by A.—On

Wittgenstein's *Philosophical Investigations*

other occasions A gives the order "this—there". At "this" he points to a building stone. And so on. [*PI*, 1, 8]

After a brief discussion of how this language will be taught, Wittgenstein returns to the question with which he began, the question raised by Augustine's and Locke's understanding of language. "Now what do the words of this language *signify*?" he asks (*PI*, 1, 10). "What is supposed to shew what they signify, if not the kind of use they have? And we have already described that. So we are asking for the expression 'This word signifies *this*' to be made part of the description. In other words the description ought to take the form: 'The word . . . . signifies . . . .' " (*PI*, 1, 10). Why do we insist that all words signify in this way? Well, we *do* after all talk about words signifying. Wittgenstein examines the cases where we properly make this a part of the description of a word. We can, as he says, "reduce the description of the use of the word 'slab' to the statement that this word signifies this object. This will be done, when, for example, it is merely a matter of removing the mistaken idea that the word 'slab' refers to the shape of building-stone that we in fact call a 'block'—but the kind of 'referring' this is, that is to say the use of these words otherwise, is already known" (*PI*, 1, 10; my translation). Likewise, we *can* say that the letters "a," "b," etc., signify numbers. We do this, for example, when we want to correct someone who mistakenly thinks that "a," "b," "c," play the part actually played in the language by "block," "slab," "pillar." "But assimilating the descriptions of the uses of words in this way cannot make the uses themselves any more like one another. For, as we see, they are absolutely unlike" (*PI*, 1, 10).

An adequate account of language, we may say, must recognize that words function in numerous ways. It foregoes the temptation to assimilate all words under one use, that of signifying.

> Think of the tools in a tool-box: there is a hammer, pliers, a saw, a screw-driver, a rule, a glue-pot, glue, nails, and screws.— The functions of words are as diverse as the functions of these objects. (And in both cases there are similarities.)
>
> Of course, what confuses us is the uniform appearance of words when we hear them spoken or meet them in script and print. For their *application* is not presented to us so clearly. Especially when we are doing philosophy! [*PI*, 1, 11]

Wittgenstein's *Philosophical Investigations*

We may think of words as instruments of another sort, to make this clearer. It is, Wittgenstein says, "like looking into the cabin of a locomotive. We see handles all looking more or less alike. (Naturally, since they are all supposed to be handled.)" (*PI*, 1, 12). But one handle is to be pulled, another cranked continuously, another is a switch with only two effective positions. Each is connected to "the rest of the mechanism," (to recall an earlier metaphor), in some way not obvious unless you know how to drive a locomotive. Our claim that all words signify something, or are symbols in a sort of communications code, is like insisting that all these handles operate the same way. No wonder, then, that we get into difficulties trying to understand language this way. "Imagine someone's saying: '*All* tools serve to modify something. Thus the hammer modifies the position of the nail, the saw the shape of the board, and so on.'—And what is modified by the rule, the glue-pot, the nails?—'Our knowledge of a thing's length, the temperature of the glue, and the solidity of the box.'——Would anything be gained by this assimilation of expressions?—" (*PI*, 1, 14).

In any language beyond the most primitive we will find different kinds of words; thus in the expanded builder's language we can distinguish the words "slab," "block," etc., from the kind of words used for numerals ("a," "b," etc.). The functions of "slab" and "block" resemble each other more than the functions of "slab" and "d," for example. But we will understand the phenomenon of language better if we do not try to make it conform to a preconceived pattern, but rather accept its multiplicity.

Reductionism

The builder's languages, both simple and expanded, consist only of orders. We should not be troubled by this fact, says Wittgenstein. "If you want to say that this shews them to be incomplete, ask yourself whether our language is complete;—whether it was so before the symbolism of chemistry and the notation of the infinitesimal calculus were incorporated in it; for these are, so to speak, suburbs of our language. (And how many houses or streets does it take before a town begins to be a town?)" In following up this metaphor, he writes, "Our language can be seen as an ancient city:

a maze of little streets and squares, of old and new houses, and of houses with additions from various periods; and this surrounded by a multitude of new boroughs with straight regular streets and uniform houses" (*PI*, 1, 18). The *Philosophical Investigations* can be seen as a record of Wittgenstein's explorations of this city, explorations in which he approaches buildings and streets now from one side, now from the other, seeing the same places again and again, but each time from a slightly different perspective.[9]

A language consisting entirely of orders is still a language, as Wittgenstein points out: "It is easy to imagine a language consisting only of . . . questions and expressions for answering yes and no." Now, Wittgenstein asks, what distinguishes one kind of sentence from another when the words of which they are composed are the same? He approaches this by asking, first, whether in the language that we have imagined, the call "slab!" is a sentence or a word. We are tempted to call it an elliptical sentence, as he says, because it seems to be a shortened form of the sentence, "Bring me a slab." "But why should I not on the contrary have called the sentence 'Bring me a slab' a *lengthening* of the sentence 'Slab!'?—Because if you shout 'Slab!' you really mean: 'Bring me a slab'.— But how do you do this: how do you *mean that* while you *say* 'Slab!'? Do you say the unshortened form to yourself?" (*PI*, 1, 19). Wittgenstein is directing our attention to the commonsense notion that some sort of mental process *accompanies* the uttering of words and gives a sentence meaning, while yet remaining independent of its expression in words.[10] He is pointing to something odd about this notion. He concludes this frustrating argument with himself as follows: "But when I call 'Slab!', then what I want is, *that he should bring me a slab!*——Certainly, but does 'wanting this' consist in thinking in some form or other a different sentence from the one you utter?—" (*PI*, 1, 19). The meaning, we begin to see, is not something separate from the words, something which exists in the head of the speaker. It is somehow embedded in the circumstances of *use*. The sentence "Slab!" is "elliptical," as he says, "not because it leaves out something that we think when we utter it, but because it is shortened—in comparison with a particular paradigm of our grammar" (*PI*, 1, 20). And that four-word paradigm, in turn, exists at least partly because our language contains a variety of other

Wittgenstein's *Philosophical Investigations*

possible expressions (from which it must be distinguished), such as "Bring *him* a slab," or "*Hand* me a slab," and so forth. It is because these possibilities exist that we speak of "Bring me a slab" as having the same sense as "Slab!" in the language we imagined. But if they have the same sense, isn't there a verbal expression for it? Wittgenstein answers: "But doesn't the fact that sentences have the same sense consist in their having the same *use*?" (*PI*, 1, 20). We will look in vain to find the meaning somewhere else.

We are asked to imagine an addition to the builder's language whereby the assistant reports on the number of slabs or blocks in such-and-such a place, by saying, for example, "Five slabs." "Now what is the difference between the report or statement 'Five slabs' and the order 'Five slabs!'?—Well, it is the part which uttering these words plays in the language-game" (*PI*, 1, 21). What differentiates a question from a statement, or an order from a report, is not just something in the words, nor is it some mysterious "meaning" in the mind of the speaker, but the totality of circumstances in which the speaker utters the words.

The point of these remarks, and the reason Wittgenstein considers this problem so fundamental to his considerations, is this: the notion that language is no more than a communications code by means of which we make statements to or ask questions of each other makes us look *elsewhere* for the thoughts or ideas, or "meanings," conveyed by language. On this understanding we have a tendency to overlook the fundamental fact that using language, or speaking, is a human activity.[11] We are tempted, if we misunderstand language in this way, to make claims such as that all questions are really statements in disguise, and thus to misunderstand the role that questioning plays in human life. We are tempted, that is, to reduce the complexity of language to one single form. But this, according to Wittgenstein, inevitably distorts language, and will not help us to understand it. In his words, "If you do not keep the multiplicity of language-games in view you will perhaps be inclined to ask questions like: 'What is a question?'— Is it the statement that I do not know such-and-such, or the statement that I wish the other person would tell me . . . .? Or is it the description of my mental state of uncertainty?—And is the cry 'Help!' such a description?" (*PI*, 1, 24). "Of course," he goes on, "it is possible to substitute the form of statement or description for the usual form of question: 'I want to know whether . . . .' or 'I am in doubt whether . . . .'—but this does not bring the different language-games any closer together."

This attack on a reductive approach to language was made more explicit in the earlier *Blue and Brown Books*. There Wittgenstein tries to explain our "craving for generality," and to show why it misleads us in these matters. "This craving for generality is the resultant of a number of tendencies connected with particular philosophical confusions" (*BB*, p. 17). "Our preoccupation with the method of science," as he puts it, is one of these.

> I mean the method of reducing the explanation of natural phe-
> nomena to the smallest possible number of primitive natural
> laws; and, in mathematics, of unifying the treatment of different
> topics by using a generalization. Philosophers constantly see the
> method of science before their eyes, and are irresistibly tempted
> to ask and answer questions in the way science does. This ten-
> dency is the real source of metaphysics, and leads the philoso-
> pher into complete darkness. [*BB*, p. 18]

Wittgenstein tries to show why the reductionist method of natural science is not appropriate to the understanding of language: reducing language to a small number of "simples," or to one model, inevitably causes us to *mis*understand it. "I want to say here that it can never be our job to reduce anything to anything, or to explain anything. Philosophy really *is* 'purely descriptive' " (*BB*, p. 18).

Language Games

We need to examine what Wittgenstein calls "language games."[12] He uses this both to describe generally "the whole, consisting of language and the actions into which it is woven," and in more restricted senses. For example, "in the practice of the use" of the builder's language, "one party calls out the words, the other acts on them" (*PI*, 1, 7). This constitutes a simple language game in itself. By means of this expression Wittgenstein emphasizes the fact that learning words means learning how to *use* them, what human beings do with them, how a particular language game is played. In this narrow sense he includes as well the very process of learning

Wittgenstein's *Philosophical Investigations*

words: in learning the builder's language, for example, "the learner *names* the objects; that is, he utters the word when the teacher points to the stone" (*PI*, 1, 7). This in itself could be considered a sort of very simple language game.

"How many kinds of sentence are there?" Wittgenstein asks. "Say assertion, question, and command?—There are *countless* kinds: countless different kinds of use of what we call 'symbols', 'words', 'sentences' " (*PI*, 1, 23). And each kind of use of words— each language game—is part of a human activity, or something human beings do:

> Review the multiplicity of language-games in the following examples, and in others:
> Giving orders, and obeying them—
> Describing the appearance of an object, or giving its measure- ments—
> Constructing an object from a description (a drawing)—
> Reporting an event—
> Speculating about an event—
> Forming and testing a hypothesis—
> Presenting the results of an experiment in tables and dia- grams—
> Making up a story; and reading it—
> Play-acting—
> Singing catches—
> Guessing riddles—
> Making a joke; telling it—
> Solving a problem in practical arithmetic—
> Translating from one language into another—
> Asking, thanking, cursing, greeting, praying.
> —It is interesting to compare the multiplicity of the tools in lan- guage and of the ways they are used, the multiplicity of kinds of word and sentence, with what logicians have said about the struc- ture of language. (Including the author of the *Tractatus Logico- Philosophicus*.) [*PI*, 1, 23]

And, we might add, including John Locke.

We have looked briefly at Wittgenstein's early "picture-theory" of language presented in the *Tractatus Logico-Philosophicus* (pp. 73–74 above). What is most important for us about this view is the claim that the only way a proposition can have meaning is by its ability to "picture" reality. Language is reduced, in the *Tractatus*, not merely to propositions, but to the kind of propositions characteristic of natural science.[13] All the other parts of language are meaningless (although there are different ways of being meaningless).[14] Hence the famous concluding remark, "Whereof one cannot speak, thereof one must be silent." The similarity with Locke lies in the claim that every word has a meaning because it "stands for" something else. For Wittgenstein, however, the class of meaningful propositions became so small as to exclude most of the statements with which Locke was concerned.

To return to language games: Learning our language means learning how to play many different language games, in which words are used in different ways. The language games are a form of human action, or activity; they are something human beings *do*, and not just something *used* in the process of doing something else. It is important to see what is entailed in this claim that language games are themselves human activities. Words are learned in language games. The meanings of words are connected to the part the words play in the various language games, or activities in which they occur. Understanding a word, we may say, is like understanding a lever in the cab of a locomotive: *fully* understanding it requires in a sense an understanding of the whole mechanism, that is, of what the mechanism is *for*.[15] Understanding the part requires some grasp of the whole of which it is a part. In the case of a language game, this entails understanding what that human activity is, what it is for, why it is played. Words—at least many words—are used in many different activities. To understand the full meaning of a word requires some grasp of all the activities, the social wholes, in which the word plays a part.

The claim that language is an activity brings out the fact that when human beings speak or use words they are *doing* something, and that speaking is a part of human life. What distinguishes human action from mere motion, or the growth of a plant, is the fact that it is potentially, at least, caring, valuing activity, activity which has meaning for human beings. The meanings of words can only be understood if we understand the purpose or ends of the human activities of which words are part. Ignoring the different language

Wittgenstein's *Philosophical Investigations*

games and their ends or purposes when seeking the meaning of a word is like trying to understand the brake lever in a locomotive without understanding what a locomotive does, or what it is for.

It is very difficult to overcome the conventional notion that words are only symbols in a communications code, that they stand for something else—thinking—which goes on inside our heads. But language is a form of, not an adjunct to, human action. Wittgenstein expresses this as follows: "It is sometimes said that animals do not talk because they lack the mental capacity. And this means: 'they do not think, and that is why they do not talk.' But—they simply do not talk. Or to put it better: they do not use language—if we except the most primitive forms of language.—Commanding, questioning, recounting, chatting, are as much a part of our natural history as walking, eating, drinking, playing" (*PI*, 1, 25).[16] Words are not signs of something else, they are themselves part of the activities in which they are learned and used. The thoughts and meanings in a language game are not, as Locke would have claimed, something independent of, or prior to, the words. The meaning is determined by the role of an expression in the language game. This is clearer in the *Blue and Brown Books*, where Wittgenstein first wrestled with the difficulties into which one is led as a result of thinking of meaning as a mental process separate from words. In one passage he examines the notion that words are signs which are in themselves lifeless, but which have the function of inducing our mental processes (that is, understanding and meaning), which in turn are "the things we really ought to be interested in" (*BB*, p. 3). We think that words are accompanied by mental pictures, which we have learned to associate with them—as if, Wittgenstein says, the action of language consists of two parts, "an inorganic part, the handling of signs, and an organic part, which we may call understanding these signs, meaning them, interpreting them, thinking" (*BB*, p. 3). What he means can be seen by thinking of the shopkeeper in the first example above. When the shopkeeper reads the slip which says "five red apples," it seems to us that a mental image of red appears to him if he understands the words. But Wittgenstein insists that we get away from the "occult appearance of the processes of thinking" (*BB*, p. 4), by replacing the mental image in every instance with the act of looking at a real object. The shopkeeper looks at a table of color samples to find "red," for

Wittgenstein's *Philosophical Investigations*

example. "If the meaning of the sign (roughly, that which is of importance about the sign) is an image built up in our minds when we see or hear the sign, then first let us adopt the method we have just described of replacing this mental image by some outward object seen, e.g. a painted or modelled image. Then why should the written sign plus the painted image be alive if the written sign alone was dead?" (*BB*, p. 5). Wittgenstein sums this up as follows: "The mistake we are liable to make could be expressed thus: We are looking for the use of a sign, but we look for it as though it were an object *co-existing* with the sign. (One of the reasons for this mistake is again that we are looking for a 'thing corresponding to a substantive')" (*BB*, p. 5). We are misled in this case by the understanding of language characteristic of Augustine and Locke, the understanding which takes words to be labels for things— objects, ideas, mixed modes, or whatever—about which we *already* have something we want to say.

Naming and Ostensive Definitions

If we return to the *Philosophical Investigations*, we find Wittgenstein continuing this line of thought. We think, he says, "that learning language consists in giving names to objects. Viz, to human beings, to shapes, to colours, to pains, to moods, to numbers, etc." (*PI*, 1, 26). This brings to mind Hobbes's words in *De Homine*: "Speech or language is the connexion of names constituted by the will of men to stand for the series of conceptions of the things about which we think. Therefore, as a name is to an idea or a conception of a thing, so is speech to the discourse of the mind" (chap. 10, p. 37). "To repeat—naming is something like attaching a label to a thing," Wittgenstein continues. "One can say that this is preparatory to the use of a word. But *what* is it a preparation *for*?" (*PI*, 1, 26). We have already seen the sort of answer he expects to this question: " 'We name things and then we can talk about them: can refer to them in talk.'—As if what we did next were given with the mere act of naming. As if there were only one thing called 'talking about a thing' " (*PI*, 1, 27). The kinds of things we do in speech are so various that they cannot be lumped together in this way:

Wittgenstein's *Philosophical Investigations*

Think of exclamations alone, with their completely different
functions.
> Water!
> Away!
> Ow!
> Help!
> Fine!
> No!

Are you inclined still to call these words "names of objects"?
[*PI*, 1, 27]

Now let us look more closely at the process of naming. We think
names are learned when we ask someone, for example, "What is
this called?" and indicate the thing we mean. The response, "This is
called . . ." is called an ostensive definition. Wittgenstein wants to
bring out something we generally do not realize about this sort of
learning of words, namely, that ostensive definitions are always
open to a kind of misunderstanding. What we overlook is the fact
that one must already know a great deal even to ask for the
definition of a word. Think of looking up words in a dictionary, for
example, and of the sort of definitions (which are not ostensive)
one finds there. We can, as Wittgenstein says, ostensively define all
sorts of things—the name of a color, of a material, of a person, a
numeral, and so forth. "The definition of the number two, 'That is
called "two" '—pointing to two nuts—is perfectly exact.—But how
can two be defined like that? The person one gives the definition to
doesn't know what one wants to call 'two'; he will suppose that
'two' is the name given to *this* group of nuts!" (*PI*, 1, 28). The ostensive definition of anything else is subject to misinterpretation of the
same kind. "He might equally well take the name of a person, of
which I gave an ostensive definition, as that of a colour, of a race,
or even of a point of the compass. That is to say: an ostensive
definition can be variously interpreted in *every* case" (*PI*, 1, 28).

Suppose, though, that we define the numeral with the following
sort of ostensive definition: " 'This *number* is called "two".' " The
use of the word "number" will show him what we are talking
about, or as Wittgenstein says, it "shews what place in language, in
grammar, we assign to the word" (*PI*, 1, 29). But then in turn we
must explain the use of "number," if the definition is to be

Wittgenstein's *Philosophical Investigations*

understood. But how can we define "number"? Apparently a whole chain of definitions will be required. "And what about the last definition in this chain? (Do not say: 'There isn't a "last" definition'. That is just as if you chose to say: 'There isn't a last house on this road; one can always build an additional one')" (*PI*, 1, 29).

It appears that we can ostensively define the numeral "two" only if the learner already knows what "number" or "numeral" means, what a number is. "So one might say: the ostensive definition explains the use—the meaning—of the word when the overall role of the word in language is clear. Thus if I know that someone means to explain a colour-word to me the ostensive definition 'That is called "sepia" ' will help me to understand the word" (*PI*, 1, 30).

It is easy to imagine going to a foreign country and learning the language, in large part, by ostensive definitions. A Frenchman might ask his English friend the name of a chess piece, for example, as they share a game. Often a stranger to the language will have to guess the meanings of these ostensive definitions, and, as Wittgenstein points out, he will be sometimes right, sometimes wrong. But this reflection on definitions is crucially important to Wittgenstein's understanding of language (and our own), because with it we begin to understand aright Augustine's description of language learning. "And now, I think, we can say: Augustine describes the learning of human language as if the child came into a strange country and did not understand the language of the country; that is, as if it already had a language, only not this one. Or again: as if the child could already *think*, only not yet speak. And 'think' would here mean something like 'talk to itself' " (*PI*, 1, 32). This is, we might say, another case of "I set up the brake by connecting rod and lever": that is, of assuming the whole of the rest of the mechanism. Augustine's description is one way we *can* learn (part of) a language, but it is not the way a child first learns to speak. Learning language the first time involves much more than learning to associate the names with the proper things; it is learning to *do* something, to participate in a human activity. Learning language is learning language games, and it involves as much "training" as explaining.[17]

The purpose of Wittgenstein's investigations up to this point might be said to have been negative or critical. He has attempted to

Wittgenstein's *Philosophical Investigations*

show why the commonsense or Augustinian picture of language is inadequate, because until that inadequacy is exposed our understanding of language is blocked. The "general notion of the meaning of a word" which we get from Augustine, Wittgenstein writes, "surrounds the working of language with a haze which makes clear vision impossible. It disperses the fog to study the phenomena of language in primitive kinds of application in which one can command a clear view of the aim and functioning of the words" (*PI*, 1, 5). After showing that Augustine's view of language does not begin to take account of anything beyond names, or beyond words which function as labels, Wittgenstein takes up in more detail the question of how names themselves work. In particular, and what is of most importance to us here, he takes up the question of whether *these* words (that is, roughly, substantives or names) stand for combinations of simpler things, ideas, or objects. Can we say, he asks, that they are somehow composite?

Simples and Composites

The doctrine that the definition of a name iterates the simple elements which together make up its meaning, we saw in the previous chapter to be characteristic of Locke. Wittgenstein's *Tractatus* propounded a similar doctrine, in which the names of primary elements of reality (which Wittgenstein called "objects")[18] "become descriptive language by being compounded together" (*PI*, 1, 46; the phrase is Wittgenstein's quotation from Socrates in the *Theaetetus*). But in the *Tractatus* Wittgenstein never said what the "object" or primary element might be. In the *Investigations* he examines the reasons why these simple elements are so elusive. Where once he was certain they had to exist, now he simply looks to see if they do exist. The "idea that names really signify simples" is indeed tempting. "But what are the simple constituent parts of which reality is composed?" he asks.

> What are the simple constituent parts of a chair?—The bits of wood of which it is made? Or the molecules, or the atoms?— "Simple" means not composite. And here the point is: in what . sense "composite"? It makes no sense at all to speak absolutely of the "simple parts of a chair". [*PI*, 1, 47]

The reason it makes no sense to speak absolutely of the simple parts of something is that the word "simple," or "composite" for that matter, takes its meaning from the language games it is used in, and "absolutely simple" is an expression in which "simple" is cut loose from its moorings. We literally do not know what you mean, if you say that. In Wittgenstein's words: "If I tell someone without further explanation: 'What I see before me now is composite', he will have the right to ask: 'What do you mean by "composite"? For there are all sorts of things that that can mean!'—The question 'Is what you see composite?' makes good sense if it is already established what kind of complexity—that is, which particular use of the word—is in question" (*PI*, 1, 47). Wittgenstein makes a joke about this. "Asking 'Is this object composite?' *outside* a particular language game is like what a boy once did, who had to say whether the verbs in certain sentences were active or passive voice, and who racked his brains over the question whether the verb 'to sleep' meant something active or passive" (*PI*, 1, 47).

For some purposes we may want to consider a table and chairs as consisting of "simples" which are pieces of wood and screws; for another purpose the simples may be the atoms which make up the materials themselves. Can we say which is the "real" table? Is one set of simples more "real" than another? Wittgenstein's understanding leads us to say that it depends on what you are going to do—if you are moving your furniture, perhaps the pieces are what you want, but if you are giving a dinner party, isn't the "essence" of a table and chairs the fact that they allow people to sit together and eat and talk? Understanding fully what a table is would certainly require knowing this just as much as knowing that it consists of screws and pieces of wood attached in such-and-such a fashion, or that it consists of atoms bonded together in a particular configuration.

But this consideration of a physical object does not satisfactorily dispose of Locke's theory of mixed modes, because we are not required to reduce complex words in the case of mixed modes to absolutely simple elements, only to component parts which we *can*, after all, recognize. And Locke's approach is doubly tempting, as we have seen, because it is powerfully reinforced by the scientific method, which understands things by taking them apart (Hobbes's

Wittgenstein's *Philosophical Investigations*

resolutive-compositive method). Really knowing the meaning of some name would seem to require knowing the parts that make up the thing named. Wittgenstein returns to the problem of composites in this form some pages later in the *Investigations*. Here he is worrying about the question of whether or not the meaning of a name is clearer to us when the name is "resolved" into component parts by analysis.

> When I say: "My broom is in the corner", —is this really a statement about the broomstick and the brush? Well, it could at any rate be replaced by a statement giving the position of the stick and the position of the brush. And this statement is surely a further analysed form of the first one. —But why do I call it "further analysed"? —Well, if the broom is there, that surely means that the stick and brush must be there, and in a particular relationship to one another; and this was as it were hidden in the sense of the first sentence, and is *expressed* in the analysed sentence. [*PI*, 1, 60]

But there is something curious about this. Someone who says the broom is in the corner surely *doesn't* mean to say, "The broomstick is in the corner, and so is the brush, and the broomstick is fixed in the brush." What, wonders Wittgenstein, would someone say if we asked him if that was what he meant? "He would probably say that he had not thought specially of the broomstick or specially of the brush at all. And that would be the *right* answer, for he meant to speak neither of the stick nor of the brush in particular." We are asked to imagine ourselves saying to someone, "Bring me the broomstick and the brush which is fitted onto it." And Wittgenstein asks: "Isn't the answer: 'Do you want the broom? Why do you put it so oddly?'——Is he going to understand the further analysed sentence better?—This sentence, one might say, achieves the same as the ordinary one, but in a more roundabout way" (*PI*, 1, 60). It is true, of course, that the intention of the speaker may be the same in both cases, and he may indeed succeed in being handed the object so he can sweep the room. In some sense the two orders may be said to have the same meaning, especially if we are differentiating them from some other order, for example one regarding the table or its component parts. But we would not in other cases consider them to have the same meaning. And to say that the

Wittgenstein's *Philosophical Investigations*

sentence in which we speak of the component parts is an "analyzed" form of the sentence "Bring me the broom" is somehow misleading. For it "readily seduces us into thinking that the former is the more fundamental form; that it alone shews what is meant by the other, and so on. For example, we think: If you have only the unanalysed form you miss the analysis; but if you know the analysed form that gives you everything.—But can I not say that an aspect of the matter is lost on you in the *latter* cases as well as the former?" (*PI*, 1, 63).

It will be worthwhile here to look at an example from politics, that is, an example of a political phenomenon of which an aspect is lost when it is reduced or broken down into more general elements. Suppose we consider the meaning of justice. (A similar kind of investigation, concerning "human excellence," is found in Plato's *Meno*, which we will discuss in chapter 7.) On first consideration, when we examine justice there appears to be a large number of particular cases of just acts and just things and just arrangements— of what common speech calls justice. We say, for example, that it is just to pay taxes, to arrest criminals, to care for aged parents. If we analyze such examples we will have difficulty bringing to light any universal elements which make each an example of justice. Are they each just because justice means giving what is deserved, what is due someone? That is a common opinion of justice, and perhaps a good guide. (For example, Polemarchus, in the *Republic*, is satisfied that "giving what is due" is the core of justice.)[19] But if justice is giving to someone what we owe (as Socrates objects), why do we think it unjust to return to a deranged man the weapon he had lent to us when in sound mind? Perhaps this suggests that the common element is "helping someone else," and not "giving what is owed." (But then why do we say it is just in some cases to kill someone in self-defense?) We have trouble finding the common element. Perhaps all these things are just, when they are, not because of some shared simple element or elements to which they can be reduced, but because of a certain participation in or contribution to a larger whole, a political community. Why do some trials and some laws strike us as unjust when courts and laws are the very locus of justice? Perhaps because there is something which stands behind our judgment in these considerations, some

Wittgenstein's *Philosophical Investigations*

notion of the ends or goals of the political community, of politics itself. In considering the vast range of political phenomena, from taxes to trials, our judgment proceeds not from the fact that they share or lack some simple element of "just-ness," but rather from their relationship to the goals we understand our political community to aim at. It is this we look to in judging the justice or injustice of a criminal sentence, of a graduated income tax, of deporting an illegal alien, or of the salary of a congressman. If we try to find justice by seeking the general factors present in all just things—if, in other words, we indulge what Wittgenstein calls our craving for generality—we will analyze these things without realizing that indeed "an aspect of the matter" is lost on us. The whole may be heterogeneous and not reducible.[20]

Names are used in various language games which may be similar, but not necessarily the same. "In what sense," Wittgenstein asks, "do the symbols of this language-game stand in need of analysis?" (*PI*, 1, 64). We might say that the flaw in Augustine's or Locke's understanding of language is once again brought to the surface here in the tendency to reduce all the ways language works to one way, to make it all conform to one pattern. If, in fact, we could reduce all complex names (to say nothing of other types of words) to parts that were more fundamental, it would be, in Wittgenstein's terms, a way of replacing one language game by another. We might say, in that case, that the one was an abbreviation of the more detailed form, an abbreviation we used for convenience. But in actual fact two such language games (one "regular" and one "analyzed") are surely different, and must be understood on their own terms. We must resist what Wittgenstein calls our "contemptuous attitude towards the particular case" (*BB*, p. 18). The observations on analyzed forms of sentences lead Wittgenstein to the end of what we may call the first major section in the progress of the *Investigations*:

> Here we come up against the great question that lies behind all these considerations.—For someone might object against me: "You take the easy way out! You talk about all sorts of language-games, but have nowhere said what the essence of a language-game, and hence of language, is: what is common to all these activities, and what makes them into language, or parts of language. So you let yourself off the very part of the investigation that once

gave you yourself most headache, the part about the *general form of propositions* and of language." [*PI*, 1, 65]

This must indeed have seemed an irony to Wittgenstein, who had thought as a young man to have finished, in the *Tractatus Logico-Philosophicus*, saying what could be said of the essence of language. Now he responds to this accusation that he has failed to show the general form of propositions with an admission of guilt: "And this is true.—Instead of producing something common to all that we call language, I am saying that these phenomena have no one thing in common which makes us use the same word for all,—but that they are *related* to one another in many different ways. And it is because of this relationship, or these relationships, that we call them all 'language'. I will try to explain this" (*PI*, 1, 65).

This is the central theme of Wittgenstein's rich understanding of language. He has found that forcing it into one pattern purchases simplicity at the cost of correct understanding. Yet how can we define language, or even recognize it, if there is no "core" meaning common to all its forms? The idea of a definition will again be a central theme in chapter 5. It will bring us back to Hobbes and Locke and their new political science by raising questions about their view of language. We have seen in chapter 4 only the critical or destructive half of Wittgenstein's later thought. It remains to be seen how, or in what sense, words *have* meanings; it is this question which we take up next.

5 Wittgenstein's Account of Meaning

We have been led by Wittgenstein to see that a proper understanding of language will be more complicated and less systematic than the understanding presented by Locke. The nature of language is accessible to us "only if we make a radical break with the idea that language always functions in one way, always serves the same purpose: to convey thoughts—which may be about houses, pains, good and evil, or anything else you please" (*PI*, 1, 304). The first step toward this understanding was to see language itself as an activity, as something bound up in human life and not an arbitrary adjunct to it. What do the parts of this activity called language have in common that makes us call them all language? At the close of the preceding chapter we found that Wittgenstein declares that there is no such core of language, no one thing shared by all the parts of which language consists. Nevertheless, we use the one word "language" to describe all the different parts. Wittgenstein must explain why we do this. The explanation comprises, in a way, the remainder of the *Philosophical Investigations*. We will once more proceed by focusing on one small portion of the work, namely, the sections which immediately follow his promise of an explanation, and try to fill out the explanation by using examples taken from elsewhere. But it must be understood that this explanation, as far as Wittgenstein is concerned, is never completed in the *Investigations* at all. And the sense of this incompleteness is itself part of the explanation, in a way that we will try to make clear.

Meaning and Family Resemblances

Wittgenstein asks us to consider, by way of example, "the proceedings that we call 'games'." What is the essence or the core of the meaning of the word "game"? What property or characteristic is common to all the things we call games? "I mean board-games, card-games, ball-games, Olympic games, and so on. What is common to them all?—Don't say: 'There *must* be something common, or they would not be called "games" '—but *look and see* whether there is anything common to all" (*PI*, 1, 66). We are urged to look into this question naively, without preconceptions. Characteristically, Wittgenstein is more interested in *understanding*, even when the direction of his inquiry seems to threaten his entire structure of knowledge, and even when the understanding he achieves appears to complicate something which at first appears simple. Years earlier he thought he had definitively explained the structure of language, with the picture theory of the *Tractatus* (see above, pp. 73–74); now he clouds that crystalline understanding for the simple reason that he sees it to have been wrong. And it was wrong, he believed, precisely because it reduced something of enormous complexity to something in principle very simple (although his explanation was not simple to grasp).

What happens when we look closely at these activities called games? "If you look at them you will not see something that is common to them *all*, but similarities, relationships, and a whole series of them at that. To repeat: don't think, but look!" (*PI*, 1, 66). As in the case of the activities which make up our language—all the things we do with words—we have trouble finding something to call the "core" of the idea of games. Wittgenstein introduces the expression "family resemblances" to describe this relationship to each other of all the things we call games. Some share certain features, and of these some features are common to still other games. They are all related as a family, although there is no single distinctive trait which identifies each as a "game."

> Look for example at board-games, with their multifarious relationships. Now pass to card-games; here you find many correspondences with the first group, but many common features drop out, and others appear. When we pass next to ball-games, much that is common is retained, but much is lost.—Are they all "amusing"? Compare chess with noughts and crosses. Or is there always winning and losing, or competition between players? Think of patience. In ball games there is winning and losing; but when a child throws his ball at the wall and catches it again, this feature has disappeared. Look at the parts played by skill and luck; and at the difference between skill in chess and skill in tennis. Think now of games like ring-a-ring-a-roses; here is the element of amusement, but how many other characteristic features have disappeared! And we can go through the many, many other groups of games in the same way; can see how similarities crop up and disappear. [*PI*, 1, 66]

Of course, the features of language are much more complicated even than this. In the case of games, as Wittgenstein examines them, we see "a complicated network of similarities overlapping and criss-crossing: sometimes overall similarities, sometimes similarities of detail" (*PI*, 1, 66). We can expect to find even greater complexity in language.

The activities we call games are related to each other not in any single way, but as members of a family, each of whom resembles others in some ways, but not in all, e.g., in build, in facial features, height, hair color, temperament, gestures, etc. " 'Games' form a family," as Wittgenstein puts it. Our concept of game is extended in the same way "as in spinning a thread we twist fibre on fibre. And the strength of the thread does not reside in the fact that some one fibre runs through its whole length, but in the overlapping of many fibres" (*PI*, 1, 67). However, a problem can arise here which is best brought out by considering the concept of number instead of game. The different kinds of numbers are related to each other by the same sort of family resemblance. But with numbers we are tempted to say something like this, which Wittgenstein anticipates: " 'All right: the concept of number is defined for you as the logical sum of these individual interrelated concepts: cardinal numbers, rational numbers, real numbers, etc.; and in the same way the concept of a game as the logical sum of a corresponding set of sub-concepts' " (*PI*, 1, 68). That is, we can imagine an exact definition of numbers or games as one in which we make a careful list of all the subordinate types, of number or of game, which together comprise the concept itself. But "it need not be so," says Wittgenstein. "For I *can* give the concept 'number' rigid limits in this way, that is, use the word 'number' for a rigidly limited concept, but I can also use it so that the extension of the concept is *not* closed by a frontier. And this is how we do use the word 'game' " (*PI*, 1, 68).

Boundaries and Precision

This idea gives us some difficulty. Can Wittgenstein mean what he appears to be saying, namely, that the concept of a game has no frontiers or boundaries? Characteristically he indicates the direction of his thought by asking questions. "How," he asks, "is the concept of a game bounded? What still counts as a game and what no longer does? Can you give the boundary? No. You can *draw* one; for none has so far been drawn. (But that never troubled you before when you used the word 'game')" (*PI*, 1, 68). Games then form not only a family, they form an open family, a family with no clear line to divide it from other concepts (sports or jokes, for example). This leads us into a tension which Wittgenstein is at pains to explore: the tension is evident in our temptation to ask how we can know what a game is at all, if the concept has no clear boundaries. If "the use of the word is unregulated, the game we play with it is unregulated," he accuses himself, and then answers: "It is not everywhere circumscribed by rules; but no more are there any rules for how high one throws the ball in tennis, or how hard; yet tennis is a game for all that and has rules too" (*PI*, 1, 68). We can admit that in one sense the use of the word "game" is unregulated—there are points where we are not guided by rules—but we can and do use the word nevertheless, and still know what a game is.[1]

Wittgenstein raises two further objections to his claim that games form a family, and then investigates their implications. We may

Wittgenstein's Account
of Meaning

consider them in turn. Suppose you tell someone what a game is by giving him examples of games. You are unable to give an exact definition, to say where the concept ends, for example, because the concept is not clearly circumscribed. Now the first objection is raised in this form: " 'But if the concept "game" is uncircumscribed like that, you don't really know what you mean by a "game".' " Wittgenstein asks the imaginary questioner a question in return: "When I give the description: 'The ground was quite covered with plants'—do you want to say I don't know what I am talking about until I can give a definition of a plant?" (*PI*, 1, 70). Most of us, of course, know what plants are, even though most of us could not give a botanist's account of them. And even botanists do not have a definition which is absolutely clear about the fringes of plant life, so to speak. If we were asked to explain the statement that the ground was covered with plants, we might, perhaps, make use of a drawing and say, "The ground looked roughly like this," as Wittgenstein suggests. "Perhaps I even say 'it looked *exactly* like this.'—Then were just *this* grass and *these* leaves there, arranged just like this? No, that is not what it means. And I should not accept any picture as exact in *this* sense" (*PI*, 1, 70). Our attention is directed here to the fact that we can say what we mean, and say it clearly, even with concepts which themselves do not have clear and distinct boundaries. And if you want to deny this, Wittgenstein hints, you will find yourself in the midst of the same sort of confusion over the concept of "exactness" as you were in over the concept "game."

Wittgenstein notes that we could describe this concept "game" as a concept with blurred edges, and then raises a second objection: "But is a blurred concept a concept at all?" That is, doesn't a concept with blurred edges somehow fall short of a perfect concept, a real concept, which ought to be clear all around? And can't we then say it isn't a real concept? Wittgenstein again questions the questioner: "Is an indistinct photograph a picture of a person at all? Is it even always an advantage to replace an indistinct picture by a sharp one? Isn't the indistinct one often exactly what we need?" (*PI*, 1, 71). If we carry a photograph of a loved one, for example, isn't a photograph which is indistinct enough to obscure facial blemishes exactly what we need? Perhaps this is only to say that even if for

Wittgenstein's Account
of Meaning

utilitarian purposes distinctness were always better, human needs transcend the utilitarian. (We have aesthetic needs and moral needs, for example.)

It is not always true that if an indistinct picture is good, a distinct one will be better, even if it *were* possible always to use distinct ones.[2] "Frege compares a concept to an area and says that an area with vague boundaries cannot be called an area at all. This presumably means that we cannot do anything with it.—But is it senseless to say: 'Stand roughly there'? Suppose that I were standing with someone in a city square and said that. As I say it I do not draw any kind of boundary, but perhaps point with my hand—as if I were indicating a particular *spot*" (*PI*, 1, 71). In a sense this is all we *can* do, for what standard of exactness are we to apply if someone complains that we are too vague? Well, we can try to indicate it more precisely, say by going over and standing where we mean the person to stand. But is that exact? (What if our feet are not the same size?) We are troubled here by the idea that we must mean something more exact than we are in practice able to indicate. But is that true? (See *PI*, 1, 87–88.)

This pointing, or saying "stand roughly there," which we do to indicate to someone where we mean him to stand, is not less exact than our intention, at least in normal cases. It is very similar to the way we would explain to someone what a game is. How would we do that, in fact? "I imagine that we should describe *games* to him, and we might add: 'This *and similar things* are called "games" ' " (*PI*, 1, 69). We give the person examples of games, describe individual games to him, without offering a general definition of the word "game." "One gives examples and intends them to be taken in a particular way.—I do not, however, mean by this that he is supposed to see in those examples that common thing which I— for some reason—was unable to express; but that he is to *employ* those examples in a particular way." Our meaning is best examined here by looking at the actions involved, and not by searching for some intention within us which we are unable to express clearly. "Here giving examples is not an *indirect* means of explaining—in default of a better. For any general definition can be misunderstood too. The point is that *this* is how we play the game. (I mean the language-game with the word 'game')" (*PI*, 1, 71). We do not teach

Wittgenstein's Account
of Meaning

someone less than we know ourselves, when we explain something this way. Somehow we feel we *ought* to be able to offer up a dictionary sort of definition of games in general, but we cannot. And this is not a failure. We can and do explain, by describing cases, and leaving our list unbounded. "And do we know any more about it ourselves? Is it only other people whom we cannot tell exactly what a game is?—But this is not ignorance. We do not know the boundaries because none have been drawn." This is curious. When we look closely here, it seems as if we have lost our grip on the concept "game." Where are its boundaries? "To repeat, we can draw a boundary—for a special purpose," writes Wittgenstein. "Does it take that to make the concept usable? Not at all! (Except for that special purpose.) No more than it took the definition: 1 pace = 75 cm. to make the measure of length 'one pace' usable. And if you want to say 'But still, before that it wasn't an exact measure', then I reply: very well, it was an inexact one.— Though you still owe me a definition of exactness" (*PI*, 1, 69).

We have observed the problematic character of exactness in pointing to a place, describing a picture, and using a measure of length. Wittgenstein now directs our attention to our commonsense idea that when we explain something to someone by giving him examples, we are in effect asking him to pick out what is common to all the examples. There is something misleading about this, something about it which does not bear close examination. Suppose we gave someone a series of pictures, each with many different colors, and told him that the color which all the pictures have in common is what we call "green." "This is a definition, and the other will get to understand it by looking for and seeing what is common to the pictures. Then he can look *at*, can point *to*, the common thing" (*PI*, 1, 72). But this gets us into difficulties as soon as we try it with definitions of other than the same shade of a color. It suggests, and misleads by suggesting, that "to have understood the definition means to have in one's mind an idea of the thing defined, and that is a sample or picture." Suppose we are talking about shapes of figures, however, or different shades of a color. Imagine we are shown various different samples of leaves and told "This is called a 'leaf.' " Then, in Wittgenstein's words, "I get an idea of the shape of a leaf, a picture of it in my mind.—But what does

Wittgenstein's Account
                                                                       of Meaning

the picture of a leaf look like when it does not shew us any particular shape, but 'what is common to all shapes of leaf'? Which shade is the 'sample in my mind' of the colour green—the sample of what is common to all shades of green?" (*PI*, 1, 73).

We can see how the picture we have formed from the first example—the example of multicolored pictures—misleads us in other examples. This recalls the discussion in chapter 2 of Hobbes's man from St. Alban's (pp. 22–23). There too the issue was the supposed existence of a conception in the mind (which Hobbes called evidence), separate from the specific examples. We are tempted to think that when we understand a definition of this type it must always mean we have a picture of, or could point to, something that the various pictures or concepts have in common. And this does not seem to be the case if we are talking about the shape of a leaf. On the other hand, we can and do recognize a leaf shape when we see one. " 'Might there not be such "general" samples?' " objects Wittgenstein's imaginary interlocutor. " 'Say a schematic leaf, or a sample of *pure* green?'—Certainly there might. But for such a schema to be understood as a *schema*, and not as the shape of a particular leaf, and for a slip of pure green to be understood as a sample of all that is greenish and not as a sample of pure green—this in turn resides in the way the samples are used." If we doubt this, we should ask ourselves what shape a sample of the color green must be, Wittgenstein suggests. If we made it rectangular, would it not be a sample of a green rectangle? "So should it be 'irregular' in shape? And what is to prevent us then from regarding it—that is, from using it—only as a sample of irregularity of shape?" (*PI*, 1, 73). The answer clearly is that nothing would prevent us from doing that. The existence of a schematic sample of shape or color depends on how we *use* it, which is what Wittgenstein is trying to bring out here.

Inarticulate Knowledge

All of these considerations are intended to reflect on the question we began with, the question about the meaning of the concept "game." They seem to point to the same disconcerting conclusion, namely, that we cannot really say what such a concept means. But

Wittgenstein's Account
of Meaning

how can we know what it means if we can't say what it means? "What does it mean to know what a game is?" Wittgenstein asks. "What does it mean, to know it and not be able to say it? Is this knowledge somehow equivalent to an unformulated definition? So that if it were formulated I should be able to recognize it as the expression of my knowledge?" (*PI*, 1, 75). We are tempted to think that if we could just find the right words for it, our knowledge could be set out clearly and distinctly. But since we cannot find just the right words, we are forced to explain the meaning of a game by giving a series of examples which somehow "hint at" the essence of "game" without ever being able to actually say it. Wittgenstein questions this way of thinking. "Isn't my knowledge, my concept of a game, completely expressed in the explanations I could give? That is, in my describing examples of various kinds of game; shewing how all sorts of other games can be constructed on the analogy of these; saying that I should scarcely include this or this among games; and so on" (*PI*, 1, 75). This is what our knowledge of what a game is consists in, no more but also no less. If our concept of a game is not defined by clear and distinct boundaries, could we not improve it by drawing them? "If someone were to draw a sharp boundary I could not acknowledge it as the one that I too always wanted to draw, or had drawn in my mind. For I did not want to draw one at all" (*PI*, 1, 76). We use the concept *despite* the fact that it seems to lack sharp boundaries, but we still feel that we know what a game is. We will see below that part of the usefulness of such a concept is precisely in its lack of these sharp boundaries, and that this is a central part of the flexibility and power of language.

We are, nevertheless, disturbed by the idea that we can know something and not be able to say it. To this uneasiness Wittgenstein comments:

Compare *knowing* and *saying*:
   how many feet high Mont Blanc is—
   how the word "game" is used—
   how a clarinet sounds.
If you are surprised that one can know something and not be able to say it, you are perhaps thinking of a case like the first. Certainly not of one like the third. [*PI*, 1, 78]

Our knowledge is in many cases an inarticulable knowledge. It cannot be proved or "tested" in these cases by our ability to give a clear explanation, although we can think of other ways to test it in many cases. (We may ask a child who says he knows how a clarinet sounds to point it out from the sounds of other instruments, for example.) We are compelled to raise an objection to this, however, on Hobbes's behalf. "Inarticulate knowledge," on Hobbes's account, is a contradiction in terms. For that is precisely what we call prudence as distinct from real knowledge, the *usefulness* of which flows from its certainty and clarity. And we must wonder, from this viewpoint, whether Wittgenstein's view would not tempt us in many cases to abandon too soon the attempt to make our knowledge secure by formulating it clearly. Wittgenstein may make us too comfortable with inarticulate knowledge, and thereby lead us to abandon scientific inquiry in cases where it might succeed. Thus Hobbes might be taken to be saying that what makes our knowledge inarticulate is a deficiency in our ordinary language; that we need to purify and clarify it so that it permits us to express our thoughts clearly, and that that is all the more reason to reject common speech in favor of precise and definite scientific language. Wittgenstein's point, however, is that not only can we not escape ambiguities and imprecision if we are to continue living as human beings,[3] but that these apparent ambiguities and imprecisions are themselves necessary to our lives and our language. If meanings were always distinct and clearly bounded, we could not use a word in new situations. We could not project our language into them (see below). (We would have to give up speaking of ethics. As Wittgenstein asserts in the *Tractatus* [6.421], "Ethics cannot be put into words," and again, "Ethics is transcendental.") We must not lose sight of the fact that speaking a language is itself an activity. We learn what sort of things to say in what sort of circumstances, which enables us to express ourselves even in new situations, where crystalline purity in meanings would preclude us from speaking because we could not know what to say. We can see, in any case, that at least some of our concepts are not limited by distinct boundaries. This is not to say they have no boundaries at all, that anything one wishes to call a game is therefore a game. The

Wittgenstein's Account
                                        of Meaning

limits which *do* more or less restrict our use of a word are a complicated subject, one to which we will turn shortly.

There is a further aspect of the meaning of a word which Wittgenstein considers at this point, and which we find in a sense most disconcerting of all. We can and do use some words, it begins to appear, as if their meanings not only are not defined by clear boundaries, but can be said not to be "fixed," in a certain sense, at all.

> Consider this example. If one says "Moses did not exist", this may mean various things. It may mean: the Israelites did not have a *single* leader when they withdrew from Egypt——or: their leader was not called Moses——or: there cannot have been any-one who accomplished all that the Bible relates of Moses——or: etc. etc.—We may say, following Russell: the name "Moses" can be defined by means of various descriptions. For example, as "the man who led the Israelites through the wilderness", "the man who lived at that time and place and was then called 'Moses' ", "the man who as a child was taken out of the Nile by Pharoah's daughter" and so on. [*PI*, 1, 79][4]

Now, Wittgenstein says, although we may define "Moses" in any of these ways, when told "Moses did not exist," we will probably still ask for clarification by asking what exactly is being denied. When we say something about Moses, then, are we always prepared to substitute "some *one* of these descriptions for 'Moses'?" Wittgenstein answers for himself: "I shall perhaps say: By 'Moses' I understand the man who did what the Bible relates of Moses, or at any rate a good deal of it. But how much? Have I decided how much must be proved false for me to give up my proposition as false? Has the name 'Moses' got a fixed and unequivocal use for me in all possible cases?" (*PI*, 1, 79). What he is pointing to here is that we often use words without fixed meanings. This results in the fact that they are open to question, if there is particular reason to raise a question.

Suppose we have given a definition in advance and then one part of it proves to be false: for example, I tell you that Nora is dead, and describe the person I mean (definition), and then it turns out that one part of the definition is mistaken. "Shall I be prepared to declare the proposition 'N is dead' false—even if it is only something which strikes me as incidental that has turned out false? But where are the bounds of the incidental?—If I had given a definition of the name in such a case, I should now be ready to alter it" (*PI*, 1, 79). The point of this is once again to attack the notion that words are always capable of clear definition, as if they were shorthand for something else (say, a list of attributes), which we might spell out if we wished. "And this can be expressed like this: I use the name 'N' without a *fixed* meaning. (But that detracts as little from its usefulness, as it detracts from that of a table that it stands on four legs instead of three and so sometimes wobbles)" (*PI*, 1, 79). We use words backed, as it were, by a whole series of "props" or meanings which we are prepared to explain if asked, and we can perhaps even do without one or two. But of course we can still use them wrongly, because at some point too many props may be removed for the word to have a use.

Language-Learning and Particular Cases

If the meaning of a word like the word "game" is neither fixed nor clearly and distinctly bounded, how do we ever learn the meaning of a word like "game" at all? Wittgenstein recommends that when we are having difficulties of the sort we have just traced, "always ask yourself: How did we *learn* the meaning of this word . . . ? From what sort of examples? in what language-games?" (*PI*, 1, 77). An examination of the process of language-learning is the remedy for many of our misconceptions about language, because an understanding of how human beings learn to participate in this activity will shed light on the activity itself.

A child is not taught the rules of grammar first, and then expected to apply them. He does not learn the principles of language at all. We can say that, for the most part, "one is not taught one's native language, one learns it," in Paul Ziff's words.[5] The child does not at first, or even for several years, ask for definitions, but simply encounters words. "Mostly, it encounters them in situations where no one is trying to teach it anything. . . . The child simply lives among persons who talk."[6] As children, we learn by hearing words used by those around us, and used in the language games or contexts in which the words are customary. This is a crucial point. We learn more "how we speak" than "what a word means." The situations in which certain words are appropriate are learned by the child: it learns the cases where one says "bye-bye" or "doggy" or "help." When a child learns such a case, that is, a situation where a word is appropriate, does it "understand" the word? Well, in a sense we want to say yes, because the child can use the word. But also we want to say no, because understanding a word really would seem to require knowing how to use it in various different contexts, not only to say "help" when the child needs to be lifted over a puddle, for example, but what help is more generally: what helping with the dishes is, how to offer a helping hand, and so forth. The child does not normally encounter isolated words, but words already in contexts, both verbal and situational. The child is confronted by human beings using language in certain *activities* or situations, where the emotions, facial expressions, etc., are as important as what is actually said. And no two situations or contexts are exactly alike. How then does the child select the features of a situation which are semantically relevant? That is difficult to say. Certainly it would be unusual for someone to tell the child what to look for, and in fact we might doubt our ability to do so. Yet somehow human beings manage to notice, even if not consciously, the features (actions, expressions, objects) of a context which are related to the words being used. Of course there are mistakes, but language-learning would be impossible if they were at all frequent.

The fact that no two contexts are exactly alike points to another feature of language: it is an open-ended system. The openness of language both requires and permits the projection into new circumstances of words and phrases learned in other, slightly different contexts. Pitkin describes one particular example of actual language-learning that is an excellent illustration of the idea of learning from cases. It involves a three-year-old child who came into her parents' bedroom one morning dragging her blanket. When her parents told her to take it back and put it on her bed, she said, "I simply can't function in the morning without my blanket." Pitkin writes,

At first her parents were astonished; they had no idea that a word like "function" was in the child's vocabulary. But then they

Wittgenstein's Account
of Meaning

recognized the expression as one the mother characteristically uses about her morning coffee, and everything seemed clear: the child had merely "picked up" the expression. Moreover, she "picked it up" well enough to use it correctly on this (almost?) appropriate occasion. Or should we say rather that something in the configuration of the situation reminded her of those other situations, involving mother and coffee, and she just found herself saying the words?[7]

Pitkin points out that while the child does know something about the word "function" at this point, we would not say she really understands "function." If we asked her what it means she could not tell us.

It seems at first glance that a child learns language by being told the names or labels of things: "doggy," "kitty," "Mom," and perhaps adjectives like "hot," or "blue." But we should by this time be suspicious of the accuracy of this view, as a result of Wittgenstein's examination of the similar picture in Augustine's *Confessions*. We can now see in what way this picture misleads us. In the blanket example above, the child did not learn what functioning is by having it pointed out by an adult. "Clearly, it was the child itself that 'looked at language and looked at the world and looked back and forth.' "[8] The child recognized a situation, a context, and used the word it thought to be appropriate to it. We will still be misled, however, if we think of the learned word as a label for a situation. Instead, we should see it not as a label at all, but as a signal in a game, an appropriate "move" to be made, to go back to Wittgenstein. What is learned is not so much what something is, as when one uses a word. The child, in short, learns to participate in language games. He learns what we human beings say to each other, in what circumstances.

The openness of language, the capacity to be projected into new situations, is not merely a useful feature: it is an essential characteristic of language, the *sine qua non*. If no two situations are exactly alike, what is it that provides the continuity which allows us to use the same word or expression in both, to recognize precisely the similarities which "count" for the appropriateness of a particular word? It is important to note that if words were confined to the exact situation in which they were first used, we could not be

Wittgenstein's Account
of Meaning

said to have a language at all. Locke, as we saw, made a similar point.[9]

The meaning of a word is learned from particular cases by the language-learning child. But this too is an inadequate formulation, because what Wittgenstein teaches us is that the meaning of a word is *constituted by* those various particular cases. The child learns the meaning of "play," for example, from the various occasions on which he hears it: "go play with Jimmy," "stop playing and come to dinner," "don't leave the playground," "let's play catch." Eventually he hears it in other contexts, and will be able himself to use the word more widely. He will hear other expressions such as "play the piano," "if you play your cards right," "we saw the O'Neill play last night," and so forth. Adults who use this word in all these ways can indeed be said to know the meaning of "play," but their knowledge is not different in kind from the child's, it is only constituted by more cases.[10] Nevertheless, language is systematic. And this is what allows us to project it into new situations. As Pitkin writes, "The individual must draw his own conclusions, abstract his own definitions from the cases he encounters; it is all up to him. And yet, it is not all up to him, for there is such a thing as making a mistake, learning wrong [*sic*]. Children do that, and then we correct them."[11] Language is characterized by a kind of tension which is responsible for both its usefulness and its power. The tension comes from the fact that a natural language[12] is both regularized—that is, characterized by rules which make it possible to say a word is used incorrectly—and at the same time is open to new contexts, is not "everywhere bounded by rules" (*PI*, 1, 84). We must now examine these characteristics in more detail. We will look at what Wittgenstein says about rules and the regularities of human life in which they are grounded.

Grammar

Wittgenstein discovers that we use the word "game" without being able to define it precisely, but nevertheless knowing what it means. He then turns to the question of the nature of his own activity: is he, by studying language philosophically, seeking a remedy for a defect in language?[13] The answer is no. It is, he says, "of the essence

Wittgenstein's Account
                                                         of Meaning

of our investigation that we do not seek to learn anything *new* by it. We want to *understand* something that is already in plain view. For *this* is what we seem in some sense not to understand" (*PI*, 1, 89). Why is it that we seem to be unable to *say* what we do after all know—for example, what a game is? "Something that we know when no one asks us, but no longer know when we are supposed to give an account of it" is, he writes, "something that we need to *remind* ourselves of" (*PI*, 1, 89).[14] The investigation of phenomena, according to Wittgenstein, is actually carried out by reminding ourselves of *"the kind of statement* that we make about phenomena": it is directed, in this sense, not so much at the phenomena themselves as "towards the *'possibilities'* of phenomena."[15] The investigation "is therefore a grammatical one" (*PI*, 1, 90). We are investigating a concept or an expression, he tells us, by examining the grammar of a word. "Grammar," he writes later, "tells us what kind of object anything is" (*PI*, 1, 373). This notion of the grammar of a word is central to his understanding of language, and to our inquiry about the meanings of words.

Wittgenstein begins to use this expression, and to explain it, in the *Blue and Brown Books*. Here Wittgenstein is examining an old philosophical question, which he traces to Socrates, in fact—the question of what knowledge is. We find out what knowledge is, he says, by looking into the language games where the word is *used*, the *circumstances* where we say "he knows" or "I know." The grammar of an expression tells us what contexts or situations the word is appropriate to. "To ask ourselves what, in the particular case we are examining, we should call 'getting to know,' " is, Wittgenstein says, merely to examine "the grammar (the use) of the word 'to know' " (*BB*, p. 23; cf. *BB*, p. 24). The grammar of a word might be said to include all the various expressions in which we can use the word, and the situations in which these are suitable. It is not simply a verbal matter, but encompasses situations, contexts, and activities in the *world*. Just as "it is part of the grammar of the word 'chair' that *this* is what we call 'to sit on a chair' " (*BB*, p. 24), we can find out something about knowledge by examining the grammar of the word "knowledge." The italicized *"this"* is meant to indicate a set of phenomena in the world, to which Wittgenstein points, as it were, in the imagination.[16] We do sometimes make

Wittgenstein's Account
of Meaning

mistakes in learning the grammar of a concept, or learn incompletely. We may know only part of the grammar of an expression, and then be surprised to find a new use as we learn more. Such learning never ceases for some expressions, especially since the grammar of a word is itself not something permanent and fixed. It may change as a word is used in new ways: what first appears as a violation of a grammatical rule gradually becomes acceptable. A child may master the grammar of a word only bit by bit, corrected only as he is detected using a word wrongly. For example, a friend who was always asked the same question by her mother on cold mornings, or after a bath, learned to use the word "robe-on" for the terry cloth garment customarily used in these circumstances. She was accustomed only to hearing, "Have you got your robe on?" or "You should have your robe on," and only when she was a teenager was this case of mistaken grammar detected by a friend and remedied. We are always vulnerable to such mistakes; that on the whole we do not make them is an indication of the complexity of an expression's grammar because it is the multiplicity of ways a word can be used which prevents us from learning from only one type of example in most cases.

Grammar tells us what kind of thing anything is because it controls the ways we can use expressions and thus relates them to our world. When, in the *Meno*,[17] Socrates tells his companion that he would define "figure" to be "that which always goes with color," he is making a statement about the grammar of these words. It is the grammar of color which tells us it is the kind of thing which always has a shape or "figure," just as, to use another example, "a 'tone' is the sort of thing that has a 'pitch'—which is to say that our concepts of 'tone' and 'pitch' are grammatically related in certain ways."[18] Again, as Wittgenstein puts it, grammar regulates "the *'possibilities'* of phenomena" (*PI*, 1, 90).

This matter may be made clearer, as well as more germane to our concern here, if we consider examples of words other than nouns we associate with physical objects. To know what a riddle is, we can say, involves mastering the grammar of "riddle," that is, the sorts of circumstances which count as "telling a riddle," "solving a riddle," "being baffled by a riddle," and so on. We learn the grammar primarily by assimilating a jumble of separate cases, cases

Wittgenstein's Account
of Meaning

where words are spoken by those around us who are not trying to teach us anything. As children we learn what a law is, for example, or what "law" means, from a great variety of expressions not all of which seem to mean the same thing. We learn that "law" is somehow connected with policemen and judges, and perhaps with paying a fine. So laws can be violated, or broken (but not repaired), or enforced, or upheld. But the law of gravity isn't enforced, nor is the law of averages. Laws are somehow like rules, but some are written, some are discovered. We learn that laws are something you can be outside of ("outlaw"), or scoff at ("scofflaw"), and they are connected to courts, and lawyers, and congressmen, to punishment, prison, and justice. They are supported by precedents and principles, and there is also the law of the land. There are good laws and bad laws, natural laws, laws which are made to be broken, and so on. When we assimilate all these usages or expressions, and many more, we find ourselves in control of the grammar which regulates our use of this complex term, and, more important, we discover that we can use the concept in new situations, can recognize new instances of laws or new uses (e.g., Parkinson's Law).

We must be careful not to think of the grammar of a word as a closed, rule-bound system. This is the same temptation we have resisted before, and now it points again to a certain tension in Wittgenstein's understanding—a sort of balancing act which keeps two opposing strains in his thought poised, with neither taking command to a point where we would call this understanding a "theory" of language. Although grammar "regulates the possibilities," that is, both permits and guides our speaking, the language is not "everywhere circumscribed by rules."[19] Wittgenstein returns again to the example of a chair:

I say "There is a chair". What if I go up to it, meaning to fetch it, and it suddenly disappears from sight?——"So it wasn't a chair, but some kind of illusion".——But in a few moments we see it again and are able to touch it and so on.——"So the chair was there after all and its disappearance was some kind of illusion".——But suppose that after a time it disappears again—or seems to disappear. What are we to say now? Have you rules ready for such cases—rules saying whether one may use the word

Wittgenstein's Account
of Meaning

"chair" to include this kind of thing? But do we miss them when we use the word "chair"; and are we to say that we do not really attach any meaning to this word, because we are not equipped with rules for every possible application of it? [*PI*, 1, 80]

That is, our grammar is open: we won't know what to say in every case. The possibilities of phenomena are regulated in the sense that we cannot come across a chair that can walk or talk or disappear, or at least if we do we shall probably wonder what to call it. "Can a machine have toothache?" asks Wittgenstein. And we want to say no, that is not possible. "Did you mean to say," he asks, "that all our past experience has shown that a machine never had toothache?" That is of course true, but he is indicating here something deeper than that. When we deny that machines can have toothaches, Wittgenstein tells us that "the impossibility of which you speak is a logical one" (*BB*, p. 16). We don't say machines cannot have toothaches because we have made an empirical generalization to that effect. Machines cannot have toothaches because nothing we could see or experience would count as a "machine having toothache." Our language precludes this possibility. It is the grammar of "machine" which tells us they are not the kind of things that have toothaches, and the grammar of "toothache" prevents our attributing one to a machine.

To return to the political example, we may find there are cases where we cannot decide whether to call something a law, and which suggest to us that our knowledge of what a law really is is incomplete. Perhaps this will cause us to look further. If we hear a dispute between two people who cannot agree on whether some law passed by Congress is really a law, we may come to realize that some laws need to be "tested" before we can know whether they are truly laws, and that this "testing" has something to do with, in some way, a judgment about whether a law accords with the broader goals of our political community. That is, whether something is a law or not may be connected with the aims of our state, or of our constitution. Thus to find out more fully what a "law" is, we cannot leave it at citing various uses; for deciding it is not merely a matter of words.

Wittgenstein's Account
of Meaning

Nature and Convention:
Wittgenstein and Locke

It is possible here to raise a serious objection, based on the following considerations. We have said that grammar tells us what kind of thing anything is, that it regulates the possibilities of phenomena, and the examples seem to bear out that claim. Now, grammar is learned from individual cases of speaking about things or speaking during activities; we learn the grammar as we learn language games. But language games to some extent seem to be arbitrary. After all, isn't it merely a matter of convention that we play this language game rather than another?[20] Couldn't we just as well have language games in which it is perfectly all right to speak of machines having toothaches? If our system of concepts is of human construction, *imposed* on a world to which we have access only by means of our senses, why could we not just as well have language games, or concepts, very different from those we know? We need only recall the suggestions to this effect by both Hobbes and Locke, which they rejected in the end, however, in favor of natural standards. Nature, we might say, though it does not give us the concepts themselves, causes us to find the concepts we have to be most "natural" or efficient. Now, for Hobbes and Locke, the notion of the "naturalness" of our concepts had as a corollary the notion that we can discover their original and precise meanings by thinking our way back to the conditions which must have existed when these concepts were needed and thus invented. Both of these notions, however, were abandoned by later thinkers, perhaps in view of the failure of attempts to recover the precise meanings (or of attempts, as Hobbes's, to restore them to use, when they were recovered).

Despite his radical critique of the understanding of language shared by Hobbes and Locke, however, Wittgenstein might be said to restore the respectability of their claim that our concepts are natural, at least to some degree. He returns again and again to this problem of the conventionality of our language games, of our grammar, and eventually leads us to a more complicated understanding of the very notion of convention. Although our language games and our grammar may be conventional, they are not

Wittgenstein's Account
of Meaning

accidental, for Wittgenstein. Rather, they are grounded in or based on characteristic ways we human beings have of living and acting together, characteristics of human beings simply. "It is only in normal cases that the use of a word is clearly prescribed; we know, are in no doubt, what to say in this or that case. The more abnormal the case, the more doubtful it becomes what we are to say. And if things were quite different from what they actually are—if there were for instance no characteristic expression of pain, of fear, of joy; if rule became exception and exception rule; or if both became phenomena of roughly equal frequency——this would make our normal language-games lose their point" (*PI*, 1, 142). So if our language games are conventional, they are conventions based on certain "very general facts of nature. (Such facts as mostly do not strike us because of their generality)" (*PI*, 2, 12, p. 230).

Wittgenstein offers numerous examples. Although weights and measures represent for us paradigms of conventionality, the *fact* that we weigh things itself depends on some "very general facts of nature." "The procedure of putting a lump of cheese on a balance and fixing the price by the turn of the scale would lose its point if it frequently happened for such lumps to suddenly grow or shrink for no obvious reason" (*PI*, 1, 142). "Why does it sound queer," Wittgenstein asks, "to say: 'For a second he felt deep grief'? Only because it so seldom happens?" (*PI*, 2, 1, p. 174). The answer of course is no, not because it is rare, but because deep grief is not the kind of thing one can feel "for a second"—whatever emotion that is, we want to say, it is not deep grief. But isn't it simply a convention that we say this about grief? Wittgenstein points to the fact that the kind of thing grief is is connected with what human beings are like, the ways they express things they feel. " 'Grief' describes a pattern which recurs, with different variations, in the weave of our life. If a man's bodily expression of sorrow and of joy alternated, say with the ticking of a clock, here we should not have the characteristic formation of the pattern of sorrow or of the pattern of joy" (*PI*, 2, 1, p. 174). Our lives, and the world, would have to be different for our concepts to change in fundamental ways. And of course it could be different, so we will admit that such things are in a sense conventional. But they are somehow, as

Wittgenstein's Account
                                                             of Meaning

Pitkin puts it, "natural conventions"; they are "not subject to renegotiation at will."[21]

But it is not sufficient to leave the matter here. We are compelled to admit that there is a range of "naturalness" here: it is not enough to say that our conventions are natural to man as man. Languages do differ, although the differences are rarely so great as to preclude translation, and it is the degree of similarity in the grammar of concepts which determines the degree to which they occupy similar places in the conceptual systems of two languages. Many concepts which are not "subject to renegotiation at will" (e.g., English religious words are mainly monotheistic) are nevertheless not "natural" to human beings.[22] The question, of course, remains, *Which* concepts are "naturally conventional," and in what degree? This must be the subject of further inquiry.

The patterns of human activity, on which our linguistic conventions are based and which in turn are grounded in "very general facts of nature," are called by Wittgenstein "forms of life." The term is not meant to be precise; we cannot make a list of all human "forms of life." It characterizes the ways human beings have of being and acting together, including all the "natural" expressions we share. It is characteristic, for example, of human beings to feel pain, or joy, or grief, and to express these in characteristic ways. The ways we express these may be said to be conventional, but they are conventions not fixed simply by custom or agreement. They are fixed, rather,

> by the nature of human life itself, the human fix itself. . . . That *that* should express understanding or boredom or anger . . . is not *necessary*: someone *may* have to be said to "understand suddenly" and then always fail to manifest the understanding five minutes later, just as someone *may* be bored by an earthquake or by the death of his child or the declaration of martial law, or *may* be angry at a pin or a cloud or a fish, just as someone may quietly (but comfortably?) sit on a chair of nails. That human beings on the whole do not respond in these ways is, therefore, seriously referred to as *conventional*; but now we are thinking of convention not as the arrangements a particular culture has found convenient. . . . Here the array of "conventions" are not patterns of life which differentiate men from one another, but those exigencies of conduct which all men share.[23]

Wittgenstein's Account
of Meaning

The regularities of convention are the foundations upon which our lives together are based. In Wittgenstein's words, "What has to be accepted, the given, is—so one could say—*forms of life*" (*PI*, 2, 11, p. 226).

The grammar of a word, then, is learned in language games which, although conventional, are not arbitrary. The connections which grammar draws for us, or allows us to draw, among our concepts are not strictly accidental. That happiness is linked to certain facial expressions, and is not normal in some circumstances; that anger is expressed in characteristic ways, and is associated with certain natural occasions for anger;[24] that pain is linked with what is called pain behavior, as well as to possible responses to someone in pain—such as pity, compassion, and so forth—all these things are indeed built into our grammar. But beyond that they are based on natural characteristics of human life on this planet, on our forms of life.[25] There is no guarantee that we will not meet with cases we don't know what to do with, as Wittgenstein often points out. And of course we can imagine different circumstances, circumstances in which our concepts would perhaps be different. Wittgenstein put it this way: "If anyone believes that certain concepts are absolutely the correct ones, and that having different ones would mean not realizing something that we realize—then let him imagine certain very general facts of nature to be different from what we are used to, and the formation of concepts different from the usual ones will become intelligible to him" (*PI*, 2, 11, p. 230).

Forms of Life and the Mistake of Reduction

What is the source of our agreement as to the concepts we use? Wittgenstein appears to be saying that our agreement comes from the grammar of an expression or concept, which we learn from language games. He imagines a critic saying to him, " 'So you are saying that human agreement decides what is true and what is false?' " As if, we might say, human beings had annual meetings to review the conventions of their grammar. But Wittgenstein answers: "It is what human beings *say* that is true and false; and they agree in the *language* they use. That is not agreement in

Wittgenstein's Account
of Meaning

opinions but in forms of life" (*PI*, 1, 241). The grammatical conventions, the language, are grounded in forms of life which human beings share, which are somehow natural to them. That is, our concepts are not "true" or "false" simply, they are part of our language; and "it is not a kind of *seeing* on our part, it is our *acting* which lies at the bottom of the language-game."[26]

The agreement as to concepts for Locke, however, *does* rest on what Wittgenstein called "a kind of seeing on our part." In chapter 3 we traced Locke's account of agreement in language to agreement in the simple ideas, which are the building blocks of all our complex ideas, and which are received passively by the mind. This is a kind of seeing: we agree, Locke says, because our minds receive the same impressions from without. As to acquiring the simple ideas, we recall Locke saying that the understanding "is merely passive; and whether or no it will have these beginnings, and as it were materials of knowledge, is not in its power" (*Essay*, 2.1.25; see also our chap. 3, p. 52). The faculty of abstraction, which isolates the simples, is shared by all of us, and this fact alone guarantees our agreement on the simple ideas. Now for Locke, this agreement meant in turn that we can in principle discover the constituent parts of our *complex* ideas—including the moral and political concepts—by progressively analyzing them into the simpler ideas on which we agree.

Wittgenstein has raised questions about this account of language and human understanding. In Wittgenstein's account of language, our concepts are not collections of simple ideas on which we agree, but, so to speak, tools in our activity of speaking, and it is this activity which constitutes our agreement. And the crucial notion here is that these activities are not reducible to something simpler; the terms we use in a language game are not necessarily constructed out of simpler elements. Wittgenstein directs us rather to look at the language game itself, and above all to its purpose, or to the place it occupies in our lives. A language game, or a game such as chess, for example, "has not only rules, but also a *point*" (*PI*, 1, 564). Wittgenstein discovers this from the fact that he is "inclined to distinguish between the essential and the inessential in a game, too," and that he does this by looking at the purpose or the goal of the activity. For Locke the various human activities, of which politics is one, are to be understood as complicated combinations

Wittgenstein's Account
of Meaning

of a few more basic activities. Politics is something we do for the sake of preserving our property or lives. The complex variety of goods or goals for the sake of which we act might be said to be reducible to two sorts, according to Locke—on the one hand, the goals which are purely conventional, or relative to each individual (beauty, art, devotion to truth); on the other, the natural goals or goods agreed on by all: those which satisfy our desire or need for comfort, security, or power. The conventional goals are not capable of being ordered or ranked, while the latter—the natural goods or goals—are reducible to one primary need, self-preservation. For Wittgenstein, however, there is no sharp distinction between these types of activities, or "forms of life." Forms of life are "what has to be accepted, the given" (*PI*, 2, 11, p. 226). "If I have exhausted the justifications I have reached bedrock and my spade is turned. Then I am inclined to say 'This is simply what I do' " (*PI*, 1, 217). We must understand a human form of life on its own terms. We do this by looking at the overall place it occupies in our lives, which means we begin by asking what its purpose or goal is. Wittgenstein's account directs us to inquire into the relations among our forms of life without necessarily seeking to reduce complicated ones to more simple or basic ones.

We are left, however, with the question of how or whether we can order or understand better the obscurely related—and sometimes contradictory—forms of life in which our concepts have their use in language games. How do we understand the notion of courage, which has a part in war but also in politics? What are the priorities? Wittgenstein does not answer this question, but through his account we learn to see it as a question. We learn that we cannot set aside the goals toward which the activities themselves claim to be directed in favor of some neutral or universal aims which lie underneath *all* our activities: the neutral or universal goals don't exist, we don't have terms for them, and we cannot invent such terms because they would have no meaning abstracted from the purposeful activities or language games in which they would find meaning. If words have meanings *in* language games, and these are part of our forms of life, we must look *at* them, and not beneath them, in order to understand what we do. If Wittgenstein is correct, our agreement is in the complicated forms of life themselves, not in

Wittgenstein's Account
of Meaning

"simple ideas" received passively by the mind. He explains the meanings of words by tracing the complicated language games in which he claims we learn them, and these language games in turn are nowhere clearly defined. We get the impression that two people using a term like "justice"—that is, what Locke calls a complex idea—may not mean quite the same thing, might use the term in different senses, or use it with different boundaries limiting their conceptions, or even no fixed boundaries at all! We are compelled to think of Hobbes's dictum, with which Locke agreed, that "one man calleth *Wisdome*, what another calleth *feare*; and one *cruelty*, what another justice; . . . And therefore such names can never be true grounds of any ratiocination" (*Leviathan*, chap. 4, pp. 109–10).

How, then, does Wittgenstein help us in any way at all to overcome the difficulties which Hobbes's insight exposes to us? How can political philosophy inquire into justice, find out what justice *is*, in such a world? Where Locke told us that what we needed was to isolate the constituent parts of such ideas and thereby compel some agreement, arrive at some certainty, regarding the political things, Wittgenstein tells us there are no constituent parts at all! If the situation seemed hopeless to the successors of Hobbes and Locke, how much worse it is after Wittgenstein, or so we may think.

We want to suggest that, conceived in the above terms, the project of understanding justice is indeed hopeless. That is, so long as we conceive of the science of political phenomena on the model of modern natural science, with its particular emphasis on explanation by reduction, we are doomed to failure. There is an alternative way of approaching politics, however. It is an alternative both pointed out and to some degree illuminated by Wittgenstein's understanding of language. It is an approach characterized by some degree of disagreement, and, to put it in the worst light, endless bickering. It is the approach which Hobbes explicitly rejected when he set down his new principles and founded his new science—that is, the approach of his predecessors. We turn to two examples of it in the next chapters.

Wittgenstein's Account
of Meaning

Aristotle's "Ethics"

The Place of Classical Political Science

We do not require Wittgenstein's account of language to tell us that Hobbes's method did not succeed, insofar as its goal was definite conceptions of the real meanings of politically relevant terms. Long before Wittgenstein's *Philosophical Investigations*, political science had ceased to understand itself as the science of what is just or unjust, strictly speaking.[1] What we may say of Wittgenstein's account is not that it teaches us to abandon what Hobbes took to be his task, but that it indicates a possible source of error in Hobbes's thought and thus reopens the debate which Hobbes thought he had settled. We must try to reconstruct the terms of the debate in order to understand the other side, and try to grasp the method which Hobbes's scientific method replaced.

Hobbes's account of the distinction between science (true knowledge) and prudence (common sense) required that he make a radical break with the classical understanding of the distinction between theoretical and practical sciences, in order to have any science of politics at all. Once certainty is made the criterion of science, it is difficult to see how there can be a science of a practical matter such as politics. Hobbes circumvents this difficulty by replacing the distinction between theoretical and practical sciences with the distinction between theoretical sciences and applied sciences. The application of Hobbes's scientific understanding of society in order to guarantee peace was understood by him to be no different from the application of geometry to solve a surveyor's problems of measurement. According to Hobbes, the absolute certainty of a theoretical science, which deals with the universal and necessary, not only does not preclude its guiding us in practice, but is what permits it to guide us. The utility and thus the justification for any science is contingent on its incontestability, or its capacity to withstand the "cavils of skeptics."[2]

According to Hobbes, the role of science or philosophy in human life is to serve practice. "The end of knowledge is power; and the use of theorems (which, among geometricians, serve for the finding out of properties) is for the construction of problems; and, lastly, the scope of all speculation is the performing of some action, or thing to be done" (*De Corpore*, 1.1.6). The utility of political science, which is the application of reason to the problems of society, might be said to be that it serves the first law which political science itself discovers: to seek peace. The utility of "moral and civil philosophy," writes Hobbes, "is to be estimated, not so much by the commodities we have by knowing these sciences, as by the calamities we receive from not knowing them" (*De Corpore*, 1.1.7). In order to be useful, a science must be indisputable. Now, Hobbes's conception of the nature of science or knowledge is closely tied to his conception of its function in human life. Theoretical science is justified by its application. Before we purify our knowledge it is not knowledge, only prudence, and as such in need of science. At the least one can say that Hobbes's moral or civil philosophy did not justify itself in practice. It may be that Hobbes is correct in his understanding of science, and wrong only in thinking that a science of justice or moral terms is possible. This might be said to be the conclusion to which later philosophers were eventually forced, on the basis of Hobbes's restriction of the use of the term science to enterprises of a certain sort, together with more than two centuries of recurring failure.

The question which we are now compelled to raise, as a result of

Aristotle's *Ethics*

the doubts posed by Wittgenstein's account of language, is whether Hobbes's restriction of the use of "science" is not itself a result of the same misunderstanding of language which led him to hope for too much from his civil philosophy. To understand the transformation in the use of "science" which Hobbes and his contemporaries accomplished, we need to examine the understanding of science which he challenged and replaced. What was the understanding of the role of science or philosophy in politics before Hobbes? What were the characteristics, in regard to method and subject, of pre-Hobbesian political science? The logical choice of subject for this examination is Aristotle, because Hobbes makes it explicit that his new science is intended to replace that of Aristotle.

We need, then, to investigate Aristotle's understanding of the place of political science or political knowledge in human life, both as to its intellectual foundations and its relation to political practice. It is well to begin by noting that Aristotle's understanding is complicated and ambiguous: the ambiguities and lacunae in his account of knowledge direct us to see what is not made explicit. One thing, however, is clear immediately: knowledge or science (*epistēmē*) is used more broadly by Aristotle than by Hobbes, although Aristotle was also aware of the narrow use.

The Problem of Political Science in Book 1 of the "Nicomachean Ethics"

The most systematic account of the epistemological and practical status of political science is to be found in books 1 and 6 of the *Nicomachean Ethics*. This account, together with points made in the *Metaphysics, Topics,* and *Posterior Analytics,* will be the basis for our inquiry. As a preliminary we may observe that there *is* a political science, according to book 1 of the *Nicomachean Ethics.* Aristotle indicates that, in general terms, it is the science of what is good for human beings (1094b5). Political science is a body of knowledge with principles and truths not necessarily demonstrable by syllogism; it remains to be seen precisely what its dependence on or relation to first principles, names, and definitions is.

There are three brief discussions of method in book 1 of the *Nicomachean Ethics* (1094b, 1095b, 1098a–1098b). Each has to do with the notion of fundamental principles, and all three leave us with the same ambiguity about the relation between fundamental principles and the investigation of ethics. The first discussion of method makes explicit the fact that political science should not be expected to be strictly demonstrable, nor its truths precise.[3] One who is educated, according to Aristotle, seeks "that degree of precision in each kind of study which the nature of the subject at hand admits" (1094b25). The strict demonstration appropriate to mathematics is here explicitly contrasted with the "merely probable" conclusions of oratory. Political science may fall somewhere in between, however. What is made clear is that political science calls for a certain degree of judgment on the part of its practitioner. Now, Aristotle continues, a man "can judge competently the things he knows," and "a good judge in each particular field is one who has been trained in it" (1094b23–1095a1). For this reason, "a young man is not equipped to be a student of politics; for he has no experience in the actions which ... form the basis and subject matter of the discussion" (1095a1–1095a3). If we scrutinize these three remarks with care, Aristotle's point turns out to be that a man is ready to be a student of something only when he is a good judge of the subject, that is, only when he already knows (gignōskei) it. The issue raised by this formulation is the status of the foundation or first principles of Aristotle's investigation. From what does the inquiry begin, if its subject must be known before we seek to know it? The first discussion of method leaves us with this quandary.

The second discussion of method takes up this qustion on the next page but one. Here Aristotle introduces the problem directly, by saying that "arguments which proceed from fundamental principles [archai] are different from arguments that lead up to them" (1095a31). He does not say which sort he is engaged in, however:[4]

> We must start with the known. But this term has two connotations: "what is known to us" and "what is known" pure and simple. Therefore, we should start perhaps from what is known to us. For that reason, to be a competent student of what is right and just, and of politics generally, one must first have received a proper upbringing in moral conduct. The acceptance of a fact as

a fact is the starting point, and if this is sufficiently clear, there will be no further need to ask why it is so. A man with this kind of background has or can easily acquire the foundations from which he must start. [1095b1–8]

The ambiguity over the two senses of "know" is a theme we will consider in detail below, in our discussion of book 6. It may suffice here to summarize Aristotle's point as follows: we must in some sense already *know* whatever it is we are inquiring into, but the inquiry will transform our knowledge. We may know something without being able to articulate it, in the sense in which we know the grammar of a word, but it is our inquiry which tells us "what kind of thing anything is" in a deeper, articulated sense.

As a consequence of this point Aristotle explicitly limits his audience to those who already know the principles of ethics, at least in the sense of understanding the code of an honorable man.[5] It will be enough, Aristotle seems to say, if we can articulate more fully for this man the nature of the principles he already knows, without questioning whether they are right. As we will see in the discussion below, this matter is more complicated. But Aristotle has a compelling reason for presenting his subject in this way.

This discussion of method also serves to indicate that the proper beginning point for inquiry is common speech or common opinions about what is good and bad, that is, the opinions common to men of good breeding. We do not yet know whether these are the fundamental principles of inquiry. They seem to be the first principles or starting points (*archai*), but perhaps first principles of another kind are the goal of the inquiry. Thus the question of the direction of investigation, with which Aristotle began, is left open.[6]

The third discussion of method occurs several pages further on (1098b). It is here that the difficulty is most openly exposed. Aristotle begins by recalling the earlier point that "one should not require precision in all pursuits alike" (1098a27), but only that degree of precision appropriate to the subject. "A carpenter and a geometrician both want to find a right angle, but they do not want to find it in the same sense: the former wants to find it to the extent to which it is useful for his work, the latter, wanting to see truth, tries to ascertain what it is and what sort of thing it is" (1098a28–33). Hobbes, we may recall, insists that understanding always relies on the same type of explanation, using the resolutive-compositive method. Aristotle, by contrast, notes that "in some instances, e.g., when dealing with fundamental principles, it is sufficient to point out convincingly that such and such is in fact the case" (1098b2). Our commonsense knowledge of the principles of ethics, then, can count as fundamental principles. Aristotle confirms this by noting that we acquire some fundamental principles "by some sort of habituation" (1098b4).[7]

We learn the fundamental principles of ethics by being brought up properly. Why then do we require Aristotle's treatise? Is it a theory of ethics which investigates the reasons for ethical principles? He insists that it is not; he is not asking why, because it is sufficient to know that something is right: "The purpose of the present study is not, as it is in other inquiries, the attainment of theoretical knowledge: we are not conducting this inquiry in order to know what virtue is, but in order to become good, else there would be no advantage in studying it" (1103b26–30). We are left wondering why he wrote the *Ethics*, in light of his claim in book 1 that one must already know what is good before he can study it. Aristotle focuses our attention on the question of the status of his enterprise by means of these three discussions of method. Is his inquiry more like that of the carpenter or the geometrician above?[8] This question is central to book 6.

Three other points about method are indicated in book 1. We have already noted Aristotle's claim that the beginning point of inquiry is common opinion, or "what we say" about the matters in question.[9] In addition, Aristotle indicates, the preliminary results of our investigation, which may be reached by logical argument (as in 1097a15–25), by induction (from particular cases to a general rule [1097a25–1097b1]), by analogy, or whatever,[10] must be tested against or examined "on the basis of the views commonly expressed about it" (1098b10). Agreement with our common opinions is one way of confirming our conclusions,[11] as Aristotle seeks to show in chapter 8 of book 1. We may say that one of Aristotle's investigative tools consists in inquiry into what Wittgenstein calls the grammar of concepts: what is good as an end, for example, must be what we praise for its own sake ("good" is connected to "praising," and in a certain way) (1101b10–1101b30). We will return to the

Aristotle's *Ethics*

question of method below. First we must try to resolve the question of why Aristotle writes the *Ethics*.

Let us turn to book 6 of the *Nicomachean Ethics*, which constitutes the single most comprehensive discussion by Aristotle of the place of the rational faculties and knowledge in human life. There is something missing, however. Aristotle neglects to mention, except obliquely, the place of the very enterprise in which he is himself engaged in the *Ethics*.

The Rational Faculties

Aristotle begins in book 6 to consider the intellectual excellences, the excellences of character having been discussed in the books immediately preceding. He offers first some "prefatory remarks about the soul" (1139a3). The soul, he begins, has two parts, rational and irrational. The former (rational, or *logos*) part of the soul has itself two parts, "one whereby we contemplate those things whose first principles are invariable, and one whereby we contemplate those things which admit of variation" (1139a7–8). These he distinguishes by name as the scientific faculty and the calculative faculty, respectively. The calculative faculty is identified with deliberating. It is important to note that the scientific and calculative faculties, as stated, are not mutually exclusive: there may be a class of things which admit of variation themselves while their "first principles" remain invariable.

It begins to appear, in the beginning of chapter 2 of book 6, that Aristotle has in mind for the calculative faculty something similar to what we have seen in Hobbes as the principle of reason itself. He appears to think reason is a kind of "reckoning" concerned only with the means to ends which are supplied independently by desire. Aristotle, however, leaves the role of the calculative faculty ambiguous here. The ground presented in chapter 1 for the distinction between the scientific and calculative faculties is in chapter 2 shifted a bit. It now appears that the former involves only intellectual truth and falsehood, whereas the latter is concerned with action or activity in the broad sense (including making· or production). The calculative faculty thus involves some sort of combination of desire and reason: "If the choice is to be good, the reasoning must be true and the desire correct; that is, reasoning must affirm what desire pursues: this then is the kind of thought and the kind of truth that is practical and concerned with action" (1139a25). This realm is distinguished from the realm of the soul's scientific faculty as follows: "On the other hand, in the kind of thought involved in theoretical knowledge and not in action or production, the good and the bad state are, respectively, truth and falsehood" (1139a25–28). We are to understand, it seems, that science is distinguished from reason concerned with action not only by the invariability of subject matter but also by the status of the reasoner as either an actor or merely a contemplator. In Aristotle's words, "Thought alone moves nothing; only thought which is directed to some end and concerned with action can do so" (1139a36–37). This in contrast to Hobbes, for whom the only distinction between scientific reason and reason concerned with action is the scientific method, which might be said to transform the latter into the former by making it incontrovertible. According to Hobbes, as we saw in chapter 2, all reasoning is "reckoning" consequences.[12] Unless secured by the scientific method (the resolutive-compositive method), this reckoning is subject to doubt; and even scientific knowledge proper remains at one remove from the phenomenal world, in a sense, because it deals with our conceptions of phenomena. Nevertheless, for Hobbes it is in principle possible to have a science of anything for which human beings have (or can invent) names or language. Aristotle, it would appear, is making a fundamental distinction between the scientific and the calculative faculties on the basis of what he believes to be a fundamental difference in the nature of the things with which each is concerned, and the difference in attitude of the reasoner. But this would not be entirely correct, for Aristotle leaves open in chapter 2 the possibility that there is something beyond these two faculties: what at first appears to be a distinction between sciences of things eternal and unchangeable, on the one hand, and the rationality of action which is concerned with the means to the ends which are supplied by virtue, on the other, begins to blur when one considers the activity in which Aristotle himself is engaged in the *Ethics*. The

Aristotle's *Ethics*

status of this activity—which is neither pure theoretical science nor simply deliberation about what to do—becomes in chapter 2 an unspoken theme which hovers over the remainder of book 6.

In chapter 3 of book 6 Aristotle begins to heighten the sense that something is missing from his account. In this and the next four chapters he considers the five ways the soul has of attaining truth: art (*technē*), science (*epistēmē*), practical wisdom (*phronēsis*), theoretical wisdom (*sophia*), and intelligence (*nous*). The reader is not given any account of why Aristotle has derived these five and not others; whatever his reason for omitting such an account, the omission has the effect of making the reader wonder precisely why he presents them as he does, and thus to consider whether they give an adequate account of the faculty of *logos* as a whole. The division Aristotle makes here, however, does not on the surface present any difficulties, and his reasons are revealed as he proceeds.

The first of the five faculties he considers is pure science (*epistēmē*). He carefully points out that he is considering it in its precise sense only, and not in any of the broader uses to which his readers might be accustomed. This caveat is worth bearing in mind. What we know scientifically, he begins, we are convinced cannot vary. The object of scientific knowledge exists by necessity; it is therefore eternal. "Moreover," he continues, "all scientific knowledge is held to be teachable, and what is scientifically knowable is capable of being learned" (1139b25–26). We cannot but recall in this connection Hobbes's great emphasis on the distinction between teaching and persuading, the former being possible in science, the latter always a sign that not knowledge but opinion is being treated. On this characteristic of scientific knowledge Hobbes and Aristotle are in agreement. Now, scientific knowledge is teachable, and all teaching is based on or proceeds from what is already known. Teaching proceeds either by induction—which arrives *at* universals—or by syllogism, which begins from universals. Scientific knowledge, according to Aristotle, is of the syllogistic type; it is a capacity "whereby we demonstrate," and here he refers the reader to his discussion in the *Posterior Analytics*, where we find a similar paragraph: "By demonstration I mean a syllogism productive of scientific knowledge" (*Post. An.*, 1.2; 71b18).[13] Thus, according to both accounts, scientific knowledge cannot stand

Aristotle's *Ethics*

entirely on its own, because "there are starting points or principles from which a syllogism [deduction] proceeds and which are themselves not arrived at by a syllogism [deduction]" (1139b30). According to Aristotle, scientific knowledge taken by itself is hypothetical in the following sense: the certainty of the knower, regarding the things he knows by syllogism, is dependent on the strength of conviction regarding the truth of the first principles from which the procedure begins. And these are not reachable by syllogism. That is, "there cannot be demonstration of the fundamental principles of demonstration, nor, consequently, scientific knowledge of scientific knowledge" (*Post. An.*, 2.19; 100b14). Science is thus in need of some assistance. "A man knows a thing scientifically when he possesses a conviction arrived at in a certain way, and when the first principles on which that conviction rests are known to him with certainty—for unless he is more certain of his first principles than of the conclusion drawn from them he will only possess the knowledge in question accidentally" (1139b35). Scientific knowledge (*epistēmē*) in the strict sense is thus concluded to be capable of demonstration, to be necessary and certain, but nevertheless incomplete or inadequate, because limited by its dependence on first principles which it is not itself able to supply. We should recall in this connection the issue with which this study began, namely, the problematic relationship between science and what Husserl called the "life-world," which led Husserl to see the need for a philosophical account of the grounding of modern science (see pp. 5–7, above). In any event, Aristotle abruptly ends his discussion of purely scientific knowledge after this limitation has been revealed. It is worth noting one more feature of his treatment: the emphasis on the teachability and learnability of *epistēmē* recalls the passage in book 1 of the *Ethics* where Aristotle warns the reader that political science is not capable of being taught to, or learned by, the young because they lack practical experiences. We are compelled to wonder, then, about the relationship between political science and science simply, the teachability of which is stressed in this account. At the very least one can say that Aristotle indicates here that political science is not a science in the strict sense.

The next chapter of book 6 of the *Ethics* considers the sort of knowledge characteristic of a craft or art (*technē*), which deals with part of the class of things that admit of variation. Thus we may be led to think that the class of things to which these were opposed initially, namely, "the things whose first principles are invariable," has been adequately dealt with in the chapter on science. Since this does not turn out to be the case, and on the assumption that the order in which Aristotle treats these rational faculties is significant, we must wonder why the discussion of *technē* follows that of *epistēmē*. One possibility is that he is dealing first with the rational faculties which are least self-sufficient. *Technē*, or what might be called technical knowledge, is characterized by the fact that it knows how to make something or bring something into being, but does not give an account of its end. The end is given; the *technē* is concerned exclusively with means. Thus not only does it not contrast sharply with pure science, *technē* is actually very much like *epistēmē* with regard to its being a procedure which conveys us, in either thought or practice, from one point (a given starting point, or given materials) to another (an end which is unquestioned).

Prudence as a Rational Faculty

Aristotle deals next with practical wisdom or prudence (*phronēsis*).[14] This comprises the second part of the rational faculty concerned with things that admit of variation, the first having been concerned with making or producing an object. Prudence is concerned with acting "with regard to things that are good and bad for human beings" (1140b7; my translation). We may thus expect practical wisdom to include or be identical with political science, and especially because the one example Aristotle gives of a man of prudence is Pericles, a great political man. This expectation is not borne out, however, and we need to discover the reasons for Aristotle's distinguishing practical wisdom or prudence from political science. We must recall that Hobbes too makes this distinction. He made it on the basis of his understanding of science and language. Aristotle's distinction is not made on the same grounds, however.

Aristotle begins with the claim that we can understand what

practical wisdom is by considering the people who are said to possess it. Why does he rely on this consideration, whereas he did not need to look at "what people say" in order to identify science or technical knowledge? He emphasizes in this way the immediate dependence of prudence on common opinion, on what poeple say in ordinary speech. We are thus alerted to the most striking difference between practical wisdom and the sorts of technical knowledge just discussed. Prudence turns out to involve a facility at deliberating about things: we speak of men having practical wisdom in some particular thing "when they calculate well with respect to some worthwhile end . . . and it follows that, in general, a man of practical wisdom is he who has the ability to deliberate" (1140a30). This rational quality is distinguished from science not simply on the basis of its method (or lack of method, as Hobbes claims), but also by its object. "No one deliberates about things that cannot be other than they are, or about actions that he cannot possibly perform" (1140a34). Practical wisdom is also distinguished from art. The former involves only action itself, whereas art aims at a product separate from the process of making. It does seem to be similar to art (or technical knowledge, or *technē*) in one important respect, however, which Aristotle considers in the very beginning. There is a sense in which prudence is an ability to get whatever one wants, a skill in acting which allows one to attain his selfish ends. Thus "it is held to be the mark of a prudent man to be able to deliberate well about what is good and advantageous for himself" (1140a25). From this perspective prudence is like art because it is concerned strictly with means. But Aristotle is careful to qualify this hint of the selfish, profitable side of prudence. He indicates that the ends of good action are not wholly open to question. That is, if practical wisdom involves means to ends which it does not itself supply, those ends are not neutral in the sense that the ends of an art may be neutral. He makes use here of the ambiguity (shared by Greek and English) in the word good (*agathos*), which can mean "profitable" in a selfish sense (good for oneself) but also carries a hint of good simply, that is, related to some more objective conception of what is really good for human beings.[15] Aristotle indicates that the ends for which practical wisdom knows the means are not neutral in the same way in which the end of a *techne* is. There is a *techne* for making weapons, and one's excellence in that *techne* is determined by the products produced. This is not true in the case of prudence, because the mere exercise of prudence is itself an excellence. "We can speak of excellence in Art, but not of excellence in prudence," according to Aristotle, but this is because in itself "prudence is an excellence or virtue" (1140b22–23). Seen from this side, it cannot be used well or badly; its use is already good because it seeks what is good for human beings.

One further point in this account of practical wisdom deserves careful scrutiny. Aristotle refers to the term for moderation (*sōphrosynē*), and explains it as etymologically derived from the words for "preserving prudence."[16] This is, he says, because moderation keeps us from forgetting what is good for us, since it prevents excesses of pleasure and pain from destroying or perverting our knowledge of the proper ends. "For pleasure and pain do not destroy or pervert all beliefs, for example, the belief that the three angles of a triangle are, or are not, together equal to two right angles, but only beliefs concerning action" (1140b14–15). That is, whatever prudence gives us, it is more vulnerable to the destructive influence of pleasures and pains than is the more technical knowledge of geometry. Perhaps it stands in need of some assistance or theoretical defense. We may wonder at the insertion of this particular example from geometry, especially followed as it is by a recurrence of the subject of first principles (which had been the main theme of the description of pure science or *epistēmē*). "The first principles of action are the end to which our acts are means; but a man corrupted by a love of pleasure or fear of pain, entirely fails to discern any first principle, and cannot see that he ought to choose and do everything as a means to this end, and for its sake" (1140b18–21). This seems to suggest—especially in light of the reference to geometry—that action as well as geometry has its own first principles, and that they may even be invariable. The only difference indicated here between the first principles of geometry and those of human action or virtue is that the latter are capable of being perverted or destroyed or forgotten. Thus they are not

Aristotle's *Ethics*

necessary in the same sense as the principles of geometry, which must be accepted if one wishes to do geometry, and one may, after all, live according to the standards merely of pleasure and pain.

The ambiguity of this account recalls the no-man's-land we discovered earlier in the beginning of book 6, where the status of Aristotle's project in the *Ethics* was brought into question. It appeared to fall somewhere between the purely contemplative scientific account of what is eternal and invariable, and the purely practical concern with making and acting as means to ends which are not themselves questioned. We have now seen the possibility that first principles may exist for human action. We are compelled to wonder if such principles are the subject of the *Ethics* itself.[17] Whether or not this is the case, such first principles are beyond the realm of purely practical wisdom or prudence, which, as he indicates, is concerned with the means to the end of living well (*eu prattein*). Virtue or morality is thus left autonomous: it is the end of human action, and from the perspective of prudence is not open to question.[18]

Aristotle has now dealt with the first three of the five rational faculties which comprise the human *logos*, and a pattern is evident in the progression. The primary link among the faculties of science, art, and prudence (*epistēmē, technē, phronēsis*) is that each is a more or less self-contained activity—since skill in each does not require further questions to be raised—and yet each is characterized by what is from a philosophical perspective an obvious limitation, not to say deficiency, namely, each fails to give an account (*logos*) of itself. Each proceeds on the basis of first principles which are themselves outside the sphere of the particular rational quality itself. The first principles of science are not guaranteed by science, the ends of an art are not given by the art itself, and the goal sought by practical wisdom is set for it by virtue. There is, moreover, a sort of ascent from the first to the third in what we might describe as the vulnerability to doubts from outside: the ends of the various arts may be the subject of disagreement more than the premises of a science, and this is manifestly even more true of the goals of action. And this leads Aristotle finally to raise the issue of the sources of first principles, at least the first principles of science. The status of the ends or first principles of action again remains in the background, an important but unspoken theme.

First Principles

The account which Aristotle offers in chapter 6 of the fourth rational faculty, intelligence (*nous*), is very brief and highly formal. It consists in the claim that science cannot itself derive its first principles, yet these principles must be known with certainty. Since they are not known as a result of any of the other rational faculties, they must be known by intelligence. One other feature inserted in this brief section deserves mention. In discussing "the faculties by which we attain truth, and by which we are never deceived both in matters which can and in those matters which cannot be other than they are" (1141a5), Aristotle omits art or *technē*, which is after all a practical skill. But he does include practical wisdom, which must thus be considered to be capable of attaining truth and not merely, as one might be tempted to think, a kind of inarticulable common-sense understanding of "the right thing to do."

The subject of the next chapter is the last of the rational faculties, which is wisdom (*sophia*). One is at first surprised to discover that this is the "most precise" (*akribestatē*) form of knowledge there is, more perfect even than pure science. The man with wisdom, or theoretical wisdom, "must not only know what follows from fundamental principles, but he must have true knowledge of the fundamental principles themselves. Accordingly, theoretical wisdom must comprise both intelligence and scientific knowledge. It is science in its consummation, as it were, the science of the things that are valued most highly" (1141a17–20). It is consequently higher than prudence (*phronēsis*) or political science (*politikē*, which literally means simply "politics"). The example Aristotle offers by way of explanation of this last point reveals that prudence is knowledge of particulars, whereas theoretical wisdom knows universal principles. Prudence for human beings involves what is good and bad for human beings, but there may be a separate prudence for other animals. Theoretical wisdom, on the contrary, deals with the whole. "Surely, if 'healthy' and 'good' mean one thing for men and another for fishes, whereas 'white' and 'straight' always mean the same, 'wise' must mean the same for everyone, but 'practically wise' will be different" (1141a23–25). It appears that the knowledge of the whole, of which Aristotle speaks here, is philosophy.

He immediately turns his attention, however, in the middle of the chapter on theoretical wisdom, back to prudence and political science. The rest of book 6, which includes six more chapters, is devoted to a further exploration of the role of practical wisdom, and the discussion is constantly shadowed by questions about the relationship between political science and practical wisdom. A sort of tension is established between, on the one hand, knowledge of general principles which may be totally useless in action, and on the other, knowledge of the principles of action which is unable to relate itself to any general principles. The latter (knowledge of the principles of action), Aristotle indicates, is prudence; and this is useful because it knows particular things. "This explains why some men who have no scientific knowledge are more adept in practical matters, especially if they have experience, than those who do have scientific knowledge. For if a person were to know that light meat is easily digested, and hence wholesome, but did not know what sort of meat is light, he will not produce health, whereas someone who knows that poultry is light and wholesome is more likely to produce health" (1141b17–20). The example would appear to demonstrate the defect of pure scientific knowledge, which is certain and deductive but lacks any grounding in experience; it also, however, reveals the fact that the man of experience may not be able to give an account of why what he knows to be true is true, and thus will be at a loss if an unfamiliar situation is encountered. The best sort of knowledge, Aristotle means to indicate, would be a combination of both: "Now, practical wisdom is concerned with action. That means that a person should have both [knowledge of universals and knowledge of particulars] or knowledge of particulars rather [than knowledge of universals]" (1141b20–23). He seems to say first that the combination would be the most desirable sort of prudence, but already we have seen that, properly speaking, prudence is only the latter—the knowledge of particulars. The man of experience, we know, is supposed to be prudent even without theoretical principles. The reader is compelled to wonder if this does not point to something beyond prudence, but different from theoretical wisdom. And in fact Aristotle concludes the chapter with the words, "Here too, it seems, there must be some supreme faculty" (1141b23; my translation). It is impossible to avoid thinking that he means political science.

The Place of Political Science

Why then is political science left in darkness, repeatedly mentioned but never focused on or defined? The reason would seem to be that the *Ethics* is a treatise on two levels: it develops the principles of virtue for men of action without questioning the foundations of virtue, and at the same time indicates a great deal about those foundations. We must recall in this context chapter 4 of book 1, where Aristotle clearly indicates that for his purposes in the *Ethics* it is enough to show what the principles of virtue are, without asking why we practice them (see above, pp. 126–27). Notwithstanding this claim, it is clear that a part of the *Ethics* is devoted to exploring the foundations of the virtues, both explaining and yet exposing the limitations of the various virtues of the human character. To consider only one example, Aristotle distinguishes genuine courage from its close relatives partly according to the *end* for which a courageous act is performed. He thus directs us to account for "why" we perform an act of courage; that is, he shows us that we practice this virtue at least for the sake of something else. In book 3, Aristotle writes that "courage is noble, and, accordingly, its end is noble, too; for a thing is defined by its end. *Thus* it is for a noble end that a courageous man endures and acts as courage demands" (1115b22–24).

The last two chapters of book 6 bring out more clearly the gap between simply acting well, on the one hand, and understanding human action, on the other. Aristotle here indicates that it is not necessary to have *knowledge* of what is noble or good or just in order to *be* noble or good or just. This may constitute a bow to virtuous men of action who would be incapable of giving a theoretical account of virtue. Yet we have observed that practical wisdom is also in need of a defense which is much closer in spirit and method to theoretical wisdom (*sophia*), and which is identical with political science, properly speaking. It is in this sense that Aristotle says that the *Ethics* is "a kind of political science" (1094b12; my translation).[19] It not only explains what things are good for human beings, but also seeks to explain why, thus bridging the gap between an autonomous virtue which can be practiced by the man of prudence without knowing why, and the realm of philosophy which requires an account of everything that is. The *Ethics*, understood this way as a kind of political science, is a theoretical defense of the virtues it at the same time outlines. The simple man of courage can be courageous simply because he knows he ought to be, and Aristotle does not teach him to doubt. But the reader who is philosophically inclined at the same time will realize that the issue is more complicated: he needs to look at the intended end, in order to judge whether it—and the action directed to it—is truly noble.

It is apparent that political science as understood by Aristotle is identical in an unqualified sense neither with prudence nor with science. Political science and prudence are very similar: they are in some sense "the same quality of mind [*hexis*] though their essence is not the same." Both are concerned with actions, with what is good and bad for man; but prudence does not comprehend its own first principles. It is also apparent that political science is not identical with theoretical wisdom (*sophia*). This is not, however, because of the distinction between things variable and things invariable, which might at first be taken to be decisive, because as we have seen, Aristotle has left an ambiguity in this apparent dichotomy. (The distinction he draws is between things whose first principles do not vary, such as mathematics, and things which do admit of variation, such as our actions. There may, as we have noted, be a kind of science of actions which vary, if their first principles are invariable.) What does separate political science from theoretical wisdom is that the former is concerned with man alone, the latter with everything that is, the whole of which man is only a part and to which what is good or bad for man may be of secondary importance (cf. 1141a30).

If political science is not prudence, not science, and not theoretical wisdom, what is it? What characterizes the enterprise in which Aristotle is engaged in the *Ethics*, which he describes as "a kind of political science"? Nowhere are the answers to these questions made explicit. But in the last two chapters of book 6 Aristotle considers this issue. He concludes the chapter preceding the last two as follows: "We have now completed our discussion of what practical and theoretical wisdom are; we have described the sphere in which each operates, and we have shown that each is the excellence of a different part of the soul" (1132b14). This should complete the plan of book 6 as it was originally stated. But Aristotle immediately goes on to "raise some questions about the usefulness of these two virtues." This is strikingly out of character in the *Ethics*, where in general no explicit attempt is made to justify a virtue on grounds of its utility. This should alert us to the importance of what follows. The problem of utility is raised, it appears, by a kind of paradoxical relationship in which theoretical and practical wisdom (*sophia* and *phronēsis*) stand to human happiness. First, theoretical wisdom, Aristotle writes, "will study none of the things that make a man happy" (1143b19). This compels us to ask what *does* study these things. Practical wisdom, Aristotle continues, is in a way "concerned with this sphere," but for what purpose do we need it? "It is true that practical wisdom deals with what is just, noble, and good for man, and it is doing such things that characterizes a man as good. But our ability to perform such actions is in no way enhanced by knowing them," since the virtues are qualities of character, acquired by habit (1143b22). Aristotle is unwilling, as we saw earlier (see above, p. 135) to claim that the exercise of virtue is dependent on reason or wisdom: virtue remains autonomous. He offers the analogy of medicine and health: one can be healthy without knowing the science of medicine. In addition, he adds, "it would seem strange if practical wisdom, though inferior to theoretical wisdom, should surpass it in authority, because that which produces a thing rules and directs it" (1143b33). This cannot help but call to mind political science or politics, the principles of ruling. Whatever we think of these questions about usefulness, it is clear that something is missing from the account up through chapter 11. A sentence from the beginning of chapter 12 underscores this. "These then are the questions we must discuss; so far we have only stated them as problems" (1143b36).

Now, Aristotle continues, each of the two separate intellectual virtues is desirable in itself, "even if neither of them produces anything." This indicates, apparently, that it is not in fact their utility which is at issue here. Nevertheless, we are told, they do in fact produce something. Theoretical wisdom produces happiness, "not as medicine produces health, but as health itself makes a person healthy" (1144a4). That is, the possession of such wisdom makes a man happy; it is an end in itself for this part of the soul.[20] Does practical wisdom produce happiness in the same way? Not precisely, because "virtue makes us aim at the right target, and practical wisdom makes us use the right means," Aristotle continues. That is, the correct parallel to theoretical wisdom, which is the excellence of one part of the soul, is for the active part of the soul not practical wisdom but *virtue*. Practical wisdom is one step further removed. And practical wisdom is not entirely necessary, because as Aristotle has just pointed out a few lines earlier, it makes no difference whether someone has practical wisdom himself or listens to others who have it (1143b30). We are thus left in some confusion as to the importance of practical wisdom for happiness.

At this point in the chapter Aristotle retraces his steps, announcing that "the argument has to be met that our ability to perform noble and just acts is in no way enhanced by practical wisdom." The dilemma here is that Aristotle does not wish to present virtue as dependent on reason, because this would subordinate virtue to the rational faculties and rob it of the autonomy which is the source of the dignity of the simply moral man.[21] Hence he usually presents virtue as determining the ends of our action, while practical wisdom is charged with seeking the means. Thus, "it is virtue which makes our choice right. It is not virtue, however, but a different capacity, which determines the steps which, in the nature of the case, must be taken to implement this choice" (1144a20). The obvious problem with this formulation, of course, is, *What is the source of virtue itself?* How do we ever know what virtue is?

Having indicated the nature of the problem he is wrestling with, Aristotle shifts the argument. "We must stop for a moment to make this point clearer," he begins. There is a capacity called "cleverness," it seems, which is "the power to perform those steps which are conducive to a goal we have set for ourselves and to attain that goal" (1144a25). It is a strictly neutral sort of calculation, very similar to Hobbes's concept of human rationality. Cleverness is distinguished from practical wisdom by the fact that the latter has as its end something noble or good, whereas cleverness in itself— what we might call technical rationality—may be used for any goal, noble or base. As far as cleverness is concerned, the goodness or badness of any action is coincidental only. Practical wisdom includes this calculating ability, but it is only practical wisdom truly when it pursues virtue. "For the syllogisms which express the principles initiating action run: 'Since the end, or the highest good, is such-and-such . . .'—whatever it may be; what it really is does not matter for our present argument" (1144a32). Clearly, however, "what it really is" is the question to which the entire *Ethics* is devoted. But from the point of view of practical wisdom, the end is a given premise from which the syllogism begins. And only the good man can judge it correctly.

Abruptly Aristotle begins a new chapter, the last chapter of book 6. The reason for the introduction of "cleverness" is now brought out. It turns out that there are really two senses of "virtue," and the lower stands in the same relation to the higher as cleverness stands to prudence. The lower sort of virtue is "natural virtue," a kind of unthinking disposition to be virtuous, which is found even in children, but which is liable to be harmful if it is not combined with "intelligence" (*nous*). "Virtue in the full sense," or the higher sort, is distinguished from the natural virtue by the fact that it has intelligence (which was earlier characerized as a knowledge of first principles, or the ends of action). The good which results from the "blind" natural virtue is a matter of accident; virtue in the full sense requires the sight of intelligence, part of the rational faculty. This distinguishing of two senses of virtue permits Aristotle to leave virtue in one sense not dependent on reason, while showing that in the the fullest sense it is closely linked to reason or practical wisdom. He strengthens the conviction that this issue is what troubles him by referring next to Socrates' contention that virtue is knowledge. This claim must be regarded with suspicion, according to Aristotle's account, because it inevitably leads to the subordination of virtue to reason, by making it impossible for the simple but good-hearted man to be virtuous. Virtue would thus be robbed of the autonomy which Aristotle wishes to leave to it. Socrates, it turns out, was "partly right and partly wrong." It is impossible to be good "in the full sense of the word" without practical wisdom—in that Socrates was right. But apparently there is another sense of good which does not require wisdom to be actualized. Virtue in the full sense is "guided by practical wisdom" (1144b25). As soon as this secret is out, however, Aristotle backs off again as the chapter draws to a close, asserting once more that "virtue determines the end, and practical wisdom makes us do what is conducive to the end" (1145a5–6). Apparently there are two senses of practical wisdom as well.

The higher kind of virtue is characterized by the fact that it is a product of right reason (*orthos logos*): it is the true knowledge of what is good for human beings. What is good for human beings— the real subject of the *Ethics*—includes theoretical wisdom, the possession of which makes men happy. Hence the knowledge which is presented in the *Ethics*, and which we have suspected to be "political science," does in fact emerge not only as the knowledge of what is good and bad for man, but also as directive of, and in a sense superior to, theoretical wisdom. Practical wisdom simply, which is on a lower level as that faculty which seeks to secure the ends to which it is directed by virtue, is concerned only with means. It cannot give direction to theoretical wisdom. But political science does direct theoretical wisdom, and this is justified by the fact that it is only through political science, truly understood, that Aristotle himself comes to know what is good for man.[22] If practical wisdom, as Aristotle says, "makes provisions to secure theoretical wisdom," one might say it knows how to do this only as a result of *political science*, which in turn knows not only how to secure theoretical wisdom, but *why*. Political science truly understood remains in the background even here, unless one reflects at each page about the activity in which Aristotle himself is engaged in writing the *Ethics*. Despite his disclaimer in book 2, chapter 2, to the effect that he writes the *Ethics* not to know what virtue is, but to become good, it is quite clear that for one audience at least the former is the central challenge;[23] and that theoretical knowledge about virtue is a desirable goal in itself is sufficiently established in book 6.

Earlier we brought up Aristotle's attempt to restrict his audience to those who already know the principles of ethics, and to exclude the young who are not familiar with politics. This restriction was made in light of his claim that one must already know how to act before one can be a good judge of the principles of ethics which Aristotle discusses. He wishes to speak, it appears, only to the gentleman, the good citizen, since he is trying to answer the question, What are the goals of human life? The gentleman knows the answer, in one sense, to this question. This requires that the perspective of the gentleman be taken as the starting point, while yet trying to see why the goals are what they are said to be. It is quickly apparent that Aristotle is reluctant to deduce the principles of virtue from their utility, since this would degrade their status to mere *means*, and thus undermine the conviction of the gentleman. This does not, however, prevent political science from inquiring as to which virtues are in fact useful, and for what; which are good or pleasant in themselves; and which partake of both. The gentleman knows, for example, that virtue includes courage and moderation, and does not need to ask *why* these are good. But Aristotle can tell us more. Moderation can be contrasted with courage, the exercise of which may not be pleasant, but is justified instead by its end—that for the sake of which it is exercised (1117a30–1117b15). Moderation, the *Ethics* tells us, is like courage in that it concerns the irrational part of the soul (1117b24), but unlike courage in that the practice of moderation is itself pleasant in a way. Yet moderation too is for the sake of something beyond. It is for the sake of freedom from the body, and from the lower part of the soul. Despite the claim that the political science of the *Ethics* inquires only into the "what" and not the "why" of the ends of human life, we see that it discovers something of the latter while it pursues the former. And this means it may discover that some virtues are not well grounded, while yet remaining necessary in some sense which, if articulated, would be destructive. In order not to undermine the conviction of the gentleman, Aristotle constantly attempts to keep in front of him the perspective of the citizen, or the political man.

Aristotle's *Ethics*

Perhaps he suspects that this perspective cannot defend itself. In contrast to Aristotle, Socrates always questions the citizen's view.[24] Socrates wants men to justify virtue: he is obstinate in his refusal to accept it without reasons. It is true that Aristotle wishes to inquire into foundations, but since he suspects—perhaps he is more certain than was Socrates—that the foundations are often arbitrary, he tries at the same time to leave the foundations undamaged, and in fact to make them a bit stronger. We cannot escape the conclusion that some virtues at least do not stand up to scrutiny, that they have no rational justification. And this is troublesome. It might be said to be the core of Hobbes's dissatisfaction. Hobbes betrays an inclination to ignore what for Aristotle are "higher" virtues—greatness of soul, etc.—because it is these which are less justifiable except as ends in themselves. Hobbes is impatient with the inability of the simply good citizen to justify his virtue with any certainty or to make his view of virtue compelling. It is better from a practical standpoint, according to Hobbes, to restrict ourselves to what we are sure of, to the "virtues" necessary to the ends we all *require*, such as peace. In this Hobbes is very persuasive: for despite whatever might be lost, we hope to make what is left that much more secure and indisputable, to buttress it against the "cavils of skeptics."

Socrates, when compared to Aristotle, may be seen to have more of the skeptical spirit of Hobbes. He pushes the gentleman for an account. By contrast, Aristotle's attempt to find a middle ground is characterized by a certain sort of indeterminacy, not to say obscurity. This is Hobbes's charge, and we may easily sympathize. Nevertheless, whatever our difficulties in accepting it, it is this middle ground which Aristotle tries to hold in the *Ethics*. The *Ethics* is "a kind of political science" because it seeks both to describe and to explain the virtues—the standards and goals—of the citizen or gentleman, while remaining within the perspective of the citizen.

The Method of Political Science

It remains for us to try to understand the method by which Aristotle's political science proceeds, in contrast especially with the

Aristotle's *Ethics*

method of Hobbes's political science. What are the "first principles" of Aristotle's political science? How are they arrived at, and how does he proceed from them?

It is important to note that Aristotle's understanding of science and Hobbes's are not wholly dissimilar: much of the *Prior Analytics* directly prefigures Hobbes's discussion of method in *De Corpore*. Aristotle, like Hobbes, makes demonstration (here *apodeixis*) a requirement for scientific knowledge. But demonstration in Aristotle's understanding includes more than strictly proof by syllogism.[25] It includes at least a second type of demonstration, the dialectical. We may see the reasons for this by the following considerations. According to some thinkers (we will have occasion to recall this when we turn to Plato's *Meno*), Aristotle says, there is no possibility of scientific knowledge, "owing to the necessity of knowing the primary premises" (*Post. An.*, 72b5). That is, if there is no way of knowing other than by syllogistic demonstration from premises, "an infinite regress is involved," because "if behind the prior stands no primary, we could not know the posterior through the prior (. . . for one cannot traverse an infinite series)" (*Post. An.*, 72b9–10). These same thinkers, according to Aristotle, go on to claim that even if

> the series terminates and there are primary premises, yet these are unknowable because incapable of demonstration, which according to them is the only form of knowledge. And since thus one cannot know the primary premises, knowledge of the conclusions which follow from them is not pure scientific knowledge nor properly knowing at all, but rests on the mere supposition that the premises are true. [*Post. An.*, 72b11–14]

This problem did not trouble Hobbes, we may recall, because, according to his account of human reason, all knowledge is hypothetical at the deepest level. For Aristotle, there is the possibility of knowledge simply, that is, knowledge which is certain without being hypothetical, because human reason is at home in the world; for Hobbes, human reason finds itself in an alien world of matter and motion, and it can know with certainty only what it constructs. Aristotle rejects the view that the only possible knowledge is the knowledge from syllogistic demonstration because that

effectively precludes any possibility of a real—that is, unhypo-
thetical—science. Either we have knowledge which is not demonstrable, then, or there is another kind of demonstration.

Both, in fact, are true according to Aristotle: we do have
knowledge which cannot be demonstrated, and if we extend the use
of the term "demonstration," we may say that there is another type
of demonstration, besides *apodeixis*, which produces knowledge.
This second type of demonstration is the dialectical.[26] The philosophical procedure of the dialectic is important to our account here
in two ways. First, it is the solution to the problem just noted, of
infinite regression or circularity in scientific demonstrations. In
philosophy, according to Aristotle, the use of dialectic is "in
relation to the ultimate bases of the principles used in the several
sciences . . . for dialectic is a process of criticism wherein lies the
path to the principles of all inquiries" (*Topics*, 101a37–101b34).
Aristotle thus recognizes the dependence of any scientific inquiry
on some "prescientific" procedure which produces the first principles of the science itself.[27] One might at first think that this is little
different from Hobbes, who did after all discuss in detail the
procedure for securing first principles. But there is an all-important
difference. In Hobbes the procedure for reaching first principles
was resolution, whereas according to Aristotle it is dialectic: "it is
through opinions generally held on the particular points that these
[principles proper to the particular science in hand] have to be
discussed, and this task belongs properly, or most appropriately, to
dialectic" (*Topics*, 101b1).[28] The foundations of sciences are understood in a radically different way by the two thinkers: Hobbes
insists that one who begins from "vulgar discourse" or common
speech will never reach the truth; on Aristotle's account, "opinions
generally held" (common speech) are *necessarily* the starting point
for any inquiry.

The second way in which dialectic is important here is that *in
itself* dialectic is a mode of reasoning (*logos*) which can produce
knowledge, and not just the foundation for knowledge. If we
extend the meaning of "demonstration," dialectic is thus a second
method of demonstrating a truth. Aristotle indicates in a passage in
the *Posterior Analytics* that we must understand at least the
possibility of using demonstration in two senses: the unqualified

sense and an extended sense wherein a knowledge is demonstrated if an argument, reasoned soundly and logically, produces conviction (*pistis*) in the hearer.[29] In the realm of political science, which is a practical science and deals with contingent matters, most conclusions will not achieve the absolute certainty of, say, the conclusions of geometry. This is not a defect of political science, for Aristotle, but simply an aspect. Dialectical reasoning, in other words, is the sort of demonstration appropriate to a practical science, in addition to being the source for the first principles of all sciences. Aristotle does not hesitate to reject some subjects as inappropriate for dialectic. It is not appropriate, for example, in geometry, where demonstration in the strict sense is required. For the use of dialectic, the appropriate subjects "should not border too closely on the sphere of demonstration, nor yet be too far removed from it: for the former cases admit of no doubt, while the latter involve difficulties too great" (*Topics*, 105a7). There are two "species" of dialectical arguments, according to Aristotle. These are induction ("a passage from individuals to universals"),[30] and reasoning, which "is an argument in which, certain things being laid down, something other than these necessarily comes about through them" (*Topics*, 100a25).[31] Dialectical reasoning begins "from opinions that are generally accepted," and "generally accepted" means "accepted by everyone or by the majority or by the philosophers" (*Topics*, 100b20). The importance of the distinction between induction and reasoning is simply this: "Induction is the more convincing and clear: it is more readily learnt by the use of the senses, and is applicable generally to the mass of men, though reasoning is more forcible and effective against contradictious people" (*Topics*, 105a16). We may take it from this that dialectical reasoning is capable of being, at least in some cases, highly compelling. Aristotle seems to have in mind the sort of argument which we associate with a clear and forceful legal brief, one that marshals all evidence to convince the reader of a point.

In Aristotle's political science the demonstration of truths is important, just as it was for Hobbes. Aristotle, however, recognizes the possibility of attaining "truth and knowledge" by a kind of demonstration which is not syllogistic.[32] The most important respect in which these approaches differ is in the starting points.

Aristotle's *Ethics*

We must recall Hobbes's claim that what was wrong with his predecessor's political science was its uncritical assumption that knowledge could be attained beginning even from common opinions. It should now be clear, however, that Aristotle's epistemological claims are not uncritical. Instead they attempt to account for our scientific knowledge by recognizing its dependence on prescientific or commonsense knowledge. One could thus say that Aristotle was sensitive to the issue which Husserl, along with others in our century, has raised concerning the foundations of modern science—and especially the foundations of the human sciences (see chap. 1 above).

The difference in starting points, though absolutely fundamental, is by no means the only difference in the two methods or approaches. It will suffice to mention only a few. Second in importance is the difference in the role of definitions. Definitions are for Hobbes the starting points, as we saw in chapter 2, because they "explicate" the simples from which syllogisms are constructed. For Aristotle, definitions are rather the goal of his enterprise, at least in the sense that an understanding of a thing is what his science seeks, and definitions are what tell us "a thing's essence" (*Topics*, 101b38). The nature of a definition is also radically different. A definition in Aristotle's science tells us what something is, first by locating it for us in a genus of things, that is, showing us what "kind" of thing it is; and second by distinguishing it from (and relating it to) other things of the same kind or members of the same genus. This is known as the "genus-differentia" definition. We will have occasion to examine such a definition in the next chapter. It cannot but remind us of the sort of linking definition which goes along with Wittgenstein's account of the grammar of a word, because such a definition defines by exploring "likeness" to and differences from other things, and hence shows us the place of a thing in our world. Hobbes, as we recall, defined by carefully analyzing a thing into its parts. In Aristotle's view, wholes are not understandable strictly by understanding parts; "the whole is not the same as the sum of its parts" because a complete account of the whole must show its relation to other wholes, as well as to the whole simply, which limits our vision.

The "whole" which we call a railroad locomotive, to recall an example used in chapter 4, is not comprehended by adding together all of its parts or "systems," such as the brake system, electrical system, driving mechanism, and so on. To really understand what a locomotive is, by Aristotle's account, we need to understand the role it plays in human life: why we build them (they are used for transportation), how they can be dangerous (they cannot stop easily), what it costs to run them, what skills it takes to operate them, and so on. Our understanding is not sufficient even when we can take one apart and put it together; unless we know how and where it fits into the human world, we do not fully understand it.

Dialectical Inquiry

Aristotle presents the steps in the method of dialectical inquiry in book 1 of the *Topics*. They may be paraphrased as follows. Begin with some problem or contradiction in the propositions of common opinion or common speech. Often this will be a problem which comes from the fact that the "supposition of some eminent philosopher" is seen to conflict with "the general opinion" (*Topics*, 104b20), but it may only be a problem resulting from our desire to discover the answer to a hypothetical problem of choice. (Aristotle offers, as an example of an ethical proposition, " 'Ought one rather to obey one's parents or the laws, if they disagree?' " [*Topics*, 105b23].) Once the proposition or problem for dialectical inquiry is established, the next step is an investigation into the senses or meanings of the various terms in it. Aristotle urges the learner again and again to "look and see whether" and "examine," with an eye to determining carefully all the various senses which a word may have, so as either to focus on the one most important for the inquiry, or to simply achieve a perspicuous understanding of the terms, and things being scrutinized. For example, he says,

> see if the actual meanings included under the same term
> themselves have different differentiae, e.g., "colour" in bodies
> and "colour" in tunes: for the differentiae of "colour" in bodies
> are "sight-piercing" and "sight-compressing," whereas "colour"
> in melodies has not the same differentiae. *Colour, then, is an ambiguous term*; for things that are the same have the same differentiae. [*Topics*, 107b26]

What is most important for us about this passage, and dozens of others in a similar spirit, is Aristotle's insistence that distinctions of meaning be drawn, and similarities explored, with a view to *understanding* something simply. He does not seek to isolate a single uncluttered meaning of a term, which somehow lies beneath the confusing surface of vulgar discourse. In fact, Aristotle takes issue with Plato partly over what he sees as the latter's attempt in this direction. In his inquiry into the meaning of the term "good" in book 1 of the *Ethics*, for example, Aristotle puts it this way:

> the term "good" has as many meanings as the word "is": it is used to describe substances, e.g., divinity and intelligence are good; qualities, e.g., the virtues are good; quantities, e.g., the proper amount is good; relatedness, e.g., the useful is good; time, e.g., the right moment is good; place, e.g., a place to live is good; and so forth. It is clear, therefore, that the good cannot be something universal, common to all cases, and single; for if it were, it would not be applicable in all categories but only in one. [1096a22–29][33]

His approach is compatible with the understanding of language offered by Wittgenstein and outlined in the previous chapters, in that it seeks a perspicuous view of a multiplicity of meanings, rather than an analysis or reduction of that multiplicity to one pure resolved meaning.[34]

Once the senses of various terms are grasped, the remaining steps of the dialectical inquiry are to examine the similarities to other related things (what Wittgenstein would call the grammatical parallels) and the differences between similar things. Courage, as Aristotle says, "is concerned with feelings of confidence and of fear," but not "with both to an equal extent" (1117a29–30). And although courage is related to fear (if we don't even know enough to be afraid of a danger, what may appear to be courage is really ignorance, says Aristotle [1117a22]), it is not related in the same way to just any fear. "Now it is true that we fear all evils, e.g., disrepute, poverty, disease, friendlessness, death. But it does not seem that a courageous man is concerned with all of these.... [A] man is not a coward if he fears insult to his wife and children, or if he fears envy or the like; nor is he courageous if he is of good cheer

when he is about to be flogged" (1115a10–23). If two things belong
to the same genus, or to two genera which are "not very much too
far apart" (*Topics*, 108a2), one should begin by eliciting "the
differences which things present to each other" (*Topics*, 107b38).
On the other hand, "likeness should be studied first, in the case of
things belonging to different genera" (*Topics*, 108a6). In addition,
such cases are more difficult, and "practice is more especially
needed in regard to terms that are far apart; for in the case of the
rest, we shall be more easily able to see in one glance the points of
likeness" (*Topics*, 108a12). The major importance of this investigation into similarities and differences—which is analogous to what
in Wittgensteinian terms we called a grammatical investigation—is
that it helps us to identify the object of inquiry: "Grammar tells us
what kind of thing anything is," Wittgenstein said. Aristotle's
formulation is scarcely different:

> The discovery of the differences of things helps us both in rea-
> sonings about sameness and difference, and also *in recognizing
> what any particular thing is* . . . It helps us in recognizing what a
> thing is because we usually distinguish the expression that is prop-
> er to the essence of each particular thing by means of the differ-
> entiae that are proper to it. [*Topics*, 108a38–108b5; emphasis
> added]

It is also useful to inquire into likenesses. This helps us, Aristotle
says, with "the rendering of definitions," because "if we are able to
see in one glance what is the same in each individual case of it, we
shall be at no loss into what genus we ought to put the object before
us when we define it: for of the common predicates that which is
most definitely in the category of essence is likely to be the genus"
(*Topics*, 108b20–23).

We may summarize what we have presented of Aristotle's
method of dialectical inquiry as follows: (1) It begins from common
speech or common opinions, and often from a contradiction
implicit in two opinions. (2) It seeks definitions which are different
in kind from Hobbes's definitions (in that they define by showing
relationships), and which play a different role in the inquiry
(because they are *ends* and not universals from which syllogisms
can be constructed). (3) It proceeds by, among other things,

eliciting relationships between different wholes, and not merely by resolving wholes into parts. (4) It seeks a perspicuous understanding rather than a reductive understanding, because (5) it is not based on the idea that knowledge can only be secured by reconstructing the combinations of ideas which are added together to make a concept. There is no denying Hobbes's accusation against this Aristotelian political science, namely, that it does not achieve the certainty or clarity, and hence the usefulness, of geometry. The issue which must be raised, however, is whether such an ideal is possible for a science of political phenomena, that is, for a science dealing with the concepts human beings use in political speech and political action.

Conclusion

The picture we have sketched of Aristotle's approach to the political world—at least insofar as dialectic is a philosophical tool in political science—must be admitted to differ drastically from Hobbes's ideal. At the same time, as we have shown, Aristotle's approach has a great deal in common with what we might imagine a political science based on Wittgenstein's understanding of language to look like. At the very least one may say that it is compatible with that understanding of language, whereas Hobbes's approach is not. This is not to say that Aristotle possessed an understanding of language anything like what Wittgenstein offers. That is doubtful, at the least. And it would be an unreasonable expectation in any case, since the overwhelming concern with language in philosophical inquiry is peculiarly modern. But the fact that we do not possess an Aristotelian critique of language is no more a decisive objection here than the fact that Wittgenstein did not write political science. Our inquiry would not be necessary if either had undertaken both tasks.

We are not comparing understandings of language only or even primarily. Our task rather is to show—and this we will try to bring out more fully in the next chapter—that a particular understanding of language is the natural accompaniment to a particular view of the world, and of a particular understanding of science and knowledge. And what is at issue in the case of Hobbes, once we have become aware of the serious problems in his understanding of naming and language, is the validity of his side of the debate with Aristotelian political science. We should not be surprised if that approach to the political world merits reconsideration, and in making this discovery we do not need or intend to claim that Aristotle and Wittgenstein would agree on very many, not to say all, philosophical issues.

For Aristotle, political science is the attempt to articulate the nature of all the phenomena of politics. It seeks to know what the political world is, both in order to act and also simply to know. To know is important because knowing is a specifically human faculty. The exercise of this faculty in reasoning and inquiring into the things which constitute our world is itself rewarding. For Hobbes, on the other hand, reason is merely a refinement of prudence, and science is fundamentally no more than the reduction of things to the framework of matter and motion which constitute them. Hobbes's science, that is, seeks to reduce politics to the framework which is supposed to lie beneath the surface of our world. Aristotle's older view can be made to appear, in contrast, as a kind of naive or unreflective contentment with mere phenomena, with the surface of things. We must, however, consider the possibility that the surface of things is the reality with which a truly political science must deal. This is not to deny that we are often fooled by appearances, or that there may be important factors in human action which lie hidden from view. It is merely to say that our access to the phenomena of the human world must necessarily be through an understanding of them which is contained in the way we think and speak about them. It may be that the effort to penetrate beneath what we can discover from the way we think and speak of them is based on a mistaken understanding of the nature of those phenomena.

In the next chapter we will examine, in Plato's *Meno*, two contrasting approaches to understanding a political term which in some ways mirror the debate we have been sketching. Among other things, this should make clear our belief that the issue between Hobbes and Aristotle is a very old, and perhaps permanent, issue in political science.

7

Plato's "Meno"

The Method of Classical Political Science

Plato's *Meno* is a dialogue concerned with, among other things, the nature of human excellence or virtue (*aretē*). But as in all the Platonic dialogues, there are many subsidiary themes. One of these, which for our purposes is the most important, is the problem of method: the problem of how to go about inquiring into the nature of excellence, or any other of the human things.[1] We will examine Plato's conception of method in the *Meno* in the light of what we now understand about the quarrel between Hobbes and the classics, and the issues in that quarrel which are raised by Wittgenstein's account of language. We should, as a result of the latter, be alert to the possibility that the method appropriate to an inquiry into the nature of human excellence is no different, strictly speaking, from the method for inquiry into the meaning of "human excellence."

Socrates confronts in the person of Meno a method, or rather a number of possible methods, which are *sophisticated* (in both the loose and the literal sense) but unreflective. Meno has been a student of Gorgias the sophist, who was rare among sophists for not claiming to teach virtue or excellence.[2] The encounter presented in the *Meno* is an encounter between a great teacher and an unteachable man. In the course of the dialogue a great deal is revealed about Meno's character. We are compelled to wonder whether this character is perhaps the natural accompaniment to the approach to knowledge which Meno presents in the dialogue. Is Meno's inability to learn what Socrates can teach related to the contrast in methods which they represent?

The Opening Scene

Meno opens the dialogue: "Can you tell me, Socrates, whether human excellence is teachable? Or if not teachable, is it acquired by training? Or if neither by training nor by learning, does it come to human beings by nature, or in some other manner?" (70a1–4).[3] Socrates does not respond directly to Meno's question but instead launches into a somewhat lengthy speech describing the general lack of wisdom in Athens, with which lack he then identifies himself, and ends by stating his own complete ignorance of the nature of human excellence. Meno is surprised, or pretends to be, and asks if he is to carry back to Thessaly this report of Socrates, namely, that Socrates does not know what human excellence is. "Not only that, my friend," replies Socrates, "but also that I have never met anyone else who knew [what human excellence is], as it seems to me." When Meno asks if this means that Socrates does not think Gorgias (Meno's teacher, whom Socrates has met) knows what excellence is, Socrates replies that he does not have a very good memory. He asks Meno to remind him what Gorgias says about virtue. Socrates thus points to a connection between his ignorance and his inferior memory; we may be led to suppose, along with Meno, that knowing what human excellence is means being able to remember something, in Meno's case to remember what Gorgias has told him.[4] Meno's reliance on the faculty of memory, which is reinforced in the Greek by the similarity between his name Meno and "remembering," or *mnēmōn*, is a persistent theme throughout the dialogue, and one to which we will return below.[5]

When Socrates asks him to say what human excellence is, Meno is immediately ready to reply. His reply, we sense right away, is somewhat naive in this context. It reflects, both in substance and in the lack of hesitation with which it is delivered, an unreflective or commonsense understanding of human excellence, except that it omits to mention piety.[6] "It is not difficult to say [what human excellence is], Socrates," Meno begins. He proceeds to name the excellence of a gentleman (*aretē andros*), and the excellence of a woman, and explains further that there is a distinct excellence appropriate to children, either female or male, an old man, and even a slave. "And there are many other excellences, so that it is not difficult to say, concerning excellence, what it is," Meno explains to Socrates. It is no surprise when Socrates is not satisfied with this first attempt by Meno to say what human excellence is. Meno has only given him a list of various excellences, and a sketchy list at that, making no attempt to relate them to each other, to account for the fact that they are all called *aretē*, or excellence.

Meno is apparently satisfied with the approach of listing, or pointing to, the multiplicity of excellences. Wittgenstein, we recall, saw the articulation of the meaning of a word in the exploration of the various senses of a word, without reducing all those senses to one "essence," without forcing the multiplicity of meanings into one rigid definition. But is Meno's answer identical to Wittgenstein's goal of a "perspicuous understanding"? Wittgenstein also seemed to say that such an understanding is more than simply a list of meanings, because the meaning of a word is not limited in that way. The approach Meno takes with excellence appears at first to be based on the same multiplicity which was so characteristic of Wittgenstein, but we need to wonder whether these two approaches are really the same.[7] Wittgenstein's understanding of language supplied us with grounds for thinking that we must start, as Meno does, from common speech; it does not require us to leave the matter there. Socrates, in any case, does not wish to leave it at a state of unexamined multiplicity.

We remember that Hobbes's rejection of the classical approach was based on the failure of that approach to settle things with certainty and clarity. The naive view with which Hobbes was dissatisfied may be said to be represented at this point by the listing of types of human excellence which Meno offers, the unreflective,

Plato's *Meno*

commonsense idea of excellence. The multiplicity of this approach, Hobbes charged, is not systematic. Socrates' first task is to bring Meno to the point of dissatisfaction which Hobbes felt with this understanding. He seeks to do this by insisting that Meno give him *one* definition of human excellence simply, and not a list of various human excellences unilluminated by any view of their relation to each other or the whole of human excellence. Socrates may suspect what will be confirmed later in the dialogue, namely, that Meno's *real* definition of excellence is something much more skeptical (and in fact we will see that it resembles Hobbes's understanding itself). There is a gentle mocking of Meno's first attempt as Socrates compares the human excellences Meno has given him to a swarm of bees, whereas what he, Socrates, wanted was the essence of bees, that is, that aspect of bees in view of which all bees are bees. With regard to human excellence, he asks Meno, What is the one aspect which all the human excellences have, in view of which they are human excellence? He wishes to find the *essence* of human excellence, it would appear, by seeing what is common to all the various meanings of the term.

To ask "what is" something is the beginning of a search for knowledge of that thing. Knowledge about something is different from right opinion in that it is anchored or connected to something else that we already know. The transformation of opinion into knowledge is accomplished by giving an account of something, by showing us the place of that something in a larger whole, which in the largest sense is our whole experience, our world. The process begins from what we opine about things, from what we commonly think or say, from common speech. But common speech points in different directions. If we simply accept this fact, or rather these different directions, without reflecting on or trying to account for them, then we do not go beyond common speech. This is the position of Meno at the beginning of the dialogue. What Socrates wants him to see is at first no more than the fact that there is a *problem* in his glib recitation of the various human excellences. How do these "parts" of human excellence fit together? How, for example, does the excellence of a child fit together with the excellence of a man, or of an old man, or a slave? Why are they all called "excellence"? The philosophic mind—that is, the mind seeking knowledge about what human excellence *is*—begins from its awareness of these questions.

Now, we must consider the possibility that the demand Socrates makes of Meno here, namely, to give him a definition of human excellence simply, is ironic. Nothing seems further from the spirit of Wittgenstein than the Platonic doctrine of the Forms, at least on the conventional understanding of Plato; and this would appear to be exactly what Socrates is hinting at in the exchange with Meno. Plato more than anyone else, according to the conventional view, taught precisely what Socrates here teaches Meno, that to understand something like human excellence is to isolate and contemplate the essence underlying all particular manifestations. This understanding of Plato, however, ignores above all the dramatic situation in the dialogues, where Socrates sometimes confronts his interlocutors as a teacher, as in the *Meno*. It is striking that Plato never has his Socrates offer a clear definition of human excellence, or rather, that he offers a number of more or less ambiguous and contradictory definitions. The *Meno* is concerned in so many places and from so many angles with the problem of definitions that it seems at least wise to remain open to the possibility that Plato was himself aware of the issue Hobbes charged the classics with ignoring, the issue of method. The *Meno* may be read as an attempt by Plato to explore the issue of definitions and meanings, both in the dramatic action and in the substantive treatment of the meaning of human excellence.[8] At this point, we only raise the possibility. We must wait and see whether Socrates has another notion of a definition, or whether his demand for the essence is serious.

The Beginning of Inquiry

To return to the dialogue, Socrates explains what he is seeking— the definition of human excellence simply—by comparing his goal to the aspect of bees in view of which they are all bees. One who is seeking knowledge about the nature of human excellence, Socrates warns, would do well to keep his eyes fixed on this common aspect, the *eidos*,[9] which goes along with *all* the various excellences.

If he were to ask Meno to identify this aspect of bees, Socrates asks, could Meno do so? Meno answers that he could. Socrates does not pursue the point further, but we are compelled to wonder whether Meno *could*, in fact, satisfy the request. There are basic types of bees—the queen, the drone, and the worker: by virtue of what quality would he, or we, say that all these types of bees are bees? This first example can be seen to contain in a sense the two fundamental alternatives for definition which will be important throughout the dialogue. One possible answer would be to identify something common to all of the types of bees, such as having four wings, or hairy bodies. But aside from a few such qualities—which are not even restricted to bees alone—and the fact that they make and eat honey, the various sorts of bees *differ* in the most important respects. What they *do* share, however (and this comprises the second possible kind of answer), is the fact of participation in a hive or social colony. Although the roles as well as the physical properties of the queen, the drones, and the workers are all different, each sort of bee contributes in some manner to the whole, and bees are commonly identified by this aspect. We would call it, however, a shared *end* rather than a shared quality.

Socrates next brings in the examples of health, size, and strength. Meno thinks that these things are the same in essence, no matter where they appear: yet when Socrates suggests that human excellence follows the same pattern, being the same insofar as it is excellence whether it appears in a child, a slave, or a man, Meno answers only that "it somehow seems to me, Socrates, that this [human excellence] is no longer the same as those others." He is apparently unaware of the second possibility contained in the bee example.

Bees are a standard metaphor for political society.[10] The metaphor might have suggested to Meno a different way of applying his first attempt to define excellence. He began by saying that there is the excellence of a man, a woman, a child, and a slave, and Socrates asked him to say what the common aspect is. The example of bees suggests that instead of searching for some quality common to all these, he could understand them all as excellences because of their common participation in, or contribution to, a whole (that is, the political community). As in the case of bees, the various "parts" of excellence could be understood to constitute excellence because of their common *end*, rather than some common quality. By moving from the example of bees—which suggests this type of definition so clearly—to the somehow different example of physical attributes (health, size, strength), Socrates is inviting Meno to focus on the nonreductive type of definition, the type which defines by looking toward a whole in which the parts participate, rather than to some quality shared by all the parts.[11] But Meno does not accept the invitation. Socrates also manages, with the example of the bees, to prepare the way for the discussion which comes up almost immediately, in which Meno says that excellence is ruling, and Socrates responds by reminding him that this does not account for the excellence of the child or of the slave. If there is a "part" of excellence which may be said to belong to a slave, it may be visible in his contribution to the political community, his role as a subordinate but necessary part of the whole. This is ignored by focusing exclusively on ruling.

We may regard the two comparisons suggested by Socrates, first the swarm of bees and then physical qualities, as attempts to get Meno started in a genuine inquiry. Such inquiry begins, characteristically for the Platonic Socrates, by eliciting the similarities and differences suggested by such comparisons. We could say that Socrates' "method" begins by exploring similarities in the "grammar" of the cases he compares. An interlocutor genuinely awake to the problems and issues—in other words an interlocutor unlike Meno—would perhaps have joined Socrates in exploring the resemblance between health, strength, and excellence by pointing out, for example, that each of these—unlike the bee-ness of bees—can be possessed by a human being to a greater or lesser degree, extending all the way to their complete absence. Health and strength, like human excellence, reveal themselves to us in what we do, in our actions; we cannot display strength in sleep, but require an opportunity to act. Strength, however, unlike human excellence, can be used for any number of purposes, not all of them good, and in that respect it is profoundly different from human excellence, which may be said to be more of a disposition than a capability. Further exploration might help Socrates to learn something about Meno's original question regarding the acquisition of excellence. Is human excellence, like size, something which, once gained, does not disappear? Or must it be constantly exercised to prevent it from slipping away, like strength? Such questions explore similarities in the grammar of the expressions: they ask what we say or think about something in numerous different contexts.

Socrates has asked Meno for an account of the whole (of human excellence), which Meno cannot give. We have next to see how Meno is forced to see the inadequacy of his original approach, and takes refuge in a certain idea of scientific method. In the process we will watch Socrates elicit, from Meno's somewhat simpleminded attempts to define human excellence, implications which are contradictory but which, by their very contradiction, reveal something fundamental about human excellence.

Two Sides of Excellence Considered

After the apparent failure of Meno to take up his half of the inquiry, Socrates returns (at 73a6) to Meno's first listing of the excellences of a man and of a woman, and focuses on a certain similarity between the descriptions. "Well then," says Socrates, "were you not saying that the excellence of a man is to manage a city well, and that of a woman to manage well the household?" Meno: "I was" (73a7). "And is it possible to manage well a city or a household, or anything else, if one does not manage moderately and justly?" Meno: "Clearly not." Socrates goes on to show that both men *and* women, and also old men and young men, whatever they do, must act justly and with moderation if they are truly good (*agathos*). Meno agrees, although his agreement seems to come strictly from the logic of the argument rather than from any deeper understanding. Socrates would appear to be directing Meno's attention to one aspect of excellence, namely, that insofar as it is something accessible to all sorts of human beings, it points toward moderation and justice. We speak of good citizens as including not only our political leaders, but the men and women who obey the laws, and who participate justly in the more mundane political processes. This "side" of human excellence or virtue is profoundly important for a man like Meno to understand, and the next exchange suggests that he does not yet see it.

Socrates again invites Meno to try to recollect what Meno himself and Gorgias say excellence is. "What else [can excellence be] but the ability to rule over human beings?" answers Meno, ignoring what has just been brought out by Socrates. We might expect Socrates here to persist in the line of argument he had begun, and ask Meno whether he would add "justly," but first he raises another objection. This objection is extremely important for our discussion of definitions. "But is the excellence of a child the same, Meno, or [the excellence] of a slave? Can the slave rule over the master, and can a slave who rules still be a slave?" That is, does not Meno's answer, that excellence is ability to rule, require that we consider excellence not as it applies to every particular sort of human being, but only to some few? Socrates does not object to the answer itself, which might offer a good beginning point for inquiry, but he brings out the fact that looking at excellence from this side would require us to abstract from another side,[12] from other aspects which would have to be included in a complete or comprehensive understanding of excellence. He will return to this theme later.

Socrates now attempts to continue his earlier line of argument, by asking Meno if he would not add "justly" to his statement. Meno agrees immediately, because, as he says, "justice is excellence"—a phrase which, in Meno's mouth, has by this time the ring of an empty slogan. This permits Socrates to pursue the point he has just hinted at about abstraction, although Meno, as we will see, does not follow. This time Socrates uses an analogy to illustrate his method. "Would you say 'excellence,' Meno, or 'an excellence'?" he asks. Meno doesn't follow. When Socrates explains, Meno responds that he means "an excellence" because justice is only one and there are others. Socrates asks him to name them. "Courage seems now to me to be excellence, and moderation and wisdom [sophia] and greatness of soul and many others," says Meno. These are the parts of excellence, it seems. But, says Socrates, "we are not able to find the one excellence which runs through them all" (74a9).

It seems likely that the analogy Socrates takes next is chosen with an eye to Meno's previous education. As a student of Gorgias he would have been trained in geometry, as will soon become apparent. If, Socrates begins, someone were to ask, "What is shape [*schēma*]?" and Meno answered "roundness," he might be asked next whether he would say roundness is "shape," or "a shape." This Meno has no trouble following. If a parallel inquiry were made about color, Socrates continues, would Meno say whiteness is "color" or "a color"? They agree he would say "a color," because there are other colors besides white. The parallel is now spelled out for Meno, but Socrates continues further, asking Meno to go ahead and answer the question "What is shape?" as *practice* for the question about excellence. Try to say, he urges, with emphasis on the repeated "try" (*peirō*). Meno responds, "No! Rather you, Socrates, say" (75b1).

Socrates' Three Definitions

The next section of the dialogue contains a clear example of the definitional approach of Socrates.[13] He agrees to try to say what *schēma* (shape or shaped surface) is, provided Meno will then attempt the same for excellence. Meno agrees. Socrates' definition of *schēma* is surprising to Meno. *Schēma*, Socrates says, is "the only thing [*ho monon tōn ontōn*] which always goes along with color." And he asks Meno whether he is satisfied with the answer, as he, Socrates, would be if Meno offered a definition of the same sort for excellence. What sort of definition has Socrates offered? It is a linking definition, drawing a connection to something else. It does not break down or resolve the term *schēma* into component parts; rather, it links the concept as a whole to another concept, another part of the phenomenal world. It links the concept to the world of common sense. It does not immediately "get behind" the phenomena, but neither is the connection obvious to us at a glance. The definition says something we *already* know or recollect once we think about it, without relying on a special method.

Meno is *not* satisfied with it. "But this is simple-minded [*euēthes*], Socrates," he objects. And he goes on to explain. What if someone were to say he did not know what color is? Then Socrates' definition would not tell him what *schēma* is. The definition Socrates has offered fails to satisfy Meno, it would appear, because it employs undefined terms. Socrates responds pedagogically, and with a barely concealed rebuke, to the effect that if he were talking to a "wise man" (there is irony in Socrates' use of this term *sophos*) (75c8) of the eristic or antagonistic sort, he would not go on until refuted, but since he is talking together in dialogue with a friend, he will instead try to explain himself further, using premises to which Meno can agree. These two possibilities for philosophical inquiry— one the eristic, the other the dialectical—are of enormous importance in this dialogue; the personalities which naturally go along with each "method" will be seen to be reflected in Meno and Socrates, respectively.

Socrates proceeds now to elicit Meno's agreement to some new terms. "There is something you call an end, or limit, or extremity?" After Socrates notes that, although these terms probably could be distinguished by Prodicus,[14] he means by them the same thing. Meno agrees. "And there is also something you call a surface [*epipedon*] and also a solid [*stereon*]?" Socrates asks, explicitly noting that these terms have the same meanings in geometry. Again Meno agrees. This allows Socrates to offer a second definition: *Schēma* is, he says, that in which a solid ends, or more concisely, "the limit of a solid [*stereou peras*]" (76a7). To this Meno's only response is to ask, "And what do you say color is, Socrates?"

Before we see how Socrates deals with this, we must examine what has just transpired. Two definitions of *schēma* have now been offered by Socrates: his own, and a second which attempts to satisfy Meno's objections. The second is clearly more "scientific"; it appears to meet Meno's requirements. This is stressed by Plato in his making geometry explicit. The terms in which *schēma* is defined on the second try are themselves technical terms in geometry. Why then did Socrates offer first the simpler definition, the definition which depended on linking the concept of *schēma* to another, familiar concept? Socrates' first definition brings out a connection between *schēma* and another concept, color. The connection reveals, at least in part, the place of *schēma* in our commonsense world, the world of phenomena. Color and shaped surface always appear together in the world; we do not find one without the other. Socrates' first definition may be said to point to the fact that his understanding of the whole, of the things (*tōn ontōn*) simply, is different from the understanding characteristic of the science of geometry. Socrates' definition connects the thing to something else; he thereby indicates the view that the whole is heterogeneous, and not a composite of universal "simples" to which it can always be reduced. We cannot but recall, in opposition to this, the resolutive-compositive method of Hobbes. Whatever geometry can reveal to us, one thing about which it has absolutely nothing to say is *color*: geometry abstracts from color. In fact, the rigor and power of geometry is in part a result of its abstraction from the world of phenomena. It is, we may say, a useful or productive understanding without being a comprehensive understanding. Geometry can tell us everything about shapes but nothing about color, even though these phenomena are never separable in the world.[15] Plato has pointed to this difference in several ways, and Meno's response to Socrates' geometric definition once again focuses our attention on color.

After chiding Meno for his demanding and hubristic attitude in the discussion, Socrates offers him a definition of color as requested. The definition is this time given "in the manner of Gorgias [*kata Gorgian*]," of which Meno approves. It is based on the claim of Gorgias (following Empedocles)[16] that there are certain "effluences" of things, and passages into which these effluences pass when they are neither too small nor too large. "And there is something you call.sight?" asks Socrates. Meno answers affirmatively. Then, explains Socrates, "color is an effluence of shaped surface, commensurate with and perceptible to sight" (76d4). Meno expresses his pleasure at this answer with high praise. "Perhaps," Socrates suggests of his answer, "it was phrased according to what is habitual with you." Not only that, he says, but a similar definition might be used for sound, odor, and many other things. He thus indicates to us that the definition is so general that it tells us very little. It is general in the sense that it reduces the variety and complexity of what appears to us in the world to an undifferentiated homogeneity. Although this sort of reduction can be very useful, especially in permitting us to manipulate data with the tools of mathematics, it also pays a price, which is the distortion of precisely the variety and complexity which also must be part of our understanding of the world.

Three definitions have now been offered by Socrates: two of

schēma,[17] and one of color, which is most pleasing to Meno. If we compare these definitions, we find a progression which reveals something about Meno's approach to understanding the meanings of the terms in question. He was not satisfied with Socrates' first definition because it relied on a connection between *schēma* and another concept—color—which, according to Meno, an interlocutor might not know. Leaving aside the question of whether anyone who understands the language at all could fail to know what "color" means, we may compare this state of affairs to Socrates' second definition. In response to Meno's claim that the first attempt used an undefined term, Socrates defined *schēma* in the style of a geometrician, using several terms which Meno had in advance admitted to understanding: "limit," "solid," "surface." There is a certain clarity in this second definition which comes from the fact that the terms employed are almost universally accepted and *used* in the same way. But the clarity is purchased only by removing oneself from ordinary speech or common sense. Meno's ready acquiescence in their use, even while he was opposed to the use of the term "color," is an indication of the sort of knowledge he seeks. The third definition, of color, goes even further. The terms of it are yet more inaccessible to the nonspecialist: the Empedoclean term "effluences" has a flavor more than merely technical, it is part of the specialized language or jargon of a particular philosophical school. Meno's immediate acceptance of the thing called "sight" in the third definition provides a further reason to wonder about his interest. Can someone who accepts "sight" without definition seriously maintain that "color" requires definition? Why is Meno ready to accept and even applaud the third definition while rejecting the first and remaining neutral with respect to the second?

All three of the definitions employ undefined terms. Socrates' first and simplest definition is least abstract, and its terms have their common or ordinary meanings. The second, geometricians' definition, abstracts from the phenomena themselves, as we have seen. It too makes use of terms which are not defined, but which are accepted as fundamental in the practice of geometry (or are reducible to others which are accepted as fundamental). The third definition uses undefined terms of both the specialized ("effluence") and ordinary ("sight") sorts, but neither is questioned by Meno. We are led to believe, by Socrates' comments, that this is because the definitions are progressively more familiar to Meno; he remembers them, or definitions like them, and he even prefers an empty formulaic definition if it is familiar and sounds "scientific." Socrates, by contrast, makes explicit his belief that "the other" (*ekeinē*) definition—presumably his first—is best. He appears to prefer an approach which sticks as closely as possible to ordinary nontechnical meanings. But we have seen that this method is open to a powerful objection: how can we get a toehold, so to speak, a base from which to begin our inquiry? With Socrates' first definition the problem is clearest, but does it not exist just as much in the case of the others, in which, though somehow hidden, the undefined terms are nevertheless present? For the moment we must leave this question, and follow Meno's second attempt to define excellence in general. The question of undefined terms will be an underlying theme in the next part of the dialogue, however, although it does not come to the surface until the end of the section (79d).

Meno's Character and the Two Types of Inquiry

In the next section of the dialogue, the character of Meno becomes a very important theme.[18] It is necessary to recall for a moment the curious rebuke Socrates gave Meno a little while back, when Meno began to sound simply argumentative. At that point (75c8; above, p. 165) Socrates implied that there are two types of inquiry, or that an inquiry like the one in which they are engaged can proceed in either of two "spirits," namely, the "eristic and antagonistic" spirit or the friendly (or erotic) "dialectical" spirit.[19] Each of these goes along with a certain method. The eristic inquiry is radically skeptical and refuses to admit undefined terms, the other tries to explain what is meant only if and when disagreement arises. Each of these methods, the *Meno* makes clear, implies a certain moral outlook, an attitude toward other human beings and the world, both in politics and in private life—as we will see. Socrates is going to unveil the full implications of these different attitudes in the next section. This will lead us into the difficult and complicated Socratic contention that virtue is knowledge. At least one side of this contention may be understood as follows: what one thinks excellence or virtue (*aretē*) is depends to a great extent on what one's conception of knowledge is, or what kind of knowledge is thought to be possible for human beings. This understanding of the connection between knowledge and virtue will be brought out more fully below.

Meno again tries to define excellence in general, this time with a quotation from an unidentified poet. "Excellence is," Meno begins, "as the poet says, 'to take delight in the high things and to master them' [*chairein te kaloisi kai dynasthai*]. And I too say this, that excellence is desiring the high things and being able to get them." In the ensuing discussion Socrates examines this statement with Meno to see if it helps them identify excellence, and in the process Socrates changes the statement in significant ways, just as Meno has already begun to reinterpret the poet's words. The manner in which the passage is altered by Socrates, with no objection from Meno, tells us a great deal about Meno's character. Meno will reveal himself to be a man who sees no distinction between the noble (*to kalon*) and the good (*ton agathon*). Socrates claims at the end of the discussion that the poet's statement has not helped them to discover excellence: if true, this may be because the distinctions crucial to understanding excellence are precisely the ones Socrates manages to blur or ignore in the inquiry. The fact that Meno is not aware of this, that he does not question the elimination of those distinctions, may explain his inability to understand excellence as well. The dialogue proceeds as follows:

Socrates takes up the statement of the poet, and in his first question to Meno he changes "the high things" (*ta kala*) to "good things" or "goods" (*agatha*), a change to which Meno readily consents. In the next few exchanges Socrates will try to show Meno that the first part of the statement, namely, that excellence is desiring good things, cannot be right because all men desire good things, or at least what they consider to be good things. It is to this end that Socrates wishes to change "high things" to "goods," since in the matter of high or noble things all men are most emphatically not alike in their desires. Whatever excellence is determined to be, common sense tells us that it is not possessed by everyone to an equal degree: the best human beings are best precisely because they have excellence. Meno is open to the change Socrates makes in part because he is sophisticated; that is, he would be prepared to agree with the view that the "high things" are only conventional anyway, and therefore not in principle different from the good things: one man's high things are another man's good things. This might also be expressed by the claim that knowledge of what is high and what is not, or knowledge of values, as we would say, is in principle impossible. With this claim goes the view that "noble" or "high" are only disguised expressions for "expedient." Expediency thus becomes the only judgment for which we have a standard.

Even if no difference between *kala* and *agatha* is admitted, however, it would be possible to argue that men differ in the *degree* to which they desire (*epithymein*) the good things. Hence Socrates' second change in Meno's statement, which consists in his substituting "willing" or "choosing" (*boulesthai*)[20] for the original "desiring." Desiring admits of degrees, whereas the verb he substitutes for it has the sense of deliberate or at least conscious choice, and therefore does not admit of degrees. The two changes Socrates makes allows him to persuade Meno to agree that since no one willingly chooses the bad things, everyone is the same in respect of willing the good things.[21]

Since excellence, as we have seen, must differentiate men, Socrates suggests to Meno that the key to excellence must be sought in the second half of Meno's statement, that is, in the ability to get the good things. "According to your definition, it would [now] appear, excellence is the ability to get hold of the good things," says Socrates. Meno agrees wholeheartedly. (This is the sort of thing he cannot help but enjoy hearing.) What good things? Socrates suggests health and wealth, and Meno adds "and to possess gold, I say, and silver, and honor in the city, and office." His enthusiasm is almost palpable: these are the goods, Plato indicates, in which Meno is most interested.

We are compelled to wonder whether Meno's preoccupation with wealth, honor, and power as the goals does not somehow go along with what he will directly reveal to be his deeper conception of knowledge, which is that it does not exist. Meno begins, as we will see, from a radical skepticism. He will come very close to claiming that we never really *know* anything, especially about what is noble or excellent, and from this it appears to follow that wealth and power are the only justifiable goals because with them we can do whatever we want. We must recall Hobbes's position here. Hobbes argues that since men cannot agree on any goals except avoiding the evil of violent death, all men seek power (in the form of wealth, or honor, because power allows them to pursue *any* good). Skepticism about the goals most men claim to believe in (the goals given by piety, tradition, etc.) seems to be the natural accompaniment to both an unrestrained selfishness and a cynicism about our ability ever to know anything beyond the "truths" which are "operational" (what is true is what works).

In response to a question from Socrates, Meno admits that it is necessary for these goods to be acquired justly and not unjustly if their possession is to constitute excellence. This small concession does not dampen Meno's enthusiasm. And further, Socrates suggests, when acquiring goods would require injustice, true excellence consists rather in *not* having them. Meno agrees.

It now appears, as Socrates demonstrates, that neither possessing nor lacking these goods is in itself excellence, but whatever is done with justice is excellence and whatever is done without it[22] is bad (*kaka*). Now, Socrates indicates, Meno appears to be saying that excellence is every action done with what he had before identified as only a part of excellence. Meno seems to think that we could know the whole by knowing a part, but can anyone, Socrates asks, who does not know what excellence is know what a part of excellence is? Socrates asks Meno to recall how, in the answer about *schēma*, they rejected any answer which employed or depended on terms which were unexamined or not agreed upon. "And rightly we rejected them, Socrates," responds Meno (79d5). Socrates: "But then, best of men, do not suppose we can explain to someone what excellence is by means of its parts, while excellence as a whole is still being sought." With this Socrates urges Meno to start all over again (for the third time) and to try to say what excellence is.

Socrates has turned Meno's original eristic objection against him, by accusing him of using undefined terms. Why has he done this, particularly in view of his later position on this issue? He may be trying to expose a defect in Meno's own understanding of scientific method by pointing to the fact that there is *no* starting place for such an inquiry which will not be open to the objection of undefined terms. Although this is true of geometry as well as of a discussion of excellence, Meno seems rather to believe that his inability to find the proper beginning is due to Socrates' trickery in dialogue. For now Meno launches into an angry and even threatening accusation of Socrates. Socrates explains that if he (as Meno claims) stuns others into ignorance, it is only because he is ignorant himself; he really does not know what excellence is. But he would be willing to join with Meno in any inquiry, since they seem to share this ignorance. Socrates might have hoped by this time to have conveyed that an inquiry into something like excellence cannot be grounded on clear definitions, but rather will have to proceed somewhat tentatively, ascending by means of connections, from ignorance to a more comprehensive understanding. He might hope, with anyone other than Meno, at least to dispense with eristic objections.

Recollection

Meno, however, responds to Socrates' suggestion that they inquire together by triumphantly asking, "And how will you inquire, Socrates, into something of which you know not at all what it is? Which of the things you do not know will you put forth as the subject of inquiry? And even if you happen to find it, how would you know that this is the thing which you did not know?" (80e). Socrates restates this "eristic argument" (*eristikon logon*) in a more general form, with which he indicates he is familiar—namely, that it is not for human beings to search for anything, neither that which they know nor that which they do not know, for if they know they do not need to search, and if they do not know they do not know what to search for. He indicates that he does not think the argument is sound, and Meno is eager to hear why. Socrates, in response, tells him a "noble truth" which he has heard from "men and women wise in divine things." This is familiar to us as the "myth of recollection." The recollection thesis, and the interrogation of the slave boy which illustrates it, are intended to help Meno and us to understand Plato's conception of the way we inquire into and have knowledge of something we do not know completely—in other words, Plato's conception of the method of philosophizing about the human things.[23] The recollection thesis, then, may be expected to shed light on the inquiry into the nature of excellence which has just been attempted, apparently unsuccessfully. We will see that the recollection thesis has certain parallels to the sort of inquiry for which we have been prepared by Wittgenstein's understanding of language.[24]

This next section of the dialogue consists of two general arguments which together are circular, a fact which will be of importance for us but is completely missed by Meno.[25] The first part consists of a story or myth, the "noble truth" Socrates has just mentioned; the second is a demonstration or illustration of the recollection thesis in the form of a dialogue between Socrates and Meno's slave boy. The noble truth teaches, according to Socrates, that the human soul is immortal and that it is born many times into this world, and also leaves this world many times. As a result of its deathlessness, the soul has seen all the things of this world and all things of the lower world many times, and hence there is nothing it does not know. It is no wonder then (*ouden thaumaston*) that, when in this world, the soul should be able to recollect (*anamnēsthēnai*) what it already once knew concerning human excellence and other things. For, he goes on, everything that exists in nature exists in kinship, and the soul has learned all things, so that there is nothing to prevent someone, if he recollects even just one thing, from recollecting everything else from that one thing, if he is courageous and does not get tired of searching. From this story Socrates draws the lesson that we should not be persuaded by the eristic objection to inquiry (which Meno had raised), but rather we should inquire actively and eagerly. He concludes by urging Meno to join him in the search for the answer to the question, What is excellence?

The story was intended to show that, as Socrates puts it, both searching and learning are altogether recollection. True learning, this would seem to mean, requires some sort of effort by the learner to recall something; it cannot occur the way we sometimes think, as if knowledge were passed to or "poured into" someone by a teacher.[26]

It is not immediately obvious how the recollection thesis contained in Socrates' story bears any relation to the problem of method which is our concern. For the moment it is enough to indicate two important features. First is its assertion that the soul somehow "knows" all things even though it does not "know" them in another, more normal sense. What is the process by which this latent knowledge is converted into true knowledge? And where is the latent knowledge before it is brought out? Second is the assertion in the story that everything in nature exists in kinship, or is related to everything else, with the result that it is possible to "recollect" the whole of nature starting from only one part. This appears to suggest that all the things that exist in or by nature constitute a whole, we may even say *the* whole, which in some way it is our goal to comprehend. This reminds us of the problem of the whole and its parts which concluded the previous section of the dialogue. But how then is it possible to know a part without knowing the whole, as Socrates asked Meno before? Is the recollection thesis intended somehow to answer that question? The second part of this section, the demonstration, will offer a resolution to these problems.

Meno has asked if Socrates can show him (*endeixasthai*) how recollection works (82a6). Socrates is willing to try, although, as he warns, "it will not be easy." He asks Meno to call one of his attendants for Socrates to demonstrate on, and a slave boy comes forward. There is only one qualification which Socrates insists on. "He is Greek and speaks Greek?" The importance of this requirement is not to be underestimated: even a slave, a young slave, apparently, will be capable of recollecting so long as he is competent in the language in which they are to converse. The emphasis on language is the more striking because the dialogue they carry on will concern not the meaning of, say, excellence, but a geometrical problem which involves only a drawing and numbers and geometrical relationships. The problem is determining the side of a square of known area, namely, eight square units. The slave has no knowledge of geometry. He does have a commonsense notion of what a square is, and he does know simple arithmetic. After telling Meno to pay attention, to see if the boy is taught the answers by Socrates or if he recollects them himself, Socrates begins to question the boy.

It is not necessary here to trace the steps of this dialogue within the dialogue. After ascertaining that the slave knows what a square is—that is, that it has four equal sides, may be of any size, and so forth—Socrates allows the boy to make an apparently confident guess as to the side of a square with an area of eight square units. After several wrong guesses, Socrates points out to Meno that the slave has now reached the point where he knows that he does not know the answer, comparing this state to the state Meno was in earlier when he accused Socrates of "numbing" him. Is he not better off now, Socrates asks, knowing his ignorance? Meno: "It seems so to me" (84b5). Then Socrates, by means of a figure drawn in the dust, carefully leads the boy through the steps necessary for him to see the answer, the length of the side of a square with an area of eight square units.[27] Now, the answer to this problem (which will show the problem to have been selected deliberately) is the square root of 8, $\sqrt{8}$, or what is called an irrational number. Euclid called such numbers *alogoi* (which in Latin would become *irrationalis*), which means unutterable, or that which cannot be said. Such a number, as in this case with the slave boy, can be *shown*, or pointed to, but its value is incapable of being stated except by the conventional notation for square roots, or in a drawing.[28] The slave boy manages to indicate the answer to this particular problem by pointing to the diagonal of a square with a side of 2 units, since the diagonal of such a square has a length of $\sqrt{8}$ and forms the side of a square with an area of 8 square units. It is only the fact that Socrates has drawn these units for him in the dust which enables him to "see" the answer. We may understand this as an analog of the problem of defining excellence; in that case too, perhaps, no clear "answer" is to be found, but something like an answer can be pointed to. There too the answer may emerge as a result of Socrates' drawing certain "lines" connecting excellence with other concepts: defining excellence is an analog in speech of the problem drawn in the dust.

Opinion and Knowledge

Socrates demonstrates to Meno that his uneducated slave boy now somehow knows the answer to this geometrical problem, without Socrates having "told" him the answer.[29] Therefore, says Socrates, the opinions must have been somehow "in him." Again Meno agrees. "Then the one who does not know certain things may have true opinions about the things he does not know?" Meno: "Apparently." The paradox expressed here contains the germ of the solution to the problem which has plagued us repeatedly in this dialogue: How can one inquire into what one does not know? Alternatively, How can one "know" the part without knowing the whole of which it is a part, and yet how can one know the whole without knowing the parts which comprise it? What is the starting point for inquiry? The slave boy, according to Socrates, somehow knew and did not know at the same time. The true opinions he had were "stirred up, as in a dream," by Socrates' questioning. And "if someone asks him these things many times and in many different ways, in the end he will know [epistēsetai] these things no less accurately than anyone else" (85c10).

The process of recollection apparently involves asking questions, or being questioned, "many times" and "in different ways," about the thing under investigation. We cannot help but recall, in this connection, the remark of Wittgenstein that philosophical problems "are solved, not by giving new information, but by arranging what we have always known" (PI, 1, 109). "The work of the philosopher," he says elsewhere, "consists in assembling reminders for a particular purpose.... The aspects of things that are most important for us are hidden because of their simplicity and familiarity. (One is unable to notice something—because it is always before one's eyes)" (PI, 1, 127, 129). Wittgenstein and Socrates appear to be speaking of the same matter. When we inquire into the nature of something—such as excellence in the Meno—we find that we do not know what it is, or rather, we cannot say what it is, though we feel we "somehow" know. At the very least it would be wrong to say we do not know what excellence is. Wittgenstein suggests that the knowledge is, in a way, contained in our language: the grammar of excellence tells us what kind of a thing it is. It does this by connecting it with other things by prescribing—largely but not wholly—the ways in which we may use it in our language games. That "knowledge" may be understood to be somehow "in" us, since by a careful and tireless inquiry we can begin to elucidate the shape of the concept, by drawing connections, exploring parallels in grammar, examining new cases. We begin with opinions about what the thing is, and anchor or jettison the opinions as we proceed in the inquiry. Such an inquiry takes the form of a dialogue: it is tentative and questioning, not deductive. The knowledge we possess at the end is only partially articulable: it is contained in the simple phrases which tell us in which directions the concept points, but for one who has not participated in the inquiry the phrase remains an empty slogan. For example, the complexities which are summed up in the formula "virtue is knowledge" are only obscurities to one who has not thought through the inquiry by which Socrates arrives at it. In some sense knowledge emerges in the *process* of inquiry and is revealed only to the *active* participant in a dialogue. Meno never participates: he waits to be told what excellence is, ignorant that its outline is being traced before his eyes both in speech and in deed. Wittgenstein remarks, "A main source of our failure to understand is that we do not *command a clear view* of the use of our words.—Our grammar is lacking in this sort of perspicuity. A perspicuous representation produces just that understanding which consists in 'seeing connexions' " (*PI*, 1, 122).

Such an approach to knowledge cannot claim, of course, to produce knowledge which is completely finished or absolutely certain. Further connections can always be traced, new circumstances imagined. And such an inquiry will always be somehow circular: it begins in our ordinary language and ends in it, without a basis outside. It begins with parts only partly known and searches for a perspicuous view of the whole, mindful always that other directions remain to be explored. Socrates' answer to the problem of parts and wholes is contained in his assertion that the slave boy somehow knows and yet does not know the answer. The status of his "true opinions" remains paradoxical at this point. We may suspect, however, that what Socrates has in mind is that opinions and knowledge are not qualitatively distinct, but rather that they are poles on a continuum, a continuum traversed in the process of "recollecting" something.

At the conclusion of Socrates' exchange with Meno about the slave's knowledge, Socrates urges Meno to confidently search for "that which you do not know, or rather, that which you do not remember." Meno: "I think you are right, Socrates; I know not how." To this Socrates replies in an uncharacteristically unironic fashion. "I think so too, Meno. I would not uphold with much confidence many things. But that we will be better men and braver and less slothful if we think one should search for that which one does not know, than if we suppose it is impossible to know and unnecessary to search for what one does not know—this I am ready to fight for strenuously, in word and in deed, whenever it is possible."[30] It was Meno, we recall, who asserted precisely that it is impossible to know and impossible to search for something one does not know (80e; above, p. 172). The implication is that this kind of skepticism goes with slothfulness and a lack of bravery in one's character, and thus touches Meno directly. And in fact we have seen something of his character already: his cynicism, his impiety, his selfishness, his devotion to "gold and silver and honor."[31] The type of inquiry which can produce knowledge for us is somehow circular, as we have seen, because it is not grounded on any outside Archimedean point of certainty. The final support for the conviction Socrates states here, the conviction that it is better to search, is no more but no less than the fact that he is prepared to fight for it. We may understand this as an acknowledgement that no cosmic guarantee is possible, that human action, in this case Socrates' action, is what lies at the base even of philosophical inquiry. Once again, Wittgenstein comes to mind: "If I have exhausted the justification, I have reached bedrock, and my spade is turned. Then I am inclined to say: 'This is simply what I do' " (PI, 1, 217).

Language and Knowledge

Knowing a language includes knowing its grammar, which we may say has "built into" it the knowledge, or partial knowledge, which we seek when we inquire about concepts like justice or excellence. We can be said to know in a sense—that is, potentially—what we do not know clearly. No new information is necessary in an inquiry into the meaning of excellence. We both know and do not know simultaneously. All the things that exist are connected in kinship. The grammar of our language may be said to relate each

Plato's *Meno*

thing to all the others directly or indirectly, so that the world of "the things which are," including the human world, forms a "whole." The connections between piety and justice, punishment and responsibility, courage and freedom, law and rulers, foreign policy and geography, virtue and knowledge—the list is endless— must be inquired into in order for us to understand ourselves and our place in the world. It is philosophy which undertakes this task, this inquiry into the "whole." It transforms opinions into knowledge by anchoring them, and this occurs when we question our opinions, or what we ordinarily say, "many times" and in "many different ways." Our starting point in the search for knowledge of the whole is our opinions, which we find by asking what "we think" something to be: we begin from common speech.[32] But philosophical knowledge transcends common speech, precisely because it is not satisfied with the unexamined and conflicting implications. Philosophy seeks to discover the whole by discovering how things fit together or by finding the place of each thing in the whole. Philosophy may even find that the whole contains fundamental tensions or contradictions. If this is the case, it seeks to reveal the roots of those fundamental contradictions, to elucidate the contradictory wholes which are indicated by the different directions in which different parts may point, or in which the same part points when considered in relation to two different things. For example, Plato seems to indicate elsewhere that courage must be understood to be subordinate to justice, and yet courage has another side which puts it, together with wisdom, into a tension with justice and the other political virtues.[33] The grammar of our language is the Wittgensteinian parallel to Socrates' understanding of the relationship among the human phenomena, that is, among excellence, courage, knowledge, justice, convention, and so on. In the Meno specifically, Socrates seeks knowledge of excellence, by beginning from common opinions and examining them dialectically, by tracing the implications of each of the partial understandings which Meno offers.

The recollection thesis was an interruption in the joint inquiry into excellence. It was presented by Socrates as an answer to the dilemma posed by an eristic and frustrated Meno, that is, the question of how it is ever possible to inquire into that which one does not know. Socrates concluded both the recollection story and the demonstration with the slave boy with the same appeal to Meno to take heart and join him in beginning again with the question, What is human excellence? Socrates' appeal is enthusiastic and hopeful. Meno, however, would rather go back instead to his original question, whether excellence is something which comes to man by teaching, or by nature, or some other way. Socrates agrees to this, although he notes that had he control of Meno as well as of himself he would first investigate what excellence is, before trying to see how it is acquired. As it turns out, he will pursue this course anyway, and even get Meno to approve it.

The Argument by Hypothesis

The remainder of the dialogue can be divided into three sections. In the first Socrates returns to his inquiry into the nature of excellence (despite Meno's request), and completes the tentative sketch of its form or *eidos*. At its conclusion we have a rough idea of the "shape" of human excellence. The second section raises a serious and perhaps decisive objection to the conclusion of the section immediately preceding. In this second section, also, the dialogue is joined by another character, who replaces Meno temporarily; this is Anytus, who will later be one of the accusers who bring Socrates to trial. Plato makes very clear in this passage how antagonistic and insulting Socrates could be, in conversation with someone like Anytus. This is one of the most dramatic passages in any of the Platonic dialogues. Anytus is provoked until he is is so enraged that he cannot or will not continue to converse, at which point Socrates turns again to Meno. The objections raised in conversation with Anytus about the conclusion of the previous section leave Meno perplexed and, perhaps for the first time, even in a state of wonder (*agamai*) (95c1) about the puzzle they now appear to be facing. The third and last section of the dialogue partially resolves the contradictory implications which have been uncovered. In the process it adds a missing piece to the discussion of method, by exploring further the tension between opinion and knowledge which was hinted at in the demonstration of recollection with the slave boy.

When Socrates and Meno begin again to inquire, they are

ostensibly going to deal with Meno's original question regarding how excellence comes to human beings. Socrates asks permission from Meno to pursue the inquiry in a different manner from before: this time he would like to examine the problem "by hypothesis" as geometricians do, that is, to make a supposition or hypothesis and then discover by examining its necessary consequences whether or not it is in fact the case.[34] The geometrical "example" he offers to illustrate this procedure involves determining whether it is possible to inscribe a triangle of specified area in a circle of specified area. The problem as stated by Socrates is so obscure that commentators have been unable to agree on what was intended.[35] One might quite reasonably conclude that the ambiguity of the formulation was intended by Plato. Whatever the geometrical problem, at least one thing is clear: the solution seems to depend on seeing whether two rectangular areas, the precise shape of which is unknown, are similar to each other. Thus the problem prepares us in advance for Socrates' next task in the inquiry, which will be to determine whether excellence (or virtue) is knowledge, while not knowing clearly what either excellence or knowledge is by itself.[36] It is also significant that Socrates suggests a geometrical method here. Such a suggestion is virtually guaranteed to provoke no objection from Meno. As we have seen, he is most comfortable with familiar techniques and the deductive rigor of geometry. And yet here he does not appear to be bothered by the remarkable ambiguity of Socrates' example.

Since we do not know what excellence is, Socrates begins, let us take as a hypothesis that it is like knowledge. Will it then be teachable or not? That is, since nothing but knowledge, as is clear to everyone (*panti dēlon*), is taught, if excellence is "like knowledge" it will be teachable, and if not, it will not be teachable. Meno voices his agreement. Socrates quickly adds, then, that the next step is to determine whether indeed excellence is knowledge or something else. He thus returns to the question he is really interested in, namely, the nature of excellence simply. Meno does not object to this shift. If we take seriously the hint in the geometrical example Socrates has just offered, we can expect not only that he will now try to see how excellence is related to knowledge, but also that the inquiry will be one in which he is trying to determine whether the two "things"—whose precise shape is unknown—are somehow "similar" to each other in extent. The method of argument "by hypothesis" has a deeper implication as well, which is connected with the problem of parts and wholes and the problem of undefined terms. Socrates appears to mean that his dialectical inquiry, which ascends from common speech or opinion to knowledge, must always be understood to proceed from a less than absolutely certain foundation, which must itself be subject to continual reexamination. He must return again and again to the beginnings, seeking a fuller and deeper knowledge, which nevertheless remains somehow tentative. The fundamental circularity of the recollection thesis may be seen as another indication of this aspect of his "method."

The argument takes shape as follows: excellence is a good thing. Good things are good for us, that is, beneficial or profitable (*ōphelimos*). The things which we call profitable to us are health, and strength, and beauty, and wealth. But such things can also be harmful (*blapton*) to us. That which determines whether they are profitable or harmful to us is the way in which they are used: used rightly they are profitable, used wrongly they are harmful. The same is true also of the goods of the soul, which include moderation (*sōphrosynē*), justice (*dikaiosynē*), courage (*andreia*), docility (*eumathia*), memory (*mnēmē*), magnificence (*megaloprepia*), and every other such thing. Of these goods—at least those which are not the same as knowledge—we may say that they are sometimes profitable, sometimes harmful. Courage, for example, can be harmful if it is used without judgment: courage without judgment is nothing but a kind of boldness. In the same way, according to Socrates' argument, each of these "things" of the soul must be guided (*hēgoumenos*) by wise judgment (*phronēsis*) if it is to be profitable, or good for us.[37] Then excellence, if it is profitable or beneficial, and if it is one of the things of the soul, must be the same as wise judgment. Such is the argument. Excellence, Meno is compelled to admit, must be wise judgment: something very much like knowledge, if not knowledge itself.[38] Insofar as wise judgment points to knowledge, it may be knowledge of two particular sorts, knowledge of ends or knowledge of means. The latter would constitute a sort of skill or *technē*. As a preliminary assumption, we can say that if it is to guide the use of the parts of excellence which are in themselves neither good nor bad, it is likely that what is indicated is a knowledge of ends.

Excellence then points to knowledge. We recall that the first discussion of excellence simply, from which emerged the problem of parts and wholes, led us to see that excellence, insofar as it is accessible to any human being—man, woman, child, slave—points to justice and moderation. In that earlier discussion, Meno raised the possibility that excellence was the ability to rule over human beings, and Socrates objected that such a definition meant ignoring the fact that we often speak of the excellence of a slave or child. Now Socrates returns to that suggestion of Meno's by considering excellence as some sort of guiding principle, that which "leads" (hēgeisthai). Considered in this way, we see that excellence points to wise judgment, which is emphatically not possessed by everyone.

Excellence, as it appears to us in this second formulation, is the excellence of only some human beings, the truly excellent ones. And this understanding of excellence comprehends the earlier one, since the justice and moderation considered earlier are now seen to be guided, in the best case, by this higher "part" of excellence which is like knowledge. Of course we should not forget the fact that some human beings who are not particularly wise are nevertheless said to be excellent or virtuous people. We must note that Socrates is much less cautious than Aristotle about presenting this side of excellence, the side which may undermine (by exposing the limitations of) the virtue or excellence of the simple good citizen (see above, chap. 6, pp. 144–45).[39] The "lower" side of excellence, which was considered first, is now seen to be incomplete.

Socrates concludes his reasoning by claiming that if excellence is wise judgment, it must not come to man by nature: the good (agathoi) are not by nature good. Whatever the merits of this claim, Meno agrees without argument. Socrates: "But if the good do not become good by nature, must they not become good through learning?" To which Meno replies that there appears to be no other alternative, because if excellence is knowledge, it must be acquired by learning. Meno is quick to assume the identity of wise judgment (phronēsis) and knowledge (epistēmē), an assumption for which the way was prepared by Socrates' casual interchanging of the terms earlier. But at this point their potential distinction becomes important. Socrates has implicitly suggested that wise judgment may be only a kind of knowledge (87c5), that is, that knowledge proper may include more than wise judgment. Now he boldly suggests to Meno that it may not be true after all that virtue is knowledge. Meno is baffled by this turn in the conversation. "What, then?" he asks. "What is it that makes you discontented with this, so that you have doubts lest excellence not be knowledge?"

Socrates now explains his reasons, beginning the *logos* in which Anytus will play so ominous a role. Socrates doubts that excellence is knowledge, it turns out, because nowhere has he ever seen teachers of it. If it were indeed knowledge it would be teachable, and this he does not retract. But something which is teachable, it is fair to assume, would have teachers and students, and Socrates says that although he has searched many times for such teachers, he has not been able to find any. Socrates proceeds by naming famous Athenian statesmen (Themistocles, Aristides, Thucydides) whom all agree to have been excellent men in the highest sense, but whose sons became men of no better than average, and often considerably inferior, character.[40] The emphasis in the argument is on the fact that these excellent fathers did everything they could to make their sons into excellent men. They invariably succeeded, it seems, in imparting to them abilities such as wrestling and horseback riding (by hiring the best teachers), but invariably failed in imparting to them the excellence they themselves possessed. The former abilities depend, of course, on knowledge of a certain sort, but it is conspicuously not the knowledge of ends, which confirms the suspicion that it is this sort which constitutes excellence. For Meno, however, for whom all knowledge is knowledge of means or technical knowledge, this distinction has no meaning.

After Anytus vents his rage by threatening Socrates, and retires from active participation in the dialogue (though he remains to witness the conversation), Socrates turns again to Meno. They are now faced with a manifest contradiction in their inquiry. On the one hand, they have established that excellence appears to point to, or even to be identical with, a certain kind of knowledge. On the other hand, since nowhere are there to be found teachers of excellence, and they have agreed that knowledge is teachable and, further, that what is teachable must have both teachers and students, it appears that excellence cannot be knowledge. Socrates asks Meno specifically about the sophists (Meno having been trained by Gorgias), and whether they may after all be the teachers of excellence. Socrates appears to believe that the sophists come closest, perhaps because they are the only teachers who ever actually claim to teach excellence. But Meno is perplexed: "I wonder very much about Gorgias, Socrates, that he is never heard to promise anything of the kind, but instead he only laughs, whenever he hears someone making such promises" (95c1–4). Even the sophists, the most famous teachers and those in a position to make the greatest claims, do not agree among themselves on this issue. Gorgias, who is one of the most renowned, makes a point of claiming to teach the means—most notably the art of rhetoric—not the ends of political action, and laughs at those whose claims are bolder. And the sophists who do claim to teach excellence, when asked to given an account of excellence, cannot do so.[41] Socrates maintains, with Meno's agreement, that men who are in such confusion about their own subject matter cannot properly be called teachers of excellence. This would include sophists and the simply excellent men, who also contradict themselves on this matter. The inescapable conclusion is that excellence is not teachable.

Knowledge and Opinion Reconsidered

Meno now finds himself in a quandary. He wonders, he says, whether there ever are good men at all, and how they could come to be good men. Meno is perhaps as close as he can ever come to genuine openness to dialectical resolution. Socrates, at least, must think something of the kind, because at this point he begins what will be the final and partially resolving treatment of the contradiction they have unearthed. Socrates reproaches himself and Meno for being worthless or uneducated (*phauloi*) because it now appears they have overlooked a crucial point in the *logos* on excellence. Socrates explains to Meno what it is they have missed: in the consideration of what it is which must guide (*hēgeisthai*) the use of the things which in themselves are either profitable or

Plato's *Meno*

harmful, they determined that this thing must be wise judgment (*phronēsis*). (The reason for his earlier use of this ambiguous term—ambiguous in that it falls between "knowledge" on the one hand and "opinions" on the other—now at last becomes apparent.) It now appears that right action can also be guided by something besides this wise judgment or knowledge. (Socrates shifts now to using "knowledge" [*epistēmē*] to make the opposition clearer.) That something is true opinion or right opinion (*orthē doxa*). If a man is to guide someone on the road to Larisa, as Socrates says, he will be just as good a guide if he "does not know" but has a true opinion of the way as he would be if, having been over the road before, he "knows" the way. The distinction between opinions (*doxa*) and knowledge (*epistēmē*), alluded to in the recollection thesis, now emerges in its full importance.[42]

Knowledge differs from true opinions, we may recall from Socrates' demonstration with the slave boy, in that it is fixed or anchored as a result of a process in which opinions are "many times" and "in different ways" examined.[43] Meno, however, apparently does not recall or else never understood this difference. Impressed by Socrates' example of the guide to Larisa, he now cannot see any difference at *all* between knowledge and true opinion, or why anyone should prefer the former to the latter. Socrates has recourse here to another simile. Right or true opinions, he says, are like the statues of Daedalus: these works are very valuable if they are fastened by chains, but unchained they have a tendency to run away and so in the unchained state they are not very valuable at all. In like manner, Socrates explains, true opinions can be "beautiful and useful" and "make for all that is good" while we have them, but they have a tendency to turn away out of the souls of human beings, and so are not very valuable unless they are "bound." This "binding" of true opinions is done by means of grounding with reasons, that is, by giving an account of them in reason. "And this, my friend Meno, is 'recollection,' as was agreed by us in what was said earlier."

Excellence, the means of acquisition of which Socrates and Meno have been seeking to discover, can now be understood to be grounded on true opinions, at least in the case of the excellent Athenians who were mentioned in Socrates' dialogue with Anytus.

Their excellence was indeed wise judgment, perhaps, but Socrates and Meno have been wrong in assuming too quickly that wise judgment (*phronēsis*) is identical with knowledge (*epistēmē*), whereas in fact it can also be based on true opinions. Thus excellence may be considered to come to men neither by teaching—since it is not knowledge—nor by nature, but by a sort of "divine dispensation": the right opinion of the statesman is similar to the pronouncements of soothsayers, in that both say many true things, but do not know what they say. The excellence of Themistocles and the other statesmen he has named could not be taught to their sons because it was not grounded on knowledge. It could not give an account of itself, but rather was based on right opinion. Men like Pericles, Aristides, and Themistocles have great excellence and "know it," we may say, but in another sense they do not know it. If they came to know it in the latter sense, their excellence itself might be transformed by the very process of "knowing." Socrates suggests that if someone capable of making a statesman of another man were to appear, he would be among the living what Homer says of Teiresias among the dead: "He alone is in his senses, and the others are flitting phantoms." We are reminded of the cave metaphor in the *Republic*, where the philosopher alone of the cave's inhabitants knows that what he sees are merely appearances, reflections of the truth of things (*Republic*, 514a2–518b5). But Socrates does not pursue this with Meno. Rather, he admonishes Meno that "we shall know the clear truth [*to saphes*] about this [presumably all that has been said] only when, before searching out the way excellence comes to human beings, we shall have attempted to discover what excellence itself is." And then he adds, as he takes his leave, that Meno should try to persuade Anytus of all that he, Meno, has been persuaded of; for this would be a service to the Athenians. Perhaps such a task could be a test for Meno, a measure of the degree to which his soul has been touched in his encounter with Socrates.

The conversation we witness in the *Meno*, and in particular the discussions related to geometry and definitions, suggest that Plato understood the nature of scientific definitions, that is, the sort of definitions on which Hobbes based his science of politics. But Plato believed there was a serious problem in such definitions, or that they are open to a decisive objection, which is that they distort the phenomena we seek to know about, because reality, and especially political reality, is not like geometry. Socrates understands scientific definitions better than Meno, who proposes them, because Socrates is aware of the objections to which such definitions are vulnerable. Socrates suggests to Meno another sort of method, one which proceeds by linking or connecting the thing being investigated to something else which is also partially known. The definition of *schēma*, as that which always accompanies color, is emphatically ungeometric, and yet reveals to us something about *schēma* which geometry can never reveal no matter how clearly *schēma* is defined, since geometry as a science has nothing to say about color. This example provided a pattern for the later attempt to link excellence with knowledge, to see the similarity of two things whose precise shape or *eidos* is itself not fully known. Plato indicates to us later that Socrates' method, to the extent to which it may be called scientific, is more like the sort of argument "by hypothesis" for which he draws a parallel from geometry later in the dialogue. The argument "by hypothesis" suggests something further about this Socratic method, namely, that it will always proceed on the basis of a fundamental hypothesis, which is a supposition in need of continual reexamination.

As to human excellence, the nature of which is explored in the *Meno* at the end, we are not wholly ignorant about it: we may say that the dialogue has partly uncovered the outlines of human excellence, its *eidos*, or shape. Excellence, or *aretē*, appears, in light of the *Meno*, to be a thing with two fundamentally different and partially contradictory sides. On the one hand, its grammar seems to be similar to the grammar of a thing like health: we say of it that it is something accessible to anyone regardless of size or wealth or sex or intelligence. In this sense, or from this side, *aretē* is deeply connected with justice. It is the excellence of the "good man," the "good citizen"; grammar suggests that this pole of *aretē* is very close to what we call "virtue," which is indeed the most common translation of the Greek *aretē*. On the other hand, however, is the excellence of the leader, or best human being. This is the second pole of the concept of *aretē*. Its grammar, as Plato tries to show, connects it again and again to knowledge, or at least to wise judgment. It is the excellence not of the citizen but of the statesman, the excellence restricted to the few (see above, pp. 182–83). This side of excellence, in fact, threatens to break away from justice completely, in the direction of tyranny or sophistry, or ultimately philosophy. (The excellence of the philosopher, in turn, somehow combines wisdom and justice on an entirely new basis, a basis connected with the erotic, but noncompetitive, social character of the philosophic life rather than with the noble ambition of the life of a statesman.) The two poles of *aretē* are not simply different; they cannot be separated. Each informs the other, and together they constitute the thing we call human excellence; that the grammar of this concept points in two partially contradictory directions is a result not of our failure to analyze it far enough, but of the nature of human language and human life simply.

In asking "what is" something, Plato, like Wittgenstein, understands that we begin from the phenomena as they come to sight for us in speech. He does not assume that the answer lies behind the scenes, where Hobbes's science seeks it. Plato examines the things by examining what we say about them, since that is where he believes they are to be found. On Plato's understanding, we are looking for things which we somehow already know, and we wish to "recollect" them. We begin from our opinions, in common speech, and seek the grounds for them, that is, seek to anchor them by giving an account of them, or of why we say what we say about the things. Exploring the grammar of a thing, for Wittgenstein, is similar to what Plato means by giving an account of a thing: both are undertaken in order to reveal the place of something in the whole, or to see "what kind of a thing anything is."

The result of this method, the method presented by Plato in the *Meno*, may be knowledge, at least knowledge of a kind (*tis epistēmē*) about the political things. It is knowledge which is tentative, always having to return and begin anew from the beginning, always checking its foundations by continually doubting them. It is, as Hobbes claimed, uncertain. Perhaps Hobbes was right to hope for more than that. But we must wonder whether more is possible.

Plato's *Meno*

8 Wittgenstein and Political Philosophy

We began from the observation that thinkers in ages prior to our own believed it was possible to have a political science of human goals or ends.[1] We sought to discover what they must have meant by "science" in order to believe what they believed. Our inquiry led directly to Hobbes, whom we discovered to have been fully self-conscious in his treatment of the question of the status of science, and who in fact believed himself to be the first to have paid the necessary attention to this question. Hobbes's understanding of science was found to rest on a particular view of language. We explored that view, partly by means of Locke's *Essay concerning Human Understanding*.

The doubts raised about Hobbes's approach, however, are not sufficient to discredit him, which is to say that they are only *doubts*. While they are not decisive, they do recommend the policy of reconsidering the method Hobbes attempted to discredit. We repeatedly uncovered similarities between the approach of Hobbes's predecessors and what we had earlier seen to be Wittgenstein's approach.

But are these similarities more than superficial? Are we justified in seeing some agreement between the classical approach to political phenomena and what Wittgenstein's teaching indicates about the way to understand our concepts? Have we not lumped together in "the classical approach" positions which themselves differ profoundly? It is necessary for us to devote some attention to these serious objections.

Philosophical Alliances Reconsidered: Plato and Aristotle

The suggestion of an alliance between such uneasy bedfellows as Plato and Aristotle, to say nothing of these two and Wittgenstein, deserves careful scrutiny. On no issue is there such wide agreement as on the fact that Aristotelian principles differ fundamentally from Platonic principles. With this general opinion we agree. But at the same time, we need to be alert to the possibility of areas of agreement between these two great thinkers; Aristotle was a student of Plato, after all.[2] However much Marx and Hegel disagree, for example, to ignore their similarities would be not only foolish but disastrous for an understanding of Marx. With regard to Plato and Aristotle, we believe an excellent case may be made that their differences are minor on the issue of starting points and on the issue of the role of philosophy generally.

Friedrich Solmsen may be taken as typical of those who see a profound difference between Plato and Aristotle on the issue of starting points. He maintains that, whereas the Platonic dialectician has "resolutely turned his back on opinion" (*doxa*), Aristotle "proceeds on the assumption that dialectic deals with arguments and propositions taken from the realm of 'opinion.'" Thus Aristotle's "disagreement with Plato, even if never allowed to come into the open, would seem to be radical."[3] What is not clear, however, is (1) that Aristotle has reduced the importance of dialectic, as Solmsen claims,[4] and (2) that Plato turns his back on *doxa*. It is difficult to see where Plato begins in dialogues, if not from the opinions of interlocutors, such as Theaetetus, Meno, or Cephalus.

A more persuasive account is offered by John H. Randall, Jr., in which Aristotle is seen as proposing that we use dialectic both to

Wittgenstein and Political Philosophy

arrive at starting points (*archai*) and to examine their correctness. Aristotle's position, according to Randall, is "an exact, analytical statement of the point of the metaphor that Plato uses, that knowledge is like remembering something, like recognizing what we have known all along. We find universals in experience."[5] In all fairness, it must be said that Solmsen also recognizes a certain similarity:

> Quite like Plato's, Aristotle's dialectic is primarily concerned with definitions, i.e. the *ti estin*, and like Plato's it reflects a genuine *dialegesthai*, a succession of questions and answers. . . . it is still as true as it was of the Platonic dialogues that a definition (or dialectical proposition) once it is put forward depends for its survival on the assent of others.[6]

The examples we possess of inquiry in Plato's dialogues do seem to begin from common speech, even if such inquiring is not content to leave the matter there. It seems fair to say that, however deeply divided Aristotle and Plato were on the issues of where inquiry ends, in the manner of how inquiry begins and proceeds there is some agreement between them.

Nevertheless, we may point to certain differences of tone which have a bearing on our concerns here. We might characterize Aristotle as more satisfied than Plato with the natural appearance of phenomena. Aristotle is more concerned to reveal each phenomenon in its detail, to supply the fullest possible articulation of its nature as we ordinarily understand it. He is more inclined to leave complexity where complexity appears, and less inclined to pursue apparent contradictions. Plato, by contrast, is more interested in knowing the place of something in the whole, and thus is more concerned with its connections to other concepts, or with what we have called its grammar. Aristotle is more concerned with language, common speech, or what we ordinarily say. As we saw in his treatment of reason in the *Ethics*, Aristotle's inclination to leave things on their own ground may have been the exercise of a philosophic prudence of his own: he allows the simply good man to stand on his own ground without reasons.

At this point it is worth noting a certain parallel difference between the positions of Hobbes and Locke. Hobbes's qualified

Wittgenstein and Political
Philosophy

admiration for Plato may be said to reflect his sharing of Plato's impatience with the ordinary articulation of phenomena. Locke is more complacent than Hobbes, more concerned to explain why what exists is legitimate and comprehensible than to find the underlying principle of political phenomena which would permit us to reorder them in some more useful way.

We are justified in finding Aristotle and Plato in agreement on one other issue of moment to this study. The certainty which is characteristic of Hobbes's method is regarded by both classical thinkers as unnecessary, not to say impossible, in political science inquiry. This may be seen from the fact that Aristotle clearly limits his audience, in the *Nicomachean Ethics*, to those who will at least not question whether virtue exists. Some agreement, at least on starting points, was thought to be necessary in order even to participate in the investigation. And Plato, as we saw in the *Meno*, distinguishes two sorts of inquiry: the dialectic, which occurs among friends and proceeds from some shared basis, and the eristic or antagonistic inquiry, where compelling proof is required in order for the participants to conclude anything. Now Hobbes, as we saw, considers this eristic and skeptical attitude endemic to any political philosophy because in that field "there is nothing not disputable, because it compareth men, and meddleth with their right and profit; in which as oft as reason is against a man, so oft will a man be against reason. And from hence it cometh, that they that have written of justice and policy in general, do all invade each other, and themselves, with contradiction" (*Elements*, Epistle Dedicatory, p. xv). The difference between the understandings of Hobbes on the one hand, and Plato and Aristotle on the other, is related to the respective understandings of the place political philosophy occupies in human life, a point we will take up below. It suffices for the moment to recall that for Hobbes such philosophy is justified only by its *usefulness*, whereas the classics, by contrast, understand that men may pursue the inquiry for its own sake.

Beyond these points we do not intend to claim a strong resemblance between the accounts offered by Plato and Aristotle. But even if some agreement between them is accepted as genuine, are we further justified in finding agreement between their approaches and the approach indicated by Wittgenstein's investigations in our

Wittgenstein and Political Philosophy

own century? Before turning to the most troublesome objection to this similarity—the fact that Wittgenstein himself never engaged in political philosophy—we need to consider a number of more detailed points of difference.

Plato and Wittgenstein

We direct our attention here to comparing Plato and Wittgenstein. We may do this because the general differences between Plato and Aristotle put Plato, for the most part, at a greater remove from Wittgenstein. Aristotle is more concerned than Plato to leave things as they are, to look and see without revising, and above all to look at what we say (see chap. 6). He is less eager to push for justification, to expose foundations which may not be fully rational, as we saw in the case of the morality of the simple good man. One could say that Aristotle's "spade reaches bedrock," to use Wittgenstein's phrase, a bit sooner than does Plato's. Hence the genuine differences regarding language and method which divide the classics from Wittgenstein are more sharply drawn by comparing Plato and Wittgenstein.

The testimony of Wittgenstein himself is the best place to begin. We do not know how seriously, or to what extent, Wittgenstein studied Plato. He makes critical references to the *Theaetetus* (see *PI*, 1, 46, 518). In that dialogue, according to Wittgenstein's reading, "when Socrates asks the question, 'what is knowledge?' he does not even regard it as a *preliminary* answer to enumerate cases of knowledge" (*BB*, p. 20; the reference is to *Theaetetus*, 1460–67c). Wittgenstein finds himself in disagreement with this position. We may inquire, however, whether it is wise to attribute to Plato the doctrine he puts in the mouth of Socrates. As for the passage to which Wittgenstein refers in the *Theaetetus*, we would be inclined to take as a preliminary answer the enumeration of cases of knowledge, just as in the *Meno* we saw such an enumeration as the statement of the perplexity from which the search for knowledge begins. Wittgenstein's disagreement with Plato in the passages to which he refers might better be described as a disagreement with positions temporarily presented by Plato's Socrates. (In *PI*, 1, 46, the passage Wittgenstein quotes even begins with Socrates' saying,

"If I make no mistake, *I have heard some people* say this . . .";
emphasis added.)[7] Here, then, Wittgenstein, in thinking he disagrees with Plato, may only be disagreeing with Socrates, or with
this particular speech of Socrates.

Nevertheless, there *are* disagreements in both method and substance between Plato and Wittgenstein. The most important as
regards language is that Wittgenstein is more tolerant of ordinary
usage than Plato. The latter may fairly be accused of a certain
impatience with the common opinions about meanings which he
usually elicits from interlocutors at the beginning of a dialogue.
Plato has his Socrates *distort* what others put forward, as he does
with Polemarchus' attempt to say what justice is in book 1 of the
Republic. Although Polemarchus' formulation is inadequate, he
clearly intends to say more than what Socrates recognizes in his
statement. Socrates argues in one direction, and succeeds in
reducing the complexity of Polemarchus' understanding to the
notion that justice is some sort of expertise, divorced from any
consideration of good intentions which Polemarchus had also
meant. Confronted with Socrates' distortion, Polemarchus is baffled. But Plato may be attempting, by means of such exchanges,
only to reveal that words, as we commonly use them, have
contradictory implications. Wittgenstein too points this out. The
difference hinges on the question of whether Plato is indicating a
need to *remedy* the defectiveness of ordinary speech. Wittgenstein
clearly does not accept this: language is " 'in order as it is.' That is
to say, we are not *striving after* an ideal, as if our ordinary vague
sentences had not yet got a quite unexceptionable sense, and a
perfect language awaited construction by us" (*PI*, 1, 98). Once we
discover that "justice" or "courage" are used in somewhat contradictory ways, what more can we do, on Wittgenstein's view?
Wittgenstein might be outraged at the way Socrates "reduces"
excellence to knowledge, or "the noble" to "the good," as we saw in
the *Meno*. But is this reduction meant to indicate that language
reform is needed, or is it an attempt by Plato to reveal certain
connections in the meanings of our words—in their grammar—
which we do not ordinarily see, but which, when exaggerated, lead
us into paradoxes? These questions we cannot hope to settle here,
and we must leave them as questions.[8]

Wittgenstein and Political
                                    Philosophy

Wittgenstein is interested in words or language more than is Plato. This goes naturally with his preoccupation with epistemological questions, which were for the classical thinkers an important but not the primary focus. In modern philosophy generally, as we saw in considering Hobbes, concern with the means of securing knowledge emerges as the central task of philosophy. As a result, concern with language has never been far from the surface of modern thought. Plato, by contrast, makes language his explicit theme only in the *Cratylus*, and there he seems to conclude that, despite its importance, language is not the key which unlocks the world to us. At the risk of distorting Plato by quoting only his Socrates, we note the latter's words near the close of the dialogue: "How real existence is to be studied or discovered is, I suspect, beyond you and me. But we may admit so much, that the knowledge of things is not to be derived from names. No, they must be studied and investigated in themselves" (*Cratylus*, 439b3–7). Although there is a genuine difference between Plato and Wittgenstein here, it may be a difference mostly in emphasis. Wittgenstein is, as we have tried to show, *not* just interested in language, or in words. He is concerned to discover what knowledge is, and he believes that the path to an understanding lies through language. But language is not just words, according to Wittgenstein. It comprises also the circumstances of their use, the world in which the words appear, as it were.

Plato searched for the ideas or forms of things, which are more than the meanings of words (although in one sense the dialogues are searches for definitions). Our words grasp reality inadequately, according to Plato. Wittgenstein, by contrast, tries to show that there is not something which stands behind the words. He therefore urges us to seek understanding not by looking behind language, but at the language games themselves in which words are used. But these two approaches are closer in spirit than they at first appear: despite the claim that the meanings of words do not supply a complete account of things, Plato nevertheless believes that speech is both the starting point and medium of inquiry; and despite his careful attention to language, Wittgenstein clearly intends his inquiry to be about things and not just about words.

The most persistent difference to be found would seem to be

what we have already noted, namely, Plato's skepticism. Plato, or at least Plato's Socrates, really is not satisfied with the contradictory implications he often uncovers in our concepts. He continues to doubt that we understand things fully, and continues to look for the account of the whole in which contradictions are resolved. In this respect Plato may be said to be closer to the skeptical spirit of Hobbes. Hobbes was impatient with ambiguity and contradiction, and sought to penetrate back to the origins of concepts in order to uncover their clear meanings. Wittgenstein seems more patient. He is prepared to tolerate ambiguity and confusion and to explore them, and even seems to teach that they are a necessary part of a living natural language. But this may not be the case. Nietzsche, in fact, maintained that such contradictory and ambiguous meanings are characteristic of the language of any culture with a long and complicated history. "Only that which has no history can be defined," as he says; concepts in history become so overlaid with layer upon layer of new meanings that they necessarily lose their clarity. At an earlier cultural stage, Nietzsche maintains, the complicated combination of meanings "must have been more easily soluble, its components more easily disassociated."[9] Plato, like Hobbes, might be said to have sought to return to a kind of natural clarity of meaning. For Nietzsche, the clarity is a matter of history, and not natural. Wittgenstein, however, forces us to wonder whether a culture where meanings were simple and clear would not have to be *very* different from ours, more like a culture of robots than a culture of human beings.

Despite these differences between Wittgenstein's and Plato's approaches,[10] their methods of inquiry are similar in two other respects, respects which in turn lead us to the real core of their differences. The first of these is the fact that both approach philosophical questions in a dialectical spirit. We mean this in the deeper sense of dialectic noted by Socrates in the *Meno*. For both Plato and Wittgenstein, philosophic inquiry is dialectical because it goes on between friends seeking truth. As such it has the tentative character, the lack of compulsion so characteristic of Wittgenstein's later philosophy, which in fact is often pursued by means of imaginary dialogues or conversations. As we saw in the *Meno*, such an approach may lead one to "see" the truth, but it does not

Wittgenstein and Political
Philosophy

compel it. We need to ask, however, whether the reasons for engaging in this dialectic were the same for Wittgenstein as for his ancient predecessors.

The second similarity involves Plato's metaphor of the cave. At least as a young man, Wittgenstein apparently accepted a principle similar to this famous Platonic teaching. He wrote to one of his friends that human existence "is like a dream. But in better hours we wake up just enough to realize that we are dreaming. Most of the time, though, we are fast asleep."[11] Philosophy seeks to penetrate a sort of fog in which most of our lives are lived, to see clearly what is only seen as in a dream most of the time. But we may wonder about this. For Plato, it is true, life is lived by most men within a horizon which prevents a true understanding of the nature of the world or themselves. That horizon is constituted by the opinions, assumptions, dogmas, which limit men's vision. Put another way, common speech gives us only an inadequate or partial grasp of reality. The task of philosophy is the escape from this linguistic cave. Wittgenstein, in contrast, seems to teach that the linguistic cave, if indeed it is a cave, must be accepted as our permanent home. The task of philosophy might be said to be to try to understand as clearly as we can what is in the cave: normally it is a cave in which we only *dream*, but in our "better hours" we wake up enough to see our situation.

We have now to consider what has so far been ignored, and what is the most obvious and most far-reaching objection to comparing these thinkers on the ground on which we have sought to compare them. Why did Wittgenstein never write a word of *political* philosophy? The answer to this question will lead us to the core of the difference between Wittgenstein and the classics, as well as reveal a fundamental similarity between Wittgenstein and the modern thinkers *against* whom we have considered him here.

Why Did Wittgenstein Write No Political Philosophy?

The discussion in chapter 6 of the place of political science or political philosophy in classical thought brought out the fact of its preeminence in philosophy simply. For both Plato and Aristotle political philosophy was necessarily in the position of preeminence because they recognized that political considerations were inextricably connected to the possibility of any philosophy whatsoever. Political philosophy is today subordinate to epistemology. We may thus translate the question of this section into the question, Why has epistemology replaced political philosophy as the queen of philosophy?

One might begin by observing that the reasons for this usurpation are themselves related to the argument of the preceding chapters. This may be seen from the following considerations: philosophy may be said to be public-spirited in varying degrees, from the essentially personal character of Wittgenstein's philosophical inquiry to the predominantly political concern of, for example, Machiavelli. The philosophy of classical thinkers was public-spirited out of necessity. Hobbes was entirely correct when he charged that the philosophy of the ancients was subversive. Purely rational inquiry was threatening to established political orders because, as Hobbes said, it taught men to question the ways of their political communities. For this reason, which the classics recognized as well as Hobbes, politics and political orders demand the attention of philosophy if philosophy is to survive. This raises the question of why philosophy should survive, if it is not useful. Or, to put it another way, why do men philosophize? In the answer to this question, Hobbes is at odds with his predecessors.

Hobbes's philosophy was public-spirited in a more primary sense. Its very *raison d'être* was utility. Philosophy must cease to be subversive, in Hobbes's view. To accomplish this, the character of politics must be altered so that political communities are not threatened by truth or rational inquiry. Politics can be made rational, as Hobbes tries to show, if we teach men to obey laws for genuine reasons (fear and self-interest) rather than out of custom, habit, belief, or superstition. That this requires a different tone in politics, i.e., less emphasis on virtue and more attention to security and "commodious living," does not bother Hobbes. The important thing is the disappearance of the subversive influence of various opposed conceptions of the virtue at which the community should aim. Since men will then have faced the truth about the reason for their living together, rational inquiry into the possible competing goals can no longer be threatening. Hence at the same moment philosophy ceases to need to worry about politics and politics about philosophic inquiry.

One might say that the transformation Hobbes sought to make would eliminate the need for philosophy to be public-spirited. And Hobbes was successful to the extent that the major problem of philosophy after Hobbes gradually became, in the succeeding two centuries, not politics, but epistemology.[12] The point of these remarks is to show why we should not be surprised, at least, that Wittgenstein wrote no political philosophy. This is a fact which is in no way striking unless one seeks, as we have here, to consider him in light of the philosophic tradition. It is partly because of Hobbes's success that philosophy is not public-spirited in the twentieth century. Wittgenstein is not unique in this respect. In one sense, Plato's thought too was not public-spirited. Plato—and this is true of classical thinkers generally—did not expect much from politics. The philosopher, according to Plato, sees "the madness of the many, and that no one who minds the business of the cities does anything healthy." And "taking all this into the calculation, he keeps quiet and minds his own business—as a man in a storm, when dust and rain are blown about by the wind, stands aside under a little wall" (*Republic*, 596c7–d8). But it is significant that this utterance of Socrates occurs in a dialogue entirely about politics, conducted with young men who are interested in politics, and whom Socrates takes very seriously. Plato took politics seriously because, as the fate of Socrates testifies, philosophy was dangerous. Since, by our time, the danger has disappeared, the private side of philosophy has emerged as most important.

This raises for us the question we passed over above: Why, if philosophy is not useful, do men philosophize? What role does philosophy play in human life, according to the thinkers we have considered here? In answering this question we come nearer to understanding the most profound difference dividing Wittgenstein from the classical thinkers, and we can uncover at least one respect in which Wittgenstein is nearer to Hobbes. For both Plato and Aristotle the philosophic life was understood to be the best type of life for a human being.[13] The pursuit of philosophy is an end in itself, rewarding not for its utility, but simply as an activity. As a consequence of this, certainty was not required in philosophic conclusions. Since philosophy seeks to know the truth about everything that exists, it inquires into the nature of politics and the political phenomena (justice, law, tyranny, etc.) as one subject among others. And for reasons we have just outlined, the subject of politics was of particular moment to philosophers anyway.

We have seen how for Hobbes, by contrast, the core of the philosophic enterprise is its utility. Curiosity or "desire, to know why, and how," according to Hobbes, is entirely natural to human beings and in fact is peculiar to them. He even seems at one point in *Leviathan* to say that the inquiring mind is rewarded by its own activity (chap. 6, p. 124). But, as it turns out, it is really "anxiety for the future time" which "disposeth men to enquire into the causes of things: because the knowledge of them, maketh men the better able to order the present to their best advantage" (chap. 11, p. 167). Since philosophy is pursued not for the sheer enjoyment of inquiry but for its utility, certainty and clarity are correspondingly more important. Whereas the public-spiritedness of classical philosophy arose from the necessity for survival of philosophy itself, Hobbes's philosophy is political or public-spirited in its very core, because it starts out to seek *peace*. That is its utility.

For Wittgenstein, three centuries later, the philosophic enterprise is pursued for reasons akin to both Hobbes's and the classics', yet different from either. In one place Wittgenstein describes philosophy as the cure for intellectual diseases, for the tormenting puzzles of the mind (*PI*, 1, 255). Although this is by no means the view of philosophy consistently presented by Wittgenstein, it indicates what is for us the most important point, namely, that philosophizing is not pursued so much as an end in itself as for its result. The result may be release from torment by conceptual problems, or it may be a kind of clarity. "Philosophy simply puts everything before us, and neither explains nor deduces anything.—Since everything lies open to view there is nothing to explain" (*PI*, 1, 126). Thus if philosophy is useful, for Wittgenstein, it is useful on a personal or individual level. For the philosophical enterprise of the classics, *certainty* was not required. Certainty of philosophical conclusions was necessary to Hobbes because it was meant to be compelling to other men, because its utility was above all political:

Wittgenstein and Political
Philosophy

it was to secure peace. Wittgenstein's philosophy is closer to Plato's and Aristotle's in respect of its uncertainty, and closer to Hobbes's in respect of its utility or usefulness.

That the problems for which Wittgenstein sought a solution in philosophy were never political problems is a fact which we are unable to explain completely, except by the reasons given above, and those reasons characterize Wittgenstein no more than most other philosophers of the last century. This may be connected to what was observed above in connection with the notion of a "linguistic cave" (p. 198). For Wittgenstein, there may not exist any natural horizon to which we can ascend by means of philosophy; there may be only a variety of "caves," and no standard for comparison. If this is the case, philosophic inqury can be concerned only with coming to understand better one's own linguistic cave; and thus political philosophy, which is the name for the enterprise of comparison, is no longer a possibility. On the other hand, perhaps it is sufficient explanation that Wittgenstein lived in a culture where philosophy does not need to pay attention to politics. But we may add the fact that for most of us, personal concerns overshadow the concerns of a political community. Because that community is so large, we rarely feel it as a community at all. Politics to most of us is a phenomenon we may ignore or not as we please. However, despite the fact that we do not offer this as a complete account of why Wittgenstein was not concerned with political philosophy, we hasten to add that his not writing political philosophy, while it may qualify the similarities between Wittgenstein and Plato or Aristotle, does not necessarily qualify the importance of what we learn about knowledge from Wittgenstein.

Conclusion

We must admit that we do not possess knowledge of the sort which Hobbes and later Locke sought, which they described as moral or political science. We have reason to think it is not possible to have this kind of knowledge. This is not news, to be sure, yet we may be permitted to hope that, by this examination of Hobbes's goal and method, we have clarified the problem of knowledge in political science. Our retracing of Hobbes's intellectual steps and our

Wittgenstein and Political
Philosophy

criticism of some of them does not mean we can return to the point from which Hobbes began. Despite our investigation of the older approach which was replaced by Hobbes's method, we quite naturally entertain certain doubts about the appropriateness of such an approach, in confronting a world so very different. Perhaps this is cause for pessimism, perhaps not. Can the historical account we have traced teach us something nonetheless?

We suggest that the understandings of knowledge and method we have surveyed can shed light on our own procedures and enrich our work as political scientists. We may be led, first of all, to moderate our habitual skepticism about knowledge not secured by scientific method. If Wittgenstein's investigations accomplished nothing else, they would be valuable simply for permitting us to question what has to many of us seemed unquestionable, namely, the idea that the only knowledge one should be willing to stand behind is scientific knowledge in the strict sense. We may doubt this, it now appears, without wholly turning away from reason to emotion or blind commitment. The moderation thus indicated suggests further that we reconsider our distinction between normative and empirical questions. The strict requirements of knowledge urged by Hobbes were intended to bring into being a true science of morality. When moral concepts did not turn out to be susceptible to investigation by his method, such concepts were eventually abandoned as an improper subject for study. We retained the strict notion of knowledge and merely restricted its focus. But we may recall Aristotle's principle that we demand of our knowledge only such exactness as is appropriate to the subject matter. We can and do know a good deal about virtues or goals, that is, about the "normative." Human goals or ends are not less empirical than laws or corrupt leaders, and we know something about the latter. Moderating our skepticism thus may permit us to include in political science many more of the considerations which are important to political actors—senators or voters alike—but which frequently have been excluded from the legitimate realm of political science.

Second, the inquiry above recommends that we seek to lessen our reliance on "models" which explain by *reducing* political phenomena to simpler elements. It may be neither necessary nor

Wittgenstein and Political
Philosophy

wise to try to "get beneath" the outward appearance or the surface of whatever we wish to understand. We may need to be more cautious about explanations which presume to construct, out of a tiny number of basic aims or drives, an account of complicated and reasoned political activity. This has often been attempted for the same reasons Hobbes himself gave when he designed the procedure, that is, because only such a method can provide the logical starting point from which compelling scientific reasoning can proceed. But we have been led to see, by Wittgenstein, that it is possible, even from a philosophical perspective, to take seriously the notion of circular inquiry. If circular inquiry is also capable of producing knowledge, the reduction to "simples" (with which, as Hobbes puts it, "passion not mistrusting," all men can agree) is not a requirement and may not be the best path to knowledge. We may do better by relating phenomena to one another in their concrete particularity than by trying to explain something by reduction to other, simpler phenomena. We may, for instance, attempt to explain political ambition by reducing it to a more fundamental human drive for power and thus see it as a complicated form of self-interest which all men share. But should we not be awake to the idea that political ambition may be different in *kind* from other human motivations? Perhaps, as some thinkers have claimed, the desire for honor must be understood on its own terms as a uniquely political motive, and as one which distinguishes men because it is rare.[14] Of course, there *are* men for whom political power gratifies only the crude sort of self-interest; but it is precisely these from whom we may wish to distinguish the truly political man, and we are precluded from doing so by an explanation which understands the more complicated or higher as reducible to the more basic or lower.

Third, we may find it wise to place less emphasis on the generality of our explanations. We need to moderate what Wittgenstein called our "contemptuous attitude towards the particular case" (*BB*, p. 18). We may seek to understand something—whether a presidential election, a Supreme Court decision, or the political constitution of Brazil—in all its concrete detail and not as a variation of more general phenomena such as voting behavior or modernization. We may indeed say, for example, that all societies

Wittgenstein and Political
Philosophy

have some sort of general process of "political socialization," and all such processes accomplish in a sense the same things, such as the inculcation of dominant values. We need to be more aware of the possibility that what is the same in all methods of political socialization may be less important and less interesting than what is different. The fact that every possible constitution is a "statement that prescribes how people, things, and events shall relate to each other within a given territorial jurisdiction"[15] may tell us less than the careful study of even one particular constitution.

Focusing on particularities and differences would also mean paying more attention to the perspective of the members of a political community themselves. We may, of course, ignore what men say about justice or what they believe it to be, and instead understand various conceptions of justice as variations of some general concept. We might understand justice in general to be any principle for the allocation of social goods: rights, punishments, material goods, or rewards. Every concept of justice, we could say, is simply a different example of this general allocative principle. A system of criminal justice allocates proper degrees of punishment to criminals, no punishment to all who should not be punished, and so on. But we need only recall Wittgenstein's parallel example of the claim that all tools serve to modify something. "Would anything be gained by this assimilation of expressions?" (PI, 1, 14). That is, do we really learn very much by seeing the general and abstract which ignores particular differences? We should be on our guard against explanations which do not really help us to understand but which make us *think* we have discovered the real essence of something.

The most serious philosophers since Hobbes have followed him[16] in the belief that the human mind is not fully at home in the world. Man's position in the cosmos is not secure, and this means that man not only needs to, but is free to, treat nature as something alien, to be mastered and controlled. That this view still dominates our thinking in subtle ways perhaps goes without saying. A recent book in political science, a sort of introductory essay, expresses it this way: in social science, "the process of model building is similar to playing an interesting game. Your opponent is reality. You are attempting to account for your opponent's behavior so that you will be able to act more intelligently. In some areas these games are played for high stakes."[17]

The rejection of the complacency with which both classical and medieval thinkers viewed man's relation to nature led the deepest thinkers to ask what sort of thing human knowledge is and to doubt its power to understand the things in the world, even with the assistance of method. Understanding was replaced by explanation and prediction as the core of knowing. They concluded, in conscious opposition to the classical view, that it is not the natural capacity for knowing which is the highest human faculty. These thinkers were aware of the alternatives and they were skeptical. The real issue, however, has drifted into a kind of haze, and we often forget that there ever was a different understanding.

We do not have sufficient grounds to reject the side taken in this controversy by Bacon, Descartes, and Hobbes. But we believe Wittgenstein's most important philosophical contribution, namely, his uncovering of the roots of modern epistemological problems, gives us cause to reconsider the entire controversy whose terms we have tried to bring to light in this study. By placing Wittgenstein in the context of the tradition of Western political philosophy in which this controversy raged, we can begin to recover what is otherwise for most of us an inaccessible alternative understanding, an understanding alien to the predominant view today. What permits this is, of course, only our willingness to step outside of that view to begin with, and this willingness in turn only comes from the sense that there is something wrong with our view. We may say that this study is for those who ask, with Husserl, where we have gone wrong. It is an attempt to show where we should look both for the source of our troubles and for an alternative understanding of the most fundamental questions.

Wittgenstein and Political
Philosophy

Notes

Chapter 1

1. Herbert Simon, *The Sciences of the Artificial* (Cambridge, Mass.: M.I.T. Press, 1969), p. 5.

2. For expressions of the two most important positions on this question, see R. H. Tawney, *Equality* (London: Unwin Books, 1964); Milton Friedman, *Capitalism and Freedom* (Chicago: University of Chicago Press, 1962).

3. That is, the questions citizens and political leaders face: What should our national goals be? Which among the policies we must choose is the most just? etc.

4. This is not to say that our knowledge should be exciting where politics is exciting, but that some of the actual and vital content of politics may be lost on, or transformed by, modern political science.

5. See Rudolph Carnap, *An Introduction to the Philosophy of Science* (New York: Basic Books, 1966), pp. 3–6, 12; Carl G. Hempel, *Aspects of Scientific Explanation* (New York: The Free Press, 1965), p. 333; and especially Israel Scheffler, "Theoretical Terms and a Modest Empiricism," in *Philosophy of Science*, ed. Arthur Danto and Sidney Morgenbesser (New York: Meridian Books, 1960), pp. 159–73.

6. Leszek Kolakowski, *Husserl and the Search for Certitude* (New Haven: Yale University Press, 1975), p. 24.

7. Pierre Duhem, *The Aim and Structure of Physical Theory*, trans. P. P. Wiener (Princeton: Princeton University Press, 1954), p. 169; cf. Ernst Mach, "The Economical Nature of Physical Inquiry," in *Philosophy of Science*, ed. J. J. Kockelmans (New York: The Free Press, 1968), pp. 174–87. One claim of Mach's is particularly appropriate here: "Physics is experience, arranged in economical order" (p. 178). See also Carnap, *Introduction*; Hempel, *Aspects*; Henri Poincaré, *The Value of Science*, trans. George Bruce Halsted (New York: Dover Publications, 1958).

8. Duhem, *Aim and Structure*, p. 172 (emphasis added).

9. Edmund Husserl, *The Crisis of European Sciences and Transcendental Phenomenology*, trans. David Carr (Evanston: Northwestern University Press, 1970), pp. 12–13.

10. Cf. Alexandre Kojève, *Introduction to the Reading of Hegel*, ed. Allan Bloom, trans. James H. Nichols, Jr. (New York: Basic Books, 1969), p. 102.

11. Hempel, for one, seems to be unaware of this implication. "So strong, indeed, is this urge [for man to know and to understand himself in his world] that in the absence of more reliable knowledge, myths are often invoked to fill the gap. But in time, many such myths give way to scientific conceptions of the what and the why of empirical phenomena" (*Aspects*, p. 333). The problem *is* brought out by Paul Feyerabend, *Against Method* (London: NLB Press, 1975).

12. Husserl, *Crisis*, pp. 6–7.

13. Ibid., pp. 68–69.

14. Ibid., p. 9.

15. Ibid., p. 281.

16. Ibid., p. 52.

17. Kolakowski, *Husserl*, pp. 28–29.

18. A currently fashionable and widely accepted moderate view holds that what was for a time regarded as exhaustive classification of all statements into factual and value is untenable; rather, it is said—though of course none would deny these two are different—that they are not exhaustive, but two of a broad spectrum of types of statements ranging from the strictly factual to purely emotive or preferential (as one's taste for artichokes). This range is related, one might say, to the degree of

intersubjective agreement which obtains on the issues involved. On this view, we can make whatever statements we want to, moral judgments, etc., so long as we recognize their status as nonfactual, as adjunct to what are *precisely* factual statements. Only the latter can be strictly said to be the statements of a science. This study will raise the possibility that this view, in even its moderate form, is mistaken.

19. For more detailed consideration of this theme, see chapter 6.

20. The claim that the method presented by Hobbes does not reflect the truth about scientific inquiry is also countered by some evidence from a modern authority, whose knowledge of science must be accorded respect. Albert Einstein wrote, "We can distinguish various kinds of theories in physics. Most of them are constructive. They attempt to build up a picture of the more complex phenomena out of the materials of a relatively simple formal scheme from which they start out. . . . Along with this most important class of theories there exists a second. . . . These employ the analytic, not the synthetic, method. The elements which form their basis and starting-point are not hypothetically constructed but empirically discovered ones, general characteristics of natural processes, principles that give rise to mathematically formulated criteria which the separate processes or the theoretical representations of them have to satisfy" (quoted in Abraham Kaplan, *The Conduct of Inquiry: Methodology for Behavioral Science* [Scranton, Pa.: Chandler Publishing Co., 1969], p. 299). See chapter 2 of this work.

21. A great deal of work is currently devoted to elucidating the connection between the Wittgensteinian (language philosophy) and Husserlian (phenomenological) approaches. See, for example, Harold A. Durfee, ed., *Analytic Philosophy and Phenomenology* (The Hague: Martinus Nijhoff, 1976).

22. But for a slightly different account, see Richard S. Peters and Henri Tajfel, "Hobbes and Hull: Metaphysicians of Behaviour," in *Hobbes and Rousseau*, ed. Maurice Cranston and Richard S. Peters (Garden City, N.Y.: Doubleday & Co., 1972), pp. 126–35.

Chapter 2

1. According to Ferdinand Tönnies there was a shift in the focus of philosophy in Hobbes's time, and this influenced Hobbes to take a mechanistic approach: "Im 17. Jahrhundert hiess Philosophie in erster Linie Naturwissenschaft, demnächst Wissenschaft schlechthin . . ."

(Ferdinand Tönnies, *Thomas Hobbes: Der Mann und der Denker* [Leipzig: A. W. Zickfeldt, 1912], p. 80). Although Tönnies is undoubtedly correct to some degree, his view fails to take account of Hobbes's own claims that what had changed in philosophy was neither its goal nor its subject, but its method, a method which for the first time promised to secure knowledge in a broad range of fields which had traditionally concerned philosophers. Cf. *De Corpore*, Epistle Dedicatory.

2. Thus science or philosophy is "the Knowledge acquired by Reasoning" either from the "Manner of the Generation of any thing to the Properties; or from the Properties, to some possible Way of Generation of the same; *to the end to bee able to produce as far as matter, and humane force permit, such Effects, as humane life requireth*" (*Leviathan*, chap. 46, p. 682; emphasis added). Cf. *De Cive*, Epistle Dedicatory, where Hobbes praises geometry for producing "whatsoever things they are in which this present age doth differ from the rude simpleness of antiquity," and then goes on to say that if "moral philosophers had as happily discharged their duty, I know not what could have been added by human industry to the completion of that happiness, which is consistent with human life."

3. Since prudence consists in much knowledge of antecedents and consequents, that is, in "taking signs from experience" or "conjecture," it is natural for Hobbes to say that "they shall conjecture best, that have most experience; because they have most signs to conjecture by; which is the reason that old men are more prudent, that is, conjecture better, *caeteris paribus*, than young" (*Elements*, 1.4.10).

4. In addition to the works discussed below, see *De Homine*, chap. 10.

5. On speech as the distinguishing feature of human beings, see Raymond Polin, *Politique et philosophie chez Thomas Hobbes* (Paris: Presses universitaires de France, 1953), pp. 5, 7, 12–13, 99. Polin argues that because speech is a human invention, we may understand Hobbes to mean that man makes himself (thus Hobbes prefigures the similar claim made by Rousseau) (pp. 24–25).

6. For a similar account of the role of propositions in scientific knowledge, the truth of which follows from the fact that the propositions are constructed from clear and well-defined names, see Tönnies, *Hobbes*, pp. 91–94; cf. Sir Leslie Stephen, *Hobbes* (Ann Arbor: University of Michigan Press, 1961), p. 95. For a critical account see J. W. N. Watkins, *Hobbes's System of Ideas: A Study in the Political Significance of Philosophical Theories* (New York: Barnes & Noble, 1965), pp. 144–47.

7. "By our several organs we have several conceptions of several qualities in the objects," Hobbes says. On the other hand, "because the image in vision consisting in colour and shape is the knowledge we have of the qualities of the object of that sense; it is no hard matter for a man to fall into this opinion, that the same colour and shape are the very qualities themselves; and for the same cause, that sound and noise are the qualities of the bell, or of the air." This would be foolish, according to Hobbes, who goes on:

> I shall therefore endeavor to make plain these four points:
> (1) That the subject wherein colour and image are inherent, is not the object or thing seen.
> (2) That that is nothing without us really which we call an image or colour.
> (3) That the said image or colour is but an apparition unto us of that motion, agitation, or alteration, which the object worketh in the brain or spirits, or some internal substance of the head.
> (4) That as in conception by vision, so also in the conceptions that arise from other senses, the subject of their inherence is not the object, but the sentient [*Elements*, 1.2.4].

See also *Leviathan*, chap. 1; cf. the account in Watkins, *Hobbes's System*, pp. 140–42.

8. Thus we might note that it also points to the dependence of even scientific knowledge on knowledge from experience, or prudence. Cf. Tönnies, *Hobbes*, pp. 92–93. This contradicts the account offered by Sheldon Wolin in *Politics and Vision* (Boston: Little, Brown & Co., 1960), pp. 249–51.

9. Cf. Tönnies, *Hobbes*, pp. 97–98: "Hobbes geht, ebenso wie Descartes, von der Tatsache aus, dass für jeden Denkenden nur seine Empfindungen, d. h. nur subjektive oder psychologische Phänomene gegeben sind; diese sind die benannten Dinge oder genauer die Dinge, denen Namen zu geben möglich ist. Wenn nun diese eingeteilt werden, so vergisst Hobbes zu erwähnen, dass schon der gemeine Menschenverstand, ja in einem gewissen Masse der noch gemeinere tierische Intellekt, vor jedem Philosophen eine solche Einteilung vollzogen hat, indem er alles sinnlich Wahrgenommene als die eigentliche oder äussere Wirklichkeit von sich getrennt empfindet und weiss; und diese Trennung kann der Philosoph nicht umhin zu wiederholen; auch in der ferneren Unterscheidung des äusseren Dinges von seinen Eigenschaften geht ihm die Sprache voraus."

10. Cf. M. M. Goldsmith, *Hobbes's Science of Politics* (New York: Columbia University Press, 1966), pp. 8–9.

11. Cf. Goldsmith, *Hobbes's Science*, p. 7; Stephen, *Hobbes*, pp. 89–90.

12. For a slightly different account of definitions, see Watkins, *Hobbes's System*, pp. 138–43. Watkins argues that Hobbes is inconsistent. Cf. also Stephen, *Hobbes*, pp. 91–92.

13. For an account which claims this to be Hobbes's meaning, see Stephen, *Hobbes*, p. 94.

14. It is necessary to clarify one point, about which a great deal of confusion has arisen. What was important about geometry for Hobbes was its method, a method used in, and essential to, any true science, but most clearly exemplified in the case of geometry. It is for this reason that he appeals to geometry, not as the only model, but as the purest. The story is of course more complicated, as will become apparent below.

15. In *De Corpore*, where Hobbes writes most extensively on philosophical method, he seems to be aware of a too-facile identification of these two sorts of definitions. Cf. Watkins, *Hobbes's System*, pp. 144–50; Goldsmith, *Hobbes's Science*, pp. 12–14.

16. Cf. the slightly different account in J. Weinberger, "Hobbes's Doctrine of Method," *American Political Science Review*, 59 (1975): 1336–53. Cf. Watkins, *Hobbes's System*, pp. 66–71.

17. Geometry does assume the existence of a line and a point. Everything else must be proven (see Euclid, *Elements*, ed. Thomas L. Heath [New York: Dover Publications, 1956], discussion by editor on p. 143). The squares with which geometry deals, of course, "exist" only in the abstract world of geometry. But at least for Euclid, the notion of a square is not invented, but rather abstracted from those four-sided approximations to squares which may be encountered in everyday life. Geometry thus seeks to discover and demonstrate the properties of abstract squares, and can do so only by showing that squares exist. We may understand this last requirement simply by considering that it is possible to define a figure which cannot exist, such as a three-sided figure with two angles greater than 90°, and which geometry cannot investigate.

18. Compare Wolin's statement: "Geometry, which served as the model for Hobbes, does not purport to test its propositions by an appeal to experience." Wolin claims that Hobbes arrived at his understanding of method largely "on the basis of a mistaken notion that the methods of geometry and science were akin" (*Politics and Vision*, p. 251). In contrast, however, see Craig Walton, "The *Philosophia Prima* of Thomas Hobbes," in *Thomas Hobbes in His Time*, ed. Ralph Ross,

Herbert W. Schneider, and Theodore Waldman (Minneapolis: University of Minnesota Press, 1974), p. 32: "Hobbes takes geometry very seriously. It provides the conceptual equipment for a theory of motion which Aristotle did not achieve. Euclid erred by bracketing actuality and merely presupposing the axioms in 'his first element.' To Hobbes, first elements should be demonstrated from their foundations in actuality.... Hobbes thus does not proceed *de more geometrico*, though he uses "mathematical science" as a synonym for rational knowledge." This interpretation has the virtue that it agrees with what Hobbes understood himself to be doing.

19. Cf. the account of Hobbes's method in Watkins, *Hobbes's System*, pp. 47–55, 66–75. Watkins carefully relates Hobbes's approach to the "Paduan methodology" of inquiry characteristic of the emerging natural science of Galileo and Harvey. He emphasizes the fact that *first principles* are the result of repeated efforts to analyze by hypothesis, that is, "that it is only gradually that we are led to the cause of an effect ... that *hypotheses* are indispensible" (p. 54).

20. We do not possess a record of how Euclid, for example, arrived at the propositions which make up his *Elements* (in which the procedure is strictly deductive). It is safe to say, however, that he did not create out of thin air the definitions from which he begins. We may, however, in the absense of such a record from Euclid, turn to Archimedes, his distinguished successor. Archimedes refers to his work in geometry as "investigations," in which he seeks to discover the relationships which hold among spheres, cones, and so on. These investigations begin from observation to ascertain the properties of geometrical bodies. Thus, he writes, in the beginning of his treatise "On the Sphere and Cylinder," "For, though these properties also were naturally inherent in the figures all along [autēi tēi physei proupērchen peri ta eirēmēna schēmata], yet they were in fact unknown to all the many able geometers who lived before Eudoxus, and *had not been observed by anyone*. Now, however, it will be open to those who possess the requisite ability to examine these discoveries of mine" (*The Works of Archimedes*, ed. T. L. Heath [Cambridge: Cambridge University Press, 1897], pp. 1–2; emphasis added). Cf. Watkins, *Hobbes's System*, pp. 66–68, 70. Goldsmith (*Hobbes's Science*, p. 47) quotes Hobbes's claim that in the practice of natural science "you must furnish yourself with as many experiments (which they call phenomenon) as you can. And supposing some motion for the cause of your phenomenon, try, if by evident consequence, without contradiction to any other manifest truth or experiment, you can derive the cause you seek for from your supposi-

tion" (*Decameron Physiologicum*, chap. 2, in Thomas Hobbes, *The English Works of Thomas Hobbes*, ed. Sir William Molesworth, 11 vols. [London: John Bohn, 1839–1845], 7:88).

21. On the reductive character of Hobbes's philosophical method, see also Tönnies, *Hobbes*, pp. 73, 89–90. "Der kritische Geist des Philosophen ist dieser Geist der Analyse, welcher alle Realität in ihre Elemente auflöst und zeigt, wie diese von selber sich zusammensetzen oder von einer über ihnen befindlichen Intelligenz zusammengesetzt und zusammengehalten werden" (pp. 89–90).

22. On the resolutive-compositive method, see *De Corpore*, 1.6.1: "The first beginnings, therefore, of knowledge, are the phantasms of sense and imagination; and that there be such phantasms we know well enough by nature; but to know why they be, or from what causes they proceed, is the work of ratiocination; which consists . . . in *composition*, and *division* or *resolution*. There is therefore no method, by which we find out the causes of things, but is either *compositive* or *resolutive*, or *partly compositive*, and *partly resolutive*. And the resolutive is commonly called *analytical* method, as the compositive is called *synthetical*."

23. On the primacy of definitions, cf. Stephen, *Hobbes*, p. 93. See also Goldsmith, *Hobbes's Science*, p. 9.

24. Although these simple conceptions exist only in our minds and not in objects, and so are in a sense arbitrary, we must note that they are not entirely arbitrary. They are in some sense "built into" the world, and not just any notion will do. Since they must enable us to explain the nature of the phenomena about which we are inquiring, arriving at them is as much a matter of discovery as it is of invention. Cf. the account in Stephen, *Hobbes*, pp. 93–94. In modern physics, for example, the notion of a neutrino is a human imposition on the world, a "simple" which is intended to supply a theoretical explanation of certain phenomena. (This is not to say that neutrinos don't "exist," or that we cannot test to see if they in fact do.) Not just any notion will satisfy the theoretical need: the concept of a neutrino, while in a sense arbitrary, must "fit" the data. Cf. the account in Polin, *Politique et philosophie*, pp. 43–52.

25. A number of commentators have argued that Hobbes was a nominalist of some sort because of his statement that there is nothing universal but names (*Leviathan*, chap. 4), but he is accused of inconsistent nominalism because he also mentions names of abstractions, which are not particular things. We may avoid the debate here since it is not germane

to our argument. See Samuel I. Mintz, *The Hunting of Leviathan* (Cambridge: Cambridge University Press, 1962), pp. 23–25; Watkins, *Hobbes's System*, pp. 104–107, 147–50; Goldsmith, *Hobbes's Science*, pp. 63–64. Cf. Dorothea Krook, "Thomas Hobbes's Doctrine of Meaning and Truth," *Philosophy* 31 (1956): 3–22.

26. We may be permitted to bypass consideration of the complicated problem of whether social sciences are in theory reducible to psychology (what Hobbes calls moral philosophy), which in turn may be reduced to physics. We may bypass this problem because Hobbes himself, after asserting the linkage just stated, goes on to say that "*Civil* and *moral philosophy* do not so adhere to one another, but that they may be severed. For the causes of the motions of the mind are known, not only by ratiocination, but also by the experience of every man that takes the pains to observe those motions within himself" (*De Corpore*, 1.6.7). Civil philosophy, in other words, or Hobbes's political science, constitutes a kind of microcosm of philosophy or science generally. Its first principles may be derived independently, by the exact same process used in "philosophy simply," as he puts it. "Therefore, not only they that have attained the knowledge of the passions and perturbations of the mind, by the synthetical *method*, and from the very first principles of philosophy," may achieve a true science of civil duties, "and all other knowledge appertaining to civil philosophy"; civil philosophy is accessible not just to these, Hobbes says, "but even they also that have not learned the first part of philosophy, namely, *geometry* and *physics*, may, not withstanding, attain the principles of civil philosophy, by the *analytical method*" (ibid.). Cf. Richard S. Peters and Henri Tajfel, "Hobbes and Hull: Metaphysicians of Behaviour," in *Hobbes and Rousseau*, ed. Maurice Cranston and Richard S. Peters (Garden City, N.Y.: Doubleday & Co., 1972).

27. To cite only the most famous example, see the argument of Thrasymachus, in Plato's *Republic*, book 1 (336b–341a). See also the speeches offered by Glaucon and Adeimantus which open book 2 (357a–367e).

28. For an account of Hobbes as an ethical relativist, and of his contemporaries' reactions, see Samuel I. Mintz, *The Hunting*, pp. 27–28.

29. For an excellent account of Hobbes's insistence that we test our political science against the commonsense political world, see Tönnies, *Hobbes*, pp. 92–94. Hobbes asserts, according to Tönnies, that "reine Wissenschaft nur möglich sei, von Gedankendingen: abstrakten Gegenständen, ideellen Ereignissen; daher auch von einem ‚politischen'

Körper, der mit keinen Sinnen wahrnehmbar ist, dessen Typus wir konstruieren. Alle diese Gedankendinge machen wir schlechthin, nämlich denkend, und können solche, die wir als der äusseren oder körperlichen Welt angehörig denken, in der Wirklichkeit—mehr oder minder auf vollkommene Weise—nachbilden; immer aber können wir wirkliche Tatsachen, *auch wenn sie, wie der Staat und wie moralische Begriffe, nur in den Gedanken der Menschen existieren, an diesen unseren Ideen messen"* (p. 93; emphasis added).

30. See chapter 6 of this work.

31. Hobbes presents his picture of a chaotic world of matter in motion, which we perceive by our senses and "order" in our own minds, in *Leviathan*, chaps. 1–3. Cf. Stephen, *Hobbes*, pp. 105–13.

32. Cf. Edwin A. Burtt, *The Metaphysical Foundations of Modern Science* (Garden City, N.Y.: Doubleday & Co., 1954), p. 134.

33. For this claim see *De Homine*, chap. 10 (see p. 29 above); cf. *De Corpore*, 3.25.1, where, as Hobbes turns to the consideration of natural phenomena, he writes: "I now enter upon the other part; which is the finding out by the appearances or effects of nature, which we know by sense, some ways and means by which they may be, I do not say they are, generated. The principles, therefore, upon which the following discourse depends, are not such as we ourselves make and pronounce in general terms, as definitions; but such, as being placed in things themselves by the Author of Nature, are by us observed in them."

34. Cf. *Leviathan*, chap. 4, p. 101. Men invented languages *"as need (the mother of all inventions) taught them"* (emphasis added).

35. See Leo Strauss, *The Political Philosophy of Hobbes* (Chicago: University of Chicago Press, 1966), pp. 151–52. For more detailed consideration of Hobbes's position, see Manfred Riedel, "Zum Verhältnis von Ontologie und politischer Theorie bei Hobbes," in *Hobbes-Forschungen*, ed. Reinhart Koselleck and Roman Schnur (Berlin: Duncker & Humblot, 1969), pp. 103–18; W. H. Greenleaf, "Hobbes: The Problem of Interpretation," in *Hobbes and Rousseau*, ed. Cranston and Peters; Goldsmith, *Hobbes's Science*, p. 39. See also Leo Strauss, "On the Basis of Hobbes's Political Philosophy," in *What is Political Philosophy* (Glencoe, Ill.: The Free Press, 1959), pp. 170–96, and *Natural Right and History* (Chicago: University of Chicago Press, 1953), pp. 166–201. Cf. note 29 above.

36. As Rousseau, for example, later claimed in the *Discourse on the Origins of Inequality*, in *The First and Second Discourses*, ed. and

trans. Roger Masters (New York: St. Martin's Press, 1964), pp. 141, 143.

37. Or structures, or functions, in another version.

Chapter 3

1. Despite Hobbes's claims, it would not be accurate to describe him as an optimist. He concedes that the final understanding of the names of the political phenomena, that is, the correct definitions and clear relationships between definitions which together comprise true political science, are not possible until philosophy itself is complete. See *De Corpore*, 1.2.16, where, after giving examples of the logical resolution of names, he adds, "I would not have any man think I deliver the forms above for a true and exact ordination of names; for this cannot be performed as long as philosophy remains imperfect."

2. See Rudolph Carnap, *An Introduction to The Philosophy of Science* (New York: Basic Books, 1966), pp. 4, 51, 52, 58–61. See also John Wilson, *Language and The Pursuit of Truth* (Cambridge: The University Press, 1969).

3. For an account of Locke's aim and accomplishment in book 3 of his *Essay* which differs in some respects from what follows, see Karl Fahrion, "Die Sprachphilosophie Lockes," in *Archiv für Geschichte der Philosophie*, n.s., vol. 26 (1912): 56–65.

4. Cf. the account in Gilbert Ryle, "John Locke on the Human Understanding," in *Locke and Berkeley*, ed. David M. Armstrong and C. B. Martin (Notre Dame, Ind.: University of Notre Dame Press, 1968), pp. 25–26. Ryle summarizes as follows: "That the evidence of particular perceptions can never be a foundation for true knowledge, that true knowledge is both completely general and completely certain and is of the type of pure mathematics . . . are doctrines which Locke's whole *Essay* is intended to establish."

5. Cf. *De Homine*, chap. 10, 2, where Hobbes describes in more detail the sense in which he means to say language was "invented": "For it is incredible that men once came together to take counsel to constitute by decree what all words and all connexions of words would signify. It is more credible, however, that at first there were few names and only of those things that were the most familiar. Thus the first man by his own will imposed names on just a few animals, namely, the ones that God led before him to look at; then on other things, as one or another species of things offered itself to his senses; these names, having been

accepted, were handed down from fathers to their sons, who also devised others."

6. See also David R. Bell, "What Hobbes Does With Words," *Philosophical Quarterly* 19 (1969): 155–58. Bell argues that Hobbes's theory of language is a direct precursor of J. L. Austin's modern theory of the language of "performative utterances." See J. L. Austin, *How to Do Things with Words*, ed. J. O. Urmson (New York: Oxford University Press, 1962). Whatever the merits of this view, it leaves untouched the account given here of Hobbes's view of science and its relationship to language. Cf. Dorothea Krook, "Thomas Hobbes's Doctrine of Meaning and Truth," *Philosophy* 31 (1956): 3–22.

7. Thus Dorothea Krook maintains Hobbes has two theories of language, a "sign functioning" theory and a theory of language as discourse. Considering Hobbes's overall purpose (to account for knowledge) and his own statements on the matter, this seems somewhat arbitrary on Krook's part, for Hobbes saw his theory of language as one consistent explanation of what language is and does. See Krook, "Hobbes's Doctrine."

8. Krook maintains that Hobbes was so radical a nominalist that he meant to say that all truths are entirely creations of men, that all definitions are wholly arbitrary. This considerably overstates his position (see above, pp. 32, 37). Men make up names to stand for thoughts, which means the *names* are arbitrary but not necessarily that thoughts are arbitrary. A proposition is a truth if the words are arranged properly, but this does not permit men (at least according to Hobbes's view) to create any truths they want. (See note 10 below.) See Krook, "Hobbes's Doctrine," pp. 4–19; cf. J. M. Brown, "A Note on Professor Oakeshott's Introduction to the Leviathan," and Krook, "Mr. Brown's Note Annotated," *Political Studies* 1 (1953): 53–64, 216–27.

9. Hobbes's friend and patron, Sir Francis Bacon, had noted this problem, and we may assume Hobbes had been exposed to Bacon's ideas. "Now words," Bacon wrote, "being commonly framed and applied according to the capacity of the vulgar, follow those lines of division which are most obvious to the vulgar understanding" (Sir Francis Bacon, *Magna Instauratio*, second part [*The New Organon*, sec. 59], in *Essays, Advancement of Learning, New Atlantis, and Other Pieces*, ed. Richard Foster Jones [New York: Odyssey Press, 1937], p. 287).

10. This attitude is characteristic of the practitioners of the emerging natural science of Hobbes's century. Galileo, for whom Hobbes had great admiration, may have profoundly influenced Hobbes on this

Notes to Pages 44–48

point. In his famous *Letters on Sunspots* Galileo challenges the view that sunspots are stars. "It is indeed true that I am quibbling over names, while I know that anyone may impose them to suit himself. So long as a man does not think that by names he can confer inherent and essential properties on things, it would make little difference whether he calls these 'stars' " (Galileo, *Letters on Sunspots*, in *Discoveries and Opinions of Galileo*, ed. Stillman Drake [Garden City, N.Y.: Doubleday & Co., 1957], p. 139). Names are entirely arbitrary. Galileo's interest is not in quibbling over what to label these phenomena. "I do not care if they are called stars. . . . But these solar stars will be different from any other stars" (quoted in Ludovico Geymonat, *Galileo Galilei* [New York: McGraw-Hill, 1957], p. 66, from Galileo, *Favor's National Ed.*, 4, 257). Call them what you will, as far as Galileo is concerned, that will in no way affect the subject of inquiry.

11. For Hobbes's account of language in general, compare the account given above with that in J. W. N. Watkins, *Hobbes's System of Ideas* (New York: Barnes & Noble, 1965), pp. 138–62; Sir Leslie Stephen, *Hobbes* (Ann Arbor: University of Michigan Press, 1961), pp. 89–97; M. M. Goldsmith, *Hobbes's Science of Politics* (New York: Columbia University Press, 1966), pp. 4–12; and Krook, "Hobbes's Doctrine."

12. It is worth noting here a certain degree of similarity with the approach of at least one modern social scientist. The following, taken from a recent book in political science, reflects a view which is by now familiar:

> In order to "know" a process, we must use symbols that we match in some way against the distribution of some aspects of the process we study. . . . [P. 5]
> A *symbol* is an order to recall from memory a particular thing or event, or a particular set of things or events. Any physical work or event that functions repeatedly as such a command can thus function as a symbol. If we use several symbols, so as to be able to recall several different things, we must connect our symbols with some operating rules. Together, the set of symbols and the set of operating rules form a *symbol system* or a model. . . .
> Any language uses such a symbol system. . . . [P. 10]
> We have seen that men think in terms of models. Their sense organs abstract the events that touch them; their memories store traces of these events as coded symbols; and they may recall them according to patterns they learned earlier, or recombine them in patterns that are new. [P. 19] (Karl Deutsch, *The Nerves of Government* [New York: The Free Press, 1966])

13. Cf. Locke's Second Letter to Stillingfleet, quoted in Fulton H. Ander-

son, *The Influence of Contemporary Science on Locke's Method and Results* (Toronto: University Library Studies, 1923), p. 20.

14. On the necessity that men share ideas, see also Sister Mary Pauline Fitts, *John Locke's Theory of Meaning: An Exposition and Critique* (Washington: Catholic University of America Press, 1960), pp. 22–23.

15. The distinction between qualities and the simple ideas which we have of them is not altogether clear in Locke's account. Ryle, in "John Locke," charges that "the term 'idea' is used by Locke in a number of completely different senses," and that this leads Locke at times into a kind of nonsense (pp. 16–25). For an attempt to clarify certain ambiguities in Locke's account of qualities, see Reginald Jackson, "Locke's Distinction Between Primary and Secondary Qualities," in *Locke and Berkeley*, ed. Armstrong and Martin, pp. 53–77. Cf. Jonathan Bennett, "Substance, Reality, and Primary Qualities," ibid., pp. 86–124; Fahrion, "Sprachphilosophie," p. 63; and note 23 below.

16. Anderson traces Locke's presentation of the theory of ideas to the influence of his good friend Robert Boyle, the chemist. Locke himself was a doctor, of course, and was passionately interested in scientific method and its application to the treatment of disease, especially because of its reliance on careful observation. Anderson argues persuasively that Locke's philosophical method was heavily influenced by the natural science outlook (in *Locke's Method*, pp. 6–14); cf. Jackson, "Locke's Distinction," pp. 56–58; John W. Yolton, "Locke's Concept of Experience," in *Locke and Berkeley*, ed. Armstrong and Martin, p. 52.

17. This passivity is, however, qualified by Locke. Despite his emphasis here on the receptive character of the mind, he speaks also of the mind *perceiving* sense impression. A certain amount of ambiguity seems inescapable here. See Anderson, *Locke's Method*, pp. 17–19; cf. Yolton, "Locke's Concept," pp. 41–44.

18. In John Locke, *An Essay concerning Human Understanding* (New York: Dover Publications, 1959), 1:144, n.

19. See *Essay*, 2.1.25. Fraser points out in note 5 (pp. 142–43) that, as regards simple ideas, Locke "does not say that they are ever 'offered' *in their simplicity*—as *isolated* sensations. Elsewhere, he implies the contrary."

20. Thus we have seen parallel accounts of this process in book 2 ("Of Ideas") and book 3 ("Of Words"). It is curious that in both accounts, and particularly in the earlier one purporting to deal with ideas themselves, and not with words, Locke introduces and explains the process of abstraction by talking about language or names rather than ideas.

One is compelled to wonder, then, whether his insistence on separating language from mental discourse is a well-founded insistence.

21. Cf. chapter 5, note 20.

22. T. H. Green accuses Locke of "playing fast and loose with 'idea' and 'quality,' " because Locke admits he will interchange the terms according to whether the powers are in the objects themselves (qualities) or "as they are sensations or perceptions in our understandings" (ideas) (*Essay*, 2.8.8). In Green's words, "An equivocation is not the less so because it is announced. It is just because Locke allows himself at his convenience to interchange the terms 'idea' and 'quality' that his doctrine is at once so plausible and so hollow" (*Hume and Locke* [New York: Thomas Y. Crowell Co., 1968], p. 13). The problem here, however, seems to be the much deeper one involving the relation of mind to the world. It is not clarified by the stricture Green places on Locke to be consistent, and the implication that Locke simply didn't grasp the problem. Cf. Winston H. F. Barnes, "Did Berkeley Misunderstand Locke?" in *Locke and Berkeley*, ed. Armstrong and Martin, pp. 78–85; Fahrion, "Sprachphilosophie," p. 63. See also note 16 above.

23. Relations, the third category of complex ideas, are subsumed under mixed modes by Locke when he discusses language, or names of these complex ideas. We are justified in doing the same here, collapsing the original three types of complex ideas into two.

24. As has been noted by many commentators on Locke's *Essay*, there is at least an apparent inconsistency (not to say a fundamental contradiction) in Locke's thought on substance. The difficulty is in the claim that the mind can have ideas only of what it experiences, and it cannot "experience" substance. The issue is outside our scope here, but of great importance for almost all subsequent British philosophy. See Fahrion, "Sprachphilosophie," pp. 56–57, 63.

25. Fitts asserts that Locke "rejects real essence as unknowable" (*Locke's Theory*, p. 31). This is clearly mistaken. Locke's point is precisely to distinguish the possibility of complete knowledge of what we make from the hypothetical knowledge to which we are limited when it comes to the natural world. Cf. W. von Leyden, "What is a Nominal Essence the Essence of?" in *John Locke: Problems and Perspectives*, ed. John W. Yolton (Cambridge: Cambridge University Press, 1969), pp. 224–33.

26. By "secondary qualities" Locke means "such qualities which in truth are nothing in the objects themselves but powers to produce various sensations in us by their primary qualities, i.e., by the bulk, figure,

texture, and motion of their insensible parts, as colours, sounds, tastes, &c." (*Essay*, 2.8.10). That is, of what is "out there," we know only that it is matter, particles of some sort, in motion: the colors we see, the sounds we hear, are secondary because they are effects *in us* of something "out there" which we cannot fully know. (Cf. Hobbes, *Leviathan*, chaps. 2, 3; Locke, *Essay*, 2.8.13, 14, 15, 16).

27. Cf. Anderson, *Locke's Method*, pp. 4–6, 12. Anderson's account emphasizes Locke's empirical inclinations, and his distrust of "vague and insignificant forms of speech."

28. *Essay*, 3.5.6 and 3.5.15; see also our discussion, pp. 62–64 above.

29. As we saw in chapter 2 above, the meanings ordained by nature were probably misapprehended in many cases by the first inventors. Confusion from religion and superstition prevented them from seeing their own need clearly. (In this sense, of course, on Locke's view a reform of language is indicated.) See below.

30. The closest Plato comes to presenting such an account is in the dialogue called the *Cratylus*, which, however, could not in any sense be called systematic. In it Plato seems to conclude that language is neither wholly natural nor wholly conventional, but rather some combination (see *Cratylus*, 385d8–e2, 390d9–e3). Aristotle's account of language must be pieced together from several of his works. See *De Interpretatione*, chap. 1; *Poetics*, especially chap. 6; and the *Rhetoric*. For an attempt to systematize Aristotle's understanding, see Miriam Therese Larkin, *Language in the Philosophy of Aristotle* (The Hague: Mouton, 1971).

Chapter 4

1. Cf. Socrates' mention of such a doctrine in Plato's *Theaetetus*, at 202a.

2. See Norman Malcolm, *Ludwig Wittgenstein: A Memoir* (New York: Oxford University Press, 1958), pp. 14–15. See also note 5 below.

3. Also, according to the *Tractatus*, "The totality of propositions is language" (4.0001). Cf. Anthony Kenny, *Wittgenstein* (London: Penguin Press, 1973), pp. 54–71; Justus Hartnack, *Wittgenstein and Modern Philosophy*, trans. Maurice Cranston (Garden City, N.Y.: Doubleday & Co., 1965), pp. 13–42; and K. T. Fann, *Wittgenstein's Conception of Philosophy* (Berkeley and Los Angeles: University of California Press, 1971), pp. 8–21.

4. Cf. *Tractatus* 3.22: "In a proposition a name is the representative of

an object." What Wittgenstein meant by "object" (*Gegenstand*) is the subject of some controversy. See note 13 below.

5. There is a large literature on the issue of the continuity or discontinuity between Wittgenstein's earlier and later philosophy. See, for example, Peter Winch, "The Unity of Wittgenstein's Philosophy," in *Studies in the Philosophy of Wittgenstein*, ed. Winch (New York: Humanities Press, 1969), pp. 1–19; Kenny, *Wittgenstein*, pp. 219–32; A. Janik and S. Toulmin, *Wittgenstein's Vienna* (New York: Simon & Schuster, 1973), pp. 13–32, 167–238; M. Engel, *Wittgenstein's Doctrine of the Tyranny of Language* (The Hague: Martinus Nijhoff, 1971), pp. 11, 27–42; Hanna F. Pitkin, *Wittgenstein and Justice* (Berkeley and Los Angeles: University of California Press, 1972), pp. 24–49.

6. For a very good and more detailed account of the development of this idea in the *Blue Book*, see Engel, *Wittgenstein's Doctrine*, pp. 15–20.

7. Though of course Hobbes would say the conception "five" is what the word stands for. This whole passage calls to mind Hobbes's insistence that a component of knowledge is *evidence*, that is, that the *meaning* of of a proposition be evident to its user. Hobbes was facing the issue that the words are nothing but signs, themselves somehow lifeless, and need mental activity to make them mean something. Cf. Engel, *Wittgenstein's Doctrine*, pp. 16–17; *Blue Book*, pp. 1–5; see below, pp. 86, 87.

8. Cf. Winch, "The Unity." Winch characterizes the tendency to look behind words for a separate realm of meanings (in elementary propositions) as looking for "what lies hidden *beneath* our normal ways of talking," and identifies this as the theme of the *Tractatus*. In the later philosophy, he says, Wittgenstein has made the "slight, but decisive" shift to looking for "what is hidden *in* our normal ways of talking" (p. 19).

9. The metaphor was used by Wittgenstein himself. He is reported to have said that "in teaching you philosophy I'm like a guide showing you how to find your way around London. . . . After I have taken you on many journeys through the city, in all sorts of directions, we shall have passed through any given street a number of times—each time traversing the street as part of a different journey. At the end of this you will know London; you will be able to find your way about like a born Londoner" (D. A. T. Gasking and A. C. Jackson, "Wittgenstein as a Teacher," in *Ludwig Wittgenstein: The Man and His Philosophy*, ed. K. T. Fann [New York: Dell, 1967], p. 51). Cf. Pitkin, *Wittgenstein*, pp. ix–xi for a similar explanation, which also quotes this remark.

10. There is already a large literature on this portion of Wittgenstein's thought. See articles by Feyerabend, Malcolm, and Strawson in *Wittgenstein: The "Philosophical Investigations"*, ed. G. Pitcher (Notre Dame, Ind.: University of Notre Dame Press, 1966).

11. For a more detailed explanation see P. F. Strawson's excellent article, "Review of Wittgenstein's *Philosophical Investigations*," in *Wittgenstein*, ed. Pitcher.

12. A detailed account of language games (*Sprachspiele*) is to be found in K. Wuchterl, *Struktur und Sprachspiel bei Wittgenstein* (Frankfurt am Main: Suhrkamp Verlag, 1969), esp. pp. 114–28, 132ff.

13. Professor T. Morawetz has called my attention to a disagreement about this matter. Morawetz holds that this view is now generally regarded as attributable to logical positivists such as Ayer, but that it was not Wittgenstein's view. It does not appear to me to be so clear. Cf. Hartnack, *Wittgenstein*, pp. 17–25, 45–57; J. Bogen, *Wittgenstein's Philosophy of Language* (New York: Humanities Press, 1972); G. E. M. Anscombe, *An Introduction to Wittgenstein's Tractatus* (Philadelphia: University of Pennsylvania Press, 1971), pp. 11–20, 25–30.

14. See A. M. Quinton, "Excerpt from 'Contemporary British Philosophy,' " in *Wittgenstein*, ed. Pitcher, pp. 7–8.

15. Cf. Strawson, "Review," p. 25. Here the importance of the purpose of what something is used *for*, is brought out. As Strawson explains it, "instead, then, of gazing at this over-simple picture of language, with its attendant assimilations, we are to look at the elements of language as instruments. We are to study their use. Only so can we solve our conceptual problems. Variants on 'use' in Wittgenstein are *'purpose'* 'function' 'role' 'part' 'application' " (emphasis added).

16. This is not to say that we cannot think without talking—we may imagine a sequence of events, presumably without articulation. But it is open to question whether we want to call this "thinking," or whether it would be better described as imagination. (Cf. Hobbes, *Leviathan*, chap. 2.) It seems unlikely that we can "think" about something without engaging in "mental speech," in some sense. Cf. Strawson, "Review," pp. 50–53.

17. This implication of Wittgenstein's thought has given rise to the impression that he was a sort of behaviorist, and meant to deny the independence of human thought or reflection by tracing it to behavioral conditioning. See C. S. Chihara and M. A. Fodor, "Operationalism and Ordinary Language: A Critique of Wittgenstein," in *Wittgenstein*, ed. Pitcher. It would appear that Noam Chomsky also

attributes such a doctrine to Wittgenstein. See Chomsky, *Cartesian Linguistics* (New York: Harper & Row, 1966), pp. 10 (where Wittgenstein is mentioned), 11–19, 59–73; notes 11, 21, 94, and above all note 114, where Chomsky refers to writers whose conclusions are "based not on observation but on a priori assumptions about what they believe must take place. Cf., e.g., the speculation on how all language 'habits' are built up by training, instruction, conditioning, and reinforcement in references cited. . . ." Here Chomsky cites Wittgenstein, along with Skinner's *Verbal Behavior*. For reasons which should be clear, this interpretation is a misunderstanding of Wittgenstein. The best discussion of this issue is to be found in Gunter Gebauer's *Wortgebrauch, Sprachbedeutung* (Munich: Bayerische Schulbuch-Verlag, 1971), pp. 71–73. Gebauer concludes, "Trotz dieser in gewissem Sinne mechanistischen Deutung der Sprache und trotz der Ablehnung der Privatsprache ist Wittgensteins Theorie der Bedeutung *nicht behavioristisch*" (p. 73; emphasis added).

18. See J. Griffin, *Wittgenstein's Logical Atomism* (Seattle: University of Washington Press, 1969) for a more detailed discussion of this issue. Cf. Bogen, *Wittgenstein's Philosophy*, pp. 55–74.

19. *Republic*, 331c–d. Polemarchus attributes the definition to Simonides. The formulation offered first by Socrates is slightly different: "As to justice, shall we so simply assert that it is the truth and giving back what a man has taken from another?"

20. See below, pp. 177, 179. One could say that Wittgenstein is here denying the naturalness of what Locke called abstraction, and implying that the (perhaps disorderly) connectedness of the whole is only obscured by scientific reductionism. I am indebted to Harvey Mansfield for this point.

Chapter 5

1. On rules, compare the account in Anthony Kenny, *Wittgenstein* (London: Penguin Press, 1973), pp. 170–77.

2. Even on utilitarian grounds an indistinct photograph may be an advantage. For example, an indistinct photograph of a policeman would be an advantage if one were teaching a child that "the policeman is our friend." If the photograph were distinct, the child might take you to mean that *only* the particular man pictured is friendly, and therefore misunderstand. A picture of a policeman with indistinct features would better convey the point that the uniform is what matters.

3. Cf. Hanna F. Pitkin, *Wittgenstein and Justice* (Berkeley and Los Angeles: University of California Press, 1972), pp. 56, 62, 90–92.

4. Wittgenstein here raises an issue with which he had wrestled in his earlier work, the issue of the distinction between names and descriptions. The problem was inherited from Gottlob Frege (see *The Basic Laws of Arithmetic* [Berkeley and Los Angeles: University of California Press, 1967], pp. 11–25), and Bertrand Russell attempted a solution by proposing the theory of definite descriptions (which would hold that the name "Moses" refers, but the descriptions of Moses are themselves propositions which are not equivalent to the proper name). See the clear discussion in Kenny, *Wittgenstein*, pp. 34–42. Cf. Justus Hartnack, *Wittgenstein and Modern Philosophy*, trans. Maurice Cranston (Garden City, N.Y.: Doubleday & Co., 1962), pp. 14–19; Hidé Ishiguro, "Use and Reference of Names," in *Studies in the Philosophy of Wittgenstein*, ed. Peter Winch (New York: Humanities Press, 1969), pp. 20–50. The latter argues persuasively that Wittgenstein disagrees with Russell even in the *Tractatus* on the question of referring.

5. Quoted in Pitkin, *Wittgenstein*, p. 55. From *Semantic Analysis* (Ithaca, N.Y.: Cornell University Press, 1960), p. 35.

6. Pitkin, *Wittgenstein*, p. 55.

7. Ibid.

8. Pitkin, *Wittgenstein*, p. 57; the quotation within is from Paul Ziff.

9. Cf. Locke, *Essay*, 2.11.9 and 3.3.3.; and above, pp. 53–54.

10. This distinction, between the child's partial or incomplete "account" of meaning and the knowledge of the adult, should not of course be mistaken for Locke's (or Hobbes's) distinction between common speech's partial knowledge and the complete account of meaning which is the goal of science. I am indebted to Harvey Mansfield for pointing this out.

11. Pitkin, *Wittgenstein*, p. 62.

12. By natural language we mean simply one which human beings live with or use in ordinary living. It is to be contrasted with an artificial language, such as a computer language (FORTRAN) or the language of a technical field. Of course the borderline may be blurred (by the more or less extensive use of originally technical language as "jargon" in daily life).

13. Wittgenstein is famous for his remark that "philosophy leaves everything as it is." (Except for our understanding, we might add.) This has

given rise to the belief that his philosophy is conservative. For such a viewpoint, see Alan Wertheimer, "Is Ordinary Language Analysis Conservative?" in *Political Theory* 4 (1976): 405–22. See also Pitkin's discussion in *Wittgenstein*, pp. 325–28, 336–40. (Cf. Karl Marx, *Theses on Feuerbach*, No. 11.) We will return to the question of Wittgenstein's understanding of philosophy in chapter 8.

14. This calls to mind Socrates' attempt, in the *Meno*, to show that the slave boy is only being "reminded" of what he somehow already knew. See chapter 7.

15. Cf. S. Morris Engel, *Wittgenstein's Doctrine of the Tyranny of Language* (The Hague: Martinus Nijhoff, 1971), pp. 35–39, 41, 133–40. Engel, whose work here is concerned mainly with the *Blue Book*, argues that Wittgenstein began, at least, with the notion that philosophical difficulties are caused only by language. His account of the difference between scientific and linguistic explanations provides a useful contrast with the account given here.

16. Learning the grammar of expressions means more than putting words together properly: it means using them in the proper situations. "Thus, the grammar of 'chair' tells us not merely *that* one 'sits on' a 'chair,' but *how* one sits on a chair. What makes it a chair is the *way* we use the object, that we sit on it in that characteristic way" (Pitkin, *Wittgenstein*, p. 118). We know because of grammar what concepts are relevant to each other. We know that "coffee" is the kind of thing which can be strong or weak, for example, while water is not. The grammar of "coffee" relates it to strong and weak. And if someone says, "I hope you like your water strong," as he serves you a glass of water, it is our knowledge of the grammar of "water" which tells us something is odd.

17. See chapter 7.

18. Pitkin, *Wittgenstein*, p. 121.

19. The problem of rules has been central to a good many interpreters of Wittgenstein's later work, especially as it raises the question of the possibility of private languages (how can there be a rule if there is no one to check on its application?). See K. T. Fann, *Wittgenstein's Conception of Philosophy* (Berkeley and Los Angeles: University of California Press, 1971), pp. 72–79, for an excellent discussion. On the notion of a private language and its connection to the idea of separate mental processes, recall the discussion of Locke's understanding of words, above, p. 56. See also Stanley Cavell, "The Availability of Wittgenstein's Later Philosophy" and "Must We Mean What We Say?"

in Cavell, *Must We Mean What We Say?* (New York: Charles Scribner's Sons, 1969), pp. 44–52, 1–43; the essays by A. J. Ayer and R. Rhees in *Wittgenstein: The "Philosophical Investigations"*, ed. G. Pitcher (Nortre Dame, Ind.: University of Notre Dame Press, 1966); and Peter Winch, *The Idea of a Social Science and Its Relation to Philosophy* (New York: Humanities Press, 1958), pp. 24–39. The Winch book has itself touched off a voluminous debate in anthropological literature. See Pitkin, *Wittgenstein*, pp. 241–63; cf. *Rationality: Key Concepts in the Social Sciences*, ed. Bryan R. Wilson (Oxford: Basil Blackwell, 1970); also Dorothy Emmet and Alasdair MacIntyre, eds., *Sociological Theory and Philosophical Analysis* (New York: Macmillan Co., 1970).

20. On the general question of the degree to which Wittgenstein is to be understood as a "conventionalist," some of the most important literature involves his understanding (or, as some critics would have it, his misunderstanding) of mathematics. In this regard, see Charles S. Chihara, "Wittgenstein and Logical Compulsion," in *Wittgenstein*, ed. Pitcher, pp. 448–68; D. S. Shwayder, "Wittgenstein on Mathematics," in *Studies*, ed. Winch, pp. 66–116. Cf. Michael Dummett, "Wittgenstein's Philosophy of Mathematics," in *Wittgenstein*, ed. Pitcher, pp. 384–447.

21. Pitkin, *Wittgenstein*, p. 138.

22. I am indebted to Thomas Pangle for the suggestion of this particular example.

23. Stanley Cavell, "Claim to Rationality" (Ph.D. diss., Harvard University), quoted in Pitkin, *Wittgenstein*, pp. 133–34. It should be noted that the very examples offered by Cavell in the passage quoted present a bit of evidence against his claim. There is no word for boredom in ancient Greek, nor, for that matter, in English before 1750 (*Oxford English Dictionary*). The concept of boredom, or ennui, has not had a general existence. The closest synonyms in ancient Greek mean something more like monotony or irritation. On the account offered by Wittgenstein, we are compelled to wonder whether people in cultures without a word for boredom did not live more exciting lives (or at least were more easily occupied).

24. An excellent discussion of this matter is to be found in J. L. Austin, "Other Minds," in Austin, *Philosophical Papers* (New York: Oxford University Press, 1970). See especially pp. 107–9.

25. Of course, one may object on the basis of some kind of cultural relativism, that these characteristic patterns are not in fact so extensive. But the fact that translation is possible so generally between even

radically different languages would appear to be prima facie evidence for Wittgenstein's point. Once again, there is a large literature in anthropology on this issue. For the conventionalist side, see Benjamin Lee Whorf, *Language, Thought, and Reality*, ed. John B. Carroll (Cambridge, Mass.: M.I.T. Press, 1967). A number of issues also arise here over the matter of the understanding of one culture by another. See Peter Winch, "Understanding a Primitive Society," in *Rationality*, ed. Bryan R. Wilson. An overall account of this issue can be found in Pitkin, *Wittgenstein*, pp. 241–63.

26. Ludwig Wittgenstein, *On Certainty*, ed. G. E. M. Anscombe and G. H. von Wright, trans. Denis Paul and G. E. M. Anscombe (New York: Harper & Row, 1969), par. 204, p. 28.

Chapter 6

1. Cf. Wilhelm Hennis, *Politik und praktische Philosophie* (Neuwied am Rhein: Hermann Luchterhand Verlag, 1963), pp. 9–23.

2. If we can have certain knowledge only of what we construct by means of syllogisms, however, it is necessary to admit that such knowledge remains always contingent. The natural world is knowable by means of the scientific languages we construct, but the meanings of our terms are a human artifice, imposed on a world permanently alien to us. In Hobbes's words, "No Discourse whatsoever, can End in absolute knowledge of Fact, past, or to come. For, as for the knowledge of Fact, it is originally, Sense; and ever after, Memory. And for the knowledge of Consequence, which I have said before is called Science, it is not Absolute, but Conditionall. No man can know by Discourse, that this, or that, is, has been, or will be; which is to know absolutely: but onely, that if This be, That is; if This has been, That has been; if This shall be, That shall be: which is to know conditionally; and that not the consequence of one thing to another; but of one name of a thing, to another name of the same thing" (*Leviathan*, chap. 7, p. 131). The predictive power of such a science—which is also, of course, the basis of its utility—is the means of testing its truth.

3. Cf. Hennis, *Politik*, p. 41. Hennis contrasts Aristotle's position in this passage with the approach of Descartes, as the founder of the modern understanding. (See pp. 41–45.) See also Otfried Höffe, *Praktische Philosophie: Das Modell des Aristoteles* (Munich: Anton Pustet, 1971), pp. 24–25, 107–25. Höffe's account is excellent. Cf. Lambert Filkuka, *Die metaphysischen Grundlagen der Ethik bei Aristoteles* (Vienna: Carl Konegen, 1895), pp. 90–91.

4. Filkuka, however, after explaining Aristotle's two concepts of method,

from first principles, and to first principles, asserts: "Für die Ethik ent-
scheidet er sich für die letztere Methode, indem ja über das Einzelne,
ob es gut oder schlecht sei, kein Zweifel ist, und aus diesen konkreten
Fällen, als dem uns Bekannteren, nun das allgemeine Prinzip hergeleitet
werden soll" (*Grundlagen*, p. 95). We find this far from clear in
Aristotle's account. Cf. J. H. Randall, *Aristotle* (New York: Columbia
University Press, 1960), pp. 42–44.

5. Cf. Hennis, *Politik*, pp. 39–40. According to Hennis we must understand the restriction of audience to be an actual *part* of the practical
   aspect of Aristotle's political science. By contrast, he notes, "In der
   modernen Erkenntnistheorie hat der Adressat der Erkenntnisse be-
   kanntlich keinen Ort. Die Wissenschaft ist eine Sache des denkenden
   Ichs, die Vermittlung der Erkenntnisse hat mit der Erkenntnis nichts zu
   tun."

6. Cf. Höffe, *Praktische Philosophie*, pp. 72–76. See also the discussion of
   starting points in Marjorie Grene, *A Portrait of Aristotle* (Chicago:
   University of Chicago Press, 1963), pp. 103–12.

7. See Ostwald's footnote to this passage in Aristotle, *Nicomachean
   Ethics*, trans. Martin Ostwald (Indianapolis: Bobbs-Merrill Co., 1962),
   p. 18.

8. Cf. Werner Jaeger, *Aristotle: Fundamentals of the History of His
   Development*, trans. Richard Robinson (London: Oxford University
   Press, 1962), pp. 85–86. Jaeger finds that Aristotle means his activity
   is more like the carpenter's activity. See also Filkuka, *Grundlagen*,
   p. 92.

9. Aristotle's reliance on expressions such as this is evident throughout
   the *Ethics*; for example, see 1097a30, 1097b15.

10. Cf. Wayne N. Thompson, *Aristotle's Deduction and Induction*
    (Amsterdam: Rodopi, 1975), pp. 89–100.

11. A similarity may be noted here to the description of "reflective
    equilibrium" in John Rawls, *A Theory of Justice* (Cambridge, Mass.:
    Harvard University Press, 1971), pp. 20–22, 48–51, 120, 432.

12. See the discussion in Hennis, *Politik*, p. 101. A connection is asserted
    between Hobbes's thought and the work of Peter Ramus (Pierre de la
    Ramée): "Indem Ramus die feine Differenzierung der aristotelischen
    Syllogismen (wissenschaftliche, dialektische, Enthymema) verwarf,
    postulierte er statt dessen die Einheit der Logik und die Gleichförmig-
    keit aller Denkoperationen. Die Erwägungen, die die Handlungen
    eines Menschen motivieren, scheinen Ramus 'logisch' von keiner
    anderen Struktur zu sein als die Kalkulationen eines Geometers."

13. The translation of the *Posterior Analytics* here is that of G. R. G. Mure in *Basic Works of Aristotle*, ed. Richard McKeon (New York: Random House, 1941).

14. See the complicated account in P. Aubenque, *La prudence chez Aristotle* (Paris: Presses universitaires de France, 1963), esp. pp. 7–30. Cf. Jaeger, *Aristotle*, pp. 81–88. Jaeger's account is criticized very carefully by Aubenque.

15. Cf. Aubenque, *La prudence*, p. 9. The author suggests that the traditional translation of *phronēsis* as "prudence," "qui a eu pour effet d'isoler assez précisément l'un des deux sens du mot, ne doit pas nous masquer ce qu'a pu avoir d'étonnant pour les auditeurs et les lecteurs d'Aristote, ni ce que peut encore avoir de problématique, l'emploi du même mot *phronēsis* dans deux acceptions aussi différentes, pour ne pas dire opposées, sans qu'aucune explication vienne justifier la coexistence de ces deux sens ou le passage de l'un à l'autre."

16. It should be noted that Plato suggests the same dubious etymology for *sōphrosynē* in *Cratylus*, 411e. See Ostwald's note in his translation of the *Ethics*, p. 153.

17. The ambiguity of the notion of prudence—as both a kind of knowledge and a virtue—is also noted by Aubenque (see note 15 above). He goes on to claim, in fact, that "l'originalité d'Aristote consiste, en réalité, dans une nouvelle conception des rapports de la théorie et de la pratique, consequence elle-même d'une rupture pour la première fois consommée dans l'univers de la théorie. Ce qui est nouveau chez lui, ce n'est pas un intérêt inedit pour l'action—Socrate ni Platon n'avaient été de purs speculatifs—, mais la découverte d'une scission a l'intérieur de la raison, et la reconnaissance de cette scission comme condition d'un nouvel intellectualism pratique" (*La prudence*, p. 144). Cf. Höffe, *Praktische Philosophie*, pp. 55–58.

18. Cf. Jaeger, *Aristotle*, pp. 83–88. See also Aubenque's discussion of Jaeger's views in *La prudence*, pp. 10–21, 26.

19. The Greek is *"hē men oun methodos toutōn epietai, politikē tis ousa."* *Politikē* is, to use Ostwald's phrase, "the science of the city-state," and is qualified by the *tis* (Ostwald, note, p. 4). *"Politikē tis"* is translated by W. D. Ross, *The Basic Works of Aristotle*, ed. McKeon, p. 936, as "political science, in one sense of that term."

20. It should be noted that it has no relation to morality, which concerns the *active* part of the soul. This would seem to leave open the possibility of happiness even for a man who does not possess moral virtue.

21. For a different interpretation, see Jaeger, *Aristotle*, pp. 82–83. Jaeger argues that Aristotle's understanding of *phronēsis*, in this connection, is actually "the public recantation of the Platonic views in the *Protrepticos*" (Aristotle's early treatise).

22. Cf. Höffe, *Praktische Philosophie*, p. 58: "Wenn [der Mensch] aber auch wissen will, warum er philosophieren soll, hat er die Ethik zu studieren."

23. Cf. Höffe, *Praktische Philosophie*, pp. 61–62: "Das sittliche Engagement spricht Aristoteles in einer Formel aus—Ziel der Abhandlung ist nicht Erkenntnis, sondern Handeln—, die als Ziel das ablehnt, was seine Ethik tatsächlich leistet: die Erkenntnis."

24. See, for example, Socrates' conversation with Cephalus and then Polemarchus in *Republic*, book 1 (330d1–336b1). Socrates' "own" account of his philosophic activity, as given in the *Apology*, offers another example. See also chapter 7 of this work. Cf. Nietzsche, *Beyond Good and Evil*, section 191.

25. One testimony to this fact is an ambiguity in translation. Some translations render both *apodeixis* and *syllogismos* from the Greek as "demonstration" in English. But demonstration in the strictest sense, for Aristotle, is *apodeixis* (*Topics*, 100a25). We use syllogism here in the modern sense, which is Hobbes's sense, of strictly logical reasoning. We will return to this below.

26. Here the word translated as demonstration is *syllogismos*. A number of articles devoted to Aristotle's understanding of dialectic in the *Topics* are collected in *Aristotle on Dialectic: The "Topics"*, ed. G. E. L. Owen (Oxford: Oxford University Press, 1968). See especially Friedrich Solmsen, "Dialectic without the Forms," pp. 49–68, and Gilbert Ryle, "Dialectic in the Academy," pp. 69–79.

27. Cf. Marjorie Grene, *A Portrait of Aristotle* (Chicago: University of Chicago Press, 1963), pp. 106–7. According to Grene, "It has often been said that Aristotle failed as a physical scientist because he was *too* empirical, because he stayed too close to the everyday world of common sense." Cf. J. H. Randall, *Aristotle* (New York: Columbia University Press, 1960), pp. 56–57.

28. On starting from opinions, see Hennis, *Politik*, pp. 88, 89–115. On the charge that such a starting point dooms the inquiry to subjectivism (Hobbes's charge), Hennis writes: "Dass die Aussage, dieses oder jenes: Tugend, Freiheit, Glück des Einzelnen, staatliche Macht, sozialer Friede oder was immer impliziere das 'eigentliche' Problem politischer Ordnungen, eine *Meinung* wiedergibt, der man andere Meinungen

entgegenstellen kann, dürfte unbestreitbar sein. Bleibt somit der Aus-
gangspunkt der politischen Wissenschaft nicht im zufällig vagen Gebiet
des Meinens verstrickt? Wir würden sagen: ja und nein. Es gibt ein
Meinen geringerer und höherer Evidenz. Es gibt sogar eine Methode
zur Gewinnung dieser höheren Evidenz" (p. 88). Cf. Solmsen, "Dialectic," pp. 49–68.

29. In the *Rhetoric*, Aristotle speaks of the kind of argument which
    produces conviction in the hearer as "a sort of demonstration
    [*apodeixis*], since we are most strongly convinced when we consider a
    thing to have been demonstrated. The orator's demonstration is an
    enthymeme, and this is, in general, the most effective of the modes of
    rhetorical proof. The enthymeme is a sort of syllogism, and the con-
    sideration of syllogisms of all kinds . . . is the business of dialectic"
    (*Rhetoric*, 1355a5; my translation).

30. This may be illustrated by Aristotle's own example, "the argument
    that supposing the skilled pilot is the most effective, and likewise the
    skilled charioteer, then in general the skilled man is the best at his
    particular task" (*Topics*, 105a12).

31. Dialectical reasoning, then, is a kind of demonstration. Aristotle does
    note that there are different degrees of demonstrative strength which
    depend on the strength of the conviction about the points from which
    the reasoning begins. See *Posterior Analytics*, 72a25–72b4; *Topics*,
    100a25.

32. This fact is noted also by Solmsen, who seems, however, to attribute
    some confusion to Aristotle in this matter. "Surely as long as dialectic
    was engaged in tracing the structure of Being it would have been
    almost a sacrilege to describe it as a technique operating on the basis
    of 'opinions.' It claimed to deal with the truth and to be a way towards
    the discovery of truth. A method relying on opinions seems to leave no
    room for *aléthé*" ("Dialectic," p. 65).

33. On the other hand, Aristotle is not satisfied simply to say the word has
    many meanings: "What, then, is the meaning of 'good' [in these
    different things]? Surely, it is not that they merely happen to have the
    same name. Do we call them 'good' because they are derived from a
    single good, or because they all aim at a single good? Or do we rather
    call them 'good' by analogy, e.g., as sight is good in the body, so
    intelligence is good in the soul, and so other things are good within
    their respective fields?" (*Ethics*, 1096b26–29).

34. We do not know whether Wittgenstein was aware of this similarity; he
    made no mention of Aristotle in his writings. See Garth Hallett, *A*

Companion to Wittgenstein's "Philosophical Investigations" (Ithaca, N.Y.: Cornell University Press, 1977).

Chapter 7

1. The usage of "things" in this manner follows the Greek, in which what we would call the noun is omitted from an expression and understood. Thus *kalos* means "noble," *ta kala* "the noble things"; *agathos* means "good," *ta agatha* "the good things," and so on. It would be difficult to avoid this usage in translating from Plato, even though we are not accustomed to it in English.

2. For Meno's background, as well as his fate after the time of the dialogue's imagined occurrence (supposed by most commentators to have been 402 B.C.), see E. Seymer Thompson, *The Meno of Plato* (Cambridge: W. Heffer & Sons, 1961; originally published by Macmillan, 1901), pp. xii–xx, lvii. See also Jacob Klein, *A Commentary on Plato's Meno* (Chapel Hill: University of North Carolina Press, 1965), pp. 35–47.

3. Translations from the Meno are my own. Where necessary for clarity, I have borrowed from translations by Klein, *Commentary*, and Benjamin Jowett, *Meno* (New York: Bobbs-Merrill Co., 1949).

4. See Thompson, *The Meno*, however, for a different view. He maintains that the fact "that Meno is a pupil of Gorgias is a mere accident" (p. lvii).

5. See Klein, *Commentary*, pp. 43–45.

6. The omission of piety and its bearing on Meno's character is also noted by Thompson, in *The Meno*, pp. xx, 85 (note 30).

7. See Martin Andic, "Inquiry and virtue in the *Meno*," in *Plato's Meno*, ed. Malcolm Brown (New York: Bobbs-Merrill Co., 1971), pp. 291–92. Andic discusses the connection between Socrates' approach and a view (which he attributes to Wittgenstein) that definitions are intelligible only on the basis of "authoritative knowledge of cases, and not cases on the basis of definitions" (p. 292). His conclusions differ from ours, partly because he appears to take Socrates' statements for Plato's views.

8. We are not alone in this reading. For an investigation of the sort of definitions Socrates is seeking, which makes use of modern theories of meaning and semantics, see Laura Grimm, *Definition in Plato's Meno*, Historisk, Filosofisk, Klasse, n.s., no. 2, Norske Videnskapps-

Akademi (Oslo: Oslo University Press, 1962). Cf. H. -P. Stahl, "Beginnings of Propositional Logic in Plato," in *Plato's Meno*, ed. M. Brown, pp. 180–97.

9. *Eidos* means in ordinary Greek literally "form" or "shape." It is, of course, usually translated in Platonic studies as "Idea." See Paul Friedländer, *Plato* (Princeton: Princeton University Press, 1973), pp. 3–31; Francis M. Cornford, *Plato's Theory of Knowledge* (New York: Bobbs-Merrill Co., 1957), pp. 4–8, 269; Klara Buchmann, "Die Stellung des Menon in der platonischen Philosophie," *Philologus*, supp. 29 (1936): 36–59, 66–73.

10. See, for example, Aristotle, *Politics*, 1253a10; Hobbes, *Leviathan*, chap. 17, pp. 225–27; Plato, *Phaedo*, 82b; *Republic*, 552c.

11. Cf. Aristotle, *Politics*, 1276b27.

12. See p. 166.

13. Grimm, however, believes Socrates, in his definitional approach, simply made a "mistake," because he made "an invalid inference from thing to concept, or from thing to word." Thus, she says, "Socrates may be said to have taken upon himself the impossible task of intending to describe the meaning of a term at the same time as he intends to give an empirical theory about things denoted by the term." Socrates' sort of definition is "a *confusion* of nominal and real definition" (*Definition*, p. 30).

14. See Plato, *Protagoras*, 337a1–c4.

15. See above, chapter 2, pp. 39–40.

16. Thus it is the type of definition characteristic of presocratic philosophy or natural philosophy, which was concerned with the study of nature (*physis*)—what we would call physics. That Socrates is familiar with this type of reductive or "scientific" definition is especially important to us here, in view of his marked lack of enthusiasm for it.

17. Socrates' own, and the narrow one conforming to Meno's objections. Cf. Klein, *Commentary*, pp. 65–67.

18. For an excellent account of what Meno's remarks reveal about his character, see Thompson, *The Meno*, pp. xix–xx. Thompson lists arrogance, self-esteem, vanity, and want of self-control. Despite this analysis, however, Thompson goes on to say of Meno: "He may have been a bad man—that was a matter of comparative indifference; he certainly was a bad *pupil*—that is a point of cardinal importance." We need to be alert to the possibility that there is some connection between these, however.

19. One commentator sees in this exchange the lesson from Plato that "Socrates reacts strongly and defensively to contentiousness or antagonism," and that he "is conscious of his tendency to respond emotionally in specific kinds of situations." See Jerome Eckstein, *The Platonic Method: An Interpretation of the Dramatic-Philosophic Aspects of the Meno* (New York: Greenwood Publishing Corp., 1968), p. 24.

20. Cf. Klein, *Commentary*, p. 75.

21. Although choosing might imply choosing well, which does in a sense admit of degrees. Thus choosing may stand somehow between "desiring" and "willing." I am indebted to Harvey Mansfield for this suggestion.

22. Or without moderation (*sōphrosynē*) or piety (*hosiotēs*), which are also mentioned.

23. Cf. Francis M. Cornford, "Anamnesis," in *Plato's Meno*, ed. M. Brown, pp. 108–27; Andic, "Inquiry and Virtue," pp. 268–73. Andic also discusses Plato's teaching in light of the *Euthydemus* and *Charmides* (pp. 274–84). For a comparison of *anamnēsis* with the midwife doctrine of the Theaetetus, see Cornford, *Plato's Theory*, pp. 2–3, 27–29. On the supposed Pythagorean influence evident in the recollection doctrine, see Buchmann, "Die Stellung des Menon," p. 73; Cornford, "Anamnesis," p. 121.

24. According to Cornford, some commentators, "wishing perhaps to transform Plato's theory into something that we can accept, reduce the doctrine of *Anamnesis* to a form in which it ceases to have any connection with the pre-existence of the soul. But Plato unquestionably believed in immortality..." (*Plato's Theory*, p. 3). We believe that what will be said below about the circularity of the recollection thesis raises at least some doubts about Cornford's position.

25. On the circularity of the recollection doctrine, see Andic, "Inquiry and Virtue," pp. 267, 299–300; cf. Marjorie Grene, *A Portrait of Aristotle* (Chicago: University of Chicago Press, 1963), pp. 103–12.

26. Cf. Klein, *Commentary*, pp. 97–98.

27. Thus there are two stages to the inquiry. Malcolm Brown suggests the theory that in the first an arithmetical approach is employed, while the second is geometrical. The first method, he says, is rigorous but produces no results: the second is methodologically "suspect" but yields the desired result (Malcolm Brown, "Plato Disapproves of the Slave-boy's Answer," in *Plato's Meno*, ed. M. Brown, pp. 200–201).

That two approaches are pursued is evident enough, but we would rather say the first one is abandoned because it is inappropriate (seeks what is not to be found), and not because Plato wishes to show that geometrical knowledge is inferior or suspect. See also note 42 below.

28. Cf. Brown, who, after expressing wonder at why Plato chose such a complicated problem instead of one where, say, the sides of the square were doubled, goes on to conclude that Plato meant to show that the method used was faulty, and that the inquiry "succeeds in finding an answer . . . only after abandoning the demand for perfect accuracy" (p. 224). But this misses the fact that the answer is perfectly accurate, only it must be pointed to because it cannot be stated.

29. And since neither Socrates nor anyone else has ever given him that knowledge, he must have possessed it always, from some earlier existence. Hence, says Socrates, "if the truth, of the things that exist is always in the soul, the soul must be deathless" (86b1). Clearly this reverses the argument of the story with which he began: there he based the claim that the soul knows all things on the fact of its immortality; here he deduces the claim for the soul's immortality from the fact that it knows all things. The circularity of the "knowledge" contained in this section should alert us to the possibility that any important knowledge about the human world may necessarily lack an Archimedean point from which it could be deduced.

30. Cf. Andic, "Inquiry and Virtue," pp. 264–74. See also Friedländer, *Plato*, pp. 189–90. Friedländer (along with M. Brown et al.) reads Socrates' qualification here not as a general doubt about "many things," but as refering specifically to his lack of belief in the recollection story or in the slave-boy demonstration. But see Cornford, *Plato's Theory*, p. 3, and note 24 above.

31. See above, pp. 168–70, and note 18.

32. Cf. Plato, *Charmides*, 158e6–159a8.

33. Cf. Plato, *Protagoras*, 349d1–350d6, 359b1–360d8.

34. See Stahl, "Beginnings," pp. 180–97. Stahl attempts to show that Plato here anticipates Stoic logic and thus modern mathematical logic.

35. See the excellent discussion of this matter, with a review of the relevant literature, in Klein, *Commentary*, pp. 206–8. But see Thompson, *The Meno*, pp. 148–49, for an attempt to make this passage coherent from a geometrical standpoint.

36. See Klein, *Commentary*, pp. 208–11.

37. It is more difficult to see how this can be in the case of justice than

with the others. Possibly Socrates would say that justice strictly applied, untempered by mercy, is sometimes cruel and thus not used wisely. Nevertheless there is something slightly outrageous about his claim and its utilitarian implications. The fact that Meno does not object may be connected to what we have already seen, namely, his skepticism about ends and the consequent preoccupation with means, or what is useful.

38. We need not deal here with the difference, although important, between wise judgment (*phronēsis*) and knowledge (epistēmē). See pp. 186–87; see also chapter 6, pp. 132–35.

39. Buchmann argues that Plato recognizes, in the *Meno*, that the connection between virtue and knowledge is not absolute. In a section devoted to "die Milderung des praktischen Intellektualismus durch die [*doxa*]," she writes that "man hat vielfach geglaubt, dass durch den Menon eine Bresche in den sokratischen Intellektualismus geschlagen sei . . . dass Platon etwa vom Menon ab auch eine Tugend anerkannte, die nicht durch reines Wissen verbürgt war" ("Die Stellung des Menon," p. 95). But see Werner Jaeger, *Aristotle* (New York: Oxford University Press, 1967), p. 84. According to Jaeger, Plato "based ethical action entirely on the knowledge of being."

40. See Thompson, *The Meno*, p. xxiii; Klein, *Commentary*, pp. 230–33. Cf. Plato, *Protagoras*, 325b4–328d2.

41. Cf. Plato, *Protagoras*.

42. Buchmann argues that the notion of right opinions was a discovery of major importance in the development of Plato's thought. See "Die Stellung des Menon," pp. 1–5, 94–97. But see also Paul Shorey, *What Plato Said* (Chicago: University of Chicago Press, Phoenix Books, abridged ed., 1965), p. 111: "It will be an economy to warn the reader here against the naive fancy that the *Meno* marks the precise point in Plato's development at which the notion of right opinion first occurred to him and brought about a revolution in his thought."

43. It is held by some commentators that all real knowledge, for Plato, is the sort of knowledge characteristic of mathematics. Thus, on Anfinn Stigen's view, Plato's understanding is based on "the reduction of all sciences to mathematics" (*The Structure of Aristotle's Thought* [Oslo: Universitetsforlaget, 1966], pp. 90–91). Cornford, who is probably the major Platonic scholar to maintain something like this, finds in the *Meno* a new conception of knowledge modeled on the knowledge of geometry and arithmetic: "Mathematical objects have all the characters which make them knowable in a way that sensible things can never

be known. They are perfect and exact, having neither more nor less content than is expressed in their definitions." As for knowledge of properties, "the properties are deduced by a rigid chain of reasoning, such that anyone who has understood the premises must see the certainty of the conclusions" (*Anamnesis*, pp. 112–13). A certain similarity to Hobbes's epistemology is evident here. But this makes us wonder why Socrates says knowledge starts from *opinions*, and is produced not by deduction but by repeated dialectical investigation.

Chapter 8

1. Cf. Jürgen Habermas, *Theory and Practice*, trans. J. Viertel (Boston: Beacon Press, 1973), pp. 42–44; and Wilhelm Hennis, *Politik und praktische Philosophie* (Berlin: Herman Luchterhand Verlag, 1963), chap. 1. In Hennis's words, "Die politische Wissenschaft hat den sie motivierenden Fragenzusammenhang aus den Augen verloren. Die wichtigsten Probleme sind ihr gestellt, aber es fehlt am Handwerkzeug, sie zu erfassen" (p. 23).

2. See the article by Roger Masters, "The Case of Aristotle's Missing Dialogues: Who Wrote the *Sophist*, the *Statesman*, and the *Politics*?" in *Political Theory* 5 (1977): 31–60.

3. Friedrich Solmsen, "Dialectic without the Forms," in *Aristotle on Dialectic*, ed. G. E. L. Owen (Oxford: Clarendon Press, 1968), p. 55.

4. Solmsen himself argues this matter in a note against Wieland, whom he quotes as writing that "für Aristoteles das Prinzipienwissen immer nur in der Weise der Doxa möglich ist" (*Die aristotelische Physik* [Göttingen, 1962], p. 221). Solmsen admits that "generally speaking, dialectical operations figure in the arguments by which Aristotle supports his 'principles,' " but he still holds that, as far as he can see, "cases of the kind are exceptional rather than typical. What may be true of the *Nicomachean Ethics* would not necessarily be true of *De Caelo* or the biological works" (Solmsen, "Dialectic," p. 54, n. 4). Cf. chapter 6, above.

5. John Herman Randall, Jr., *Aristotle* (New York: Columbia University Press, 1960), p. 45.

6. Solmsen, "Dialectic," p. 52.

7. For positions on language variously expressed by Socrates, not all of which could be read as Plato's views, see also *Cratylus*, 421e, 431b, 439b–c.

8. It is interesting to point out in this connection a passage from Norman Malcolm's memoir of Wittgenstein: "Wittgenstein once observed in a lecture that there is a similarity between his conception of philosophy (e.g. 'the problems are solved, not by giving new information, but by arranging what we have always known'. . .; 'the work of the philosopher consists in assembling reminders for a particular purpose'. . .) and the Socratic doctrine that knowledge is reminiscence: although he believed that there were also other things involved in the latter" (Norman Malcolm, *Ludwig Wittgenstein: A Memoir* [New York: Oxford University Press, 1972], p. 51).

9. Friedrich Nietzsche, *The Geneology of Morals*, "Second Essay," section 13, in *The Birth of Tragedy and The Geneology of Morals*, trans. Francis Golffing (Garden City, N.Y.: Doubleday & Co., 1956), p. 212. I am indebted to Mr. T. Paterson for directing me to this passage.

10. We must also note here the possible bearing of the fundamental transformation in our philosophical orientation accomplished by Kant, whose thought deeply influenced Wittgenstein (see Allan Janik and Stephen Toulmin, *Wittgenstein's Vienna* [New York: Simon & Schuster, 1973], pp. 223–31). The Kantian aspects of Wittgenstein's approach—the sense of his uncovering of the limits of human reason or speech, and the historical or anthropological flavor of his examination of forms of life—which of course contrast with Plato, have perhaps been underemphasized in this study because Kant was not a point of reference. On the other hand, overattention to these aspects has often obscured the serious naturalist or anticonventionalist bearing of Wittgenstein's thought. I am indebted to David Greenstone for raising this point.

11. *Letters from Ludwig Wittgenstein* (Oxford: Basil Blackwell, 1967), p. 7; also quoted in Anthony Kenny, *Wittgenstein* (London: Penguin Press, 1973), p. 3.

12. One may observe a progression, in this regard, from Hobbes and Locke through Rousseau, Hume, Kant, and Hegel to Nietzsche and the major twentieth century philosophers (Husserl, Wittgenstein, Heidegger, and Whitehead, to name only four), who wrote almost nothing directly about politics.

13. See chapter 6 above, esp. pp. 143–45, where this notion is discussed in the context of Aristotle's activity in the *Ethics*.

14. Alexis de Tocqueville, *Democracy in America*, ed. J. P. Mayer, trans. George Lawrence (Garden City, N.Y.: Doubleday & Co., 1969), p. 510.

15. Wayne L. Francis, *Formal Models of American Politics: An* duction (New York: Harper & Row, 1972), p. 115.

16. Along with Bacon and Descartes, one must add.

17. Francis, *Formal Models*, p. 9.

Bibliography

Primary Sources

Archimedes. *The Works of Archimedes*. Translated and edited by T. L. Health. Cambridge: Cambridge University Press, 1897.

Aristotle. *The Basic Works of Aristotle*. Various translators. Edited by Richard McKeon. New York: Random House, 1941.

———. *Nicomachean Ethics*. Translated by Martin Ostwald. Indianapolis: Bobbs-Merrill Co., Liberal Arts Press, 1962.

———. *The Nicomachaean Ethics*. Bilingual edition, with a translation by H. Rackham. Loeb Classical Library, Aristotle, vol. 19. London: William Heinemann, 1934.

Bacon, Francis. *Essays, Advancement of Learning, New Atlantis, and Other Pieces*. Edited by Richard Foster Jones. New York: Odyssey Press, 1937.

———. *Francis Bacon: A Selection of His Works*. Edited by Sidney Warhaft. Toronto: Macmillan of Canada, 1965.

Euclid. *The Thirteen Books of Euclid's Elements*. Translated by Sir Thomas L. Heath. 2d ed. 3 vols. New York: Dover Publications, 1956.

Galileo. *Discoveries and Opinions of Galileo*. Translated by Stillman Drake. Garden City, N.Y.: Doubleday & Co., Doubleday Anchor Books, 1957.

Hobbes, Thomas. *De Cive* or *The Citizen*. Edited by Sterling P. Lamprecht. New York: Appleton-Century-Crofts, 1949.

_____. *De Corpore*. Vol. 1. The English Works of Thomas Hobbes of Malmesbury, edited by Sir William Molesworth. 11 vols. London: John Bohn, 1839–1845.

_____. *De Homine*. Translated by Charles T. Wood, T. S. K. Scott-Craig, and Bernard Gert. Man and Citizen, edited by Bernard Gert. Garden City, N.Y.: Doubleday & Co., Doubleday Anchor Books, 1972.

_____. *The Elements of Law Natural and Politic*. Edited by Ferdinand Tönnies. London: Frank Cass & Co., 1969.

_____. *The English Works of Thomas Hobbes of Malmesbury*. Edited by Sir William Molesworth. 11 vols. London: John Bohn, 1839–1845.

_____. *Leviathan*. Edited by C. B. Macpherson. Harmondsworth, England: Penguin Books, 1968.

Locke, John. *An Essay concerning Human Understanding*. Edited by Alexander Campbell Fraser. 2 vols. New York: Dover Publications, 1959.

_____. *Essays on the Law of Nature*. Translated and edited by W. von Leyden. Oxford: Oxford University Press, 1958.

_____. *The Second Treatise of Government*. Edited by Thomas P. Peardon. Indianapolis: Bobbs-Merrill Co., Library of Liberal Arts, 1952.

Plato. *The Collected Dialogues of Plato Including the Letters*. Various translators. Edited by Edith Hamilton and Huntington Cairns. Princeton: Princeton University Press, Bollingen Series, 1961.

_____. *Meno*. Translated by W. K. C. Guthrie. Plato's Meno with Essays, edited by Malcolm Brown. Indianapolis: Bobbs-Merrill Co., 1971.

_____. *Platonis Opera*. Edited by John Burnet. 5 vols. Oxford: Oxford University Press, 1903.

_____. *The Republic of Plato*. Translated by Allan Bloom. New York: Basic Books, 1968.

Wittgenstein, Ludwig. *The Blue and Brown Books*. 2d ed. New York: Harper & Row, 1965.

_____. *Lectures and Conversations on Aesthetics, Psychology, and Religious Belief*. Edited by Cyril Barrett. Berkeley and Los Angeles: University of California Press, 1972.

_____. *Notebooks 1914–1916*. Bilingual edition, with a translation by G. E. M. Anscombe. Edited by G. H. von Wright and G. E. M. Anscombe. New York: Harper & Row, 1969.

_____. *On Certainty*. Bilingual edition, with a translation by Denis Paul and G. E. M. Anscombe. Edited by G. E. M. Anscombe and G. H. von Wright. New York: Harper & Row, 1972.

_____. *Philosophical Investigations*. Bilingual edition, with a translation by G. E. M. Anscombe. Oxford: Basil Blackwell, 1968.

_____. *Remarks on the Foundations of Mathematics*. Bilingual edition, with a translation by G. E. M. Anscombe. Edited by G. H. von Wright, R. Rhees, and G. E. M. Anscombe. Cambridge, Mass.: M.I.T. Press, 1967.

_____. *Tractatus Logico-Philosophicus*. Bilingual edition, with a translation by D. F. Pears and B. F. McGuiness. 2d ed. London: Routledge & Kegan Paul, 1971.

_____. *Zettel*. Bilingual edition, with a translation by G. E. M. Anscombe. Edited by G. E. M. Anscombe and G. H. von Wright. Berkeley and Los Angeles: University of California Press, 1970.

Secondary Sources

Alston, William P. *Philosophy of Language*. Englewood Cliffs, N.J.: Prentice-Hall, 1964.

Anderson, Fulton Henry. *The Influence of Contemporary Science on Locke's Method and Results*. Toronto: University Library Studies, 1923.

Andic, Martin. "Inquiry and virtue in the Meno." In *Plato's Meno with Essays*, edited by Malcolm Brown. Indianapolis: Bobbs-Merrill Co., 1971.

Anscombe, G. E. M. *An Introduction to Wittgenstein's Tractatus*. Philadelphia: University of Pennsylvania Press, 1971.

Arleth, Emil. *Die metaphysischen Grundlagen der aristotelischen*

Ethik. Prague: Carl Bellmann, 1903.

Armstrong, D. M., and Martin, C. B., eds. *Locke and Berkeley: A Collection of Critical Essays*. Notre Dame, Ind.: University of Notre Dame Press, 1968.

Aubenque, Pierre. *La prudence chez Aristotle*. Paris: Presses universitaires de France, 1963.

Austin, J. L. *How to Do Things with Words*. New York: Oxford University Press, 1965.

————. *Philosophical Papers*. Edited by J. O. Urmson and G. J. Warnock. 2d ed. Oxford: Oxford University Press, 1961.

Ayer, Alfred Jules. *Language, Truth and Logic*. New York: Dover Publications, n.d.

Bambrough, R. "Universals and Family Resemblances." In *Wittgenstein*, edited by G. Pitcher. Notre Dame, Ind.: University of Notre Dame Press, 1966.

Barnes, Winston H. F. "Did Berkeley Misunderstand Locke?" In *Locke and Berkeley*, edited by D. M. Armstrong and C. B. Martin. Notre Dame, Ind.: University of Notre Dame Press, 1968.

Bell, David R. "What Hobbes Does with Words." *Philosophical Quarterly* 19 (1969): 155–58.

Bennett, Jonathan. "Substance, Reality, and Primary Qualities." In *Locke and Berkeley*, edited by D. M. Armstrong and C. B. Martin. Notre Dame, Ind.: University of Notre Dame Press, 1968.

Bogen, James. *Wittgenstein's Philosophy of Language: Some Aspects of Its Development*. New York: Humanities Press, 1972.

Brown, J. M. "A Note on Professor Oakeshott's Introduction to the Leviathan." *Political Studies* 1 (1953): 53–64.

Brown, Malcolm, ed. *Plato's Meno with Essays*. Indianapolis: Bobbs-Merrill Co., 1971.

————. "Plato Disapproves of the Slave-Boy's Answer." In *Plato's Meno with Essays*, edited by Malcolm Brown. Indianapolis: Bobbs-Merrill Co., 1971.

Buchmann, Klara. "Die Stellung des Menon in der platonischen Philosophie." *Philologus* supp. vol. 29, no. 3 (1936): 1–102.

Burtt, Edwin Arthur. *The Metaphysical Foundations of Modern Physical Science*. Rev. ed. Garden City, N.Y.: Doubleday & Co., Doubleday Anchor Books, 1954.

Carnap, Rudolf. *An Introduction to the Philosophy of Science.* Edited by Martin Gardner. New York: Basic Books, 1966.

Carroll, John B. *Language and Thought.* Englewood Cliffs, N.J.: Prentice-Hall, 1964.

Cavell, Stanley. "The Availability of Wittgenstein's Later Philosophy." In *Must We Mean What We Say?* edited by Stanley Cavell. New York: Charles Scribner's Sons, 1969.

_____. "The Claim to Rationality: Knowledge and the Basis of Morality." Ph.D. diss., Harvard University, 1961–2.

_____. *Must We Mean What We Say?: A Book of Essays.* New York: Charles Scribner's Sons, 1969.

_____. "Must We Mean What We Say?" In *Must We Mean What We Say?* edited by Stanley Cavell. New York: Charles Scribner's Sons, 1969.

Chihara, Charles S., and Fodor, M. A. "Operationalism and Ordinary Language: A Critique of Wittgenstein." In *Wittgenstein*, edited by G. Pitcher. Notre Dame, Ind.: University of Notre Dame Press, 1966.

Chihara, Charles S. "Wittgenstein and Logical Compulsion." In *Wittgenstein*, edited by G. Pitcher. Notre Dame, Ind.: University of Notre Dame Press, 1966.

Chomsky, Noam. *Aspects of the Theory of Syntax.* Cambridge, Mass.: M.I.T. Press, 1965.

_____. *Cartesian Linguistics: A Chapter in the History of Rationalist Thought.* New York: Harper & Row, 1966.

_____. *Language and Mind.* New York: Harcourt, Brace & World, 1968.

Cornford, F. M., "Anamnesis." In *Plato's Meno with Essays*, edited by Malcolm Brown. Indianapolis: Bobbs-Merrill Co., 1971.

Cranston, Maurice, and Peters, Richard S., eds. *Hobbes and Rousseau: A Collection of Critical Essays.* Garden City, N.Y.: Doubleday & Co., Doubleday Anchor Books, 1972.

Dante, Arthur, and Morgenbesser, Sidney, eds. *Philosophy of Science.* New York: New American Library, Meridian Books, 1960.

Dean, Leonard F., and Wilson, Kenneth G., eds. *Essays on Language and Usage.* 2d ed. New York: Oxford University Press, 1963.

Deutsch, Karl. *Nerves of Government*. New York: The Free Press, 1966.

Dummett, Michael. "Wittgenstein's Philosophy of Mathematics." In *Wittgenstein*, edited by G. Pitcher. Notre Dame, Ind.: University of Notre Dame Press, 1966.

Easton, David. *A Framework for Political Analysis*. Englewood Cliffs, N.J.: Prentice-Hall, 1965.

————. *The Political System: An Inquiry into the State of Political Science*. New York: Alfred A. Knopf, 1953.

Edel, Abraham. *Science and the Structure of Ethics*. International Encyclopedia of Unified Science, vol. 2, no. 3. Chicago: University of Chicago Press, 1961.

Emmet, Dorothy, and MacIntyre, Alasdair, eds. *Sociological Theory and Philosophical Analysis*. New York: Macmillan Co., 1970.

The Encyclopedia of Philosophy, s.v. "Induction," by Max Black.

Engel, S. Morris. *Wittgenstein's Doctrine of the Tyranny of Language: An Historical and Critical Examination of His Blue Book*. The Hague: Martinus Nijhoff, 1971.

Fahrion, Karl. "Die Sprachphilosophie Lockes," *Archiv für Geschichte der Philosophie*, n.s., vol. 26 (1912): 56–65.

Fann, K. T., ed. *Ludwig Wittgenstein: The Man and His Philosophy*. New York: Dell, 1967.

————. *Wittgenstein's Conception of Philosophy*. Berkeley and Los Angeles: University of California Press, 1971.

Farrington, Benjamin. *The Philosophy of Francis Bacon*. Chicago: University of Chicago Press, Phoenix Books, 1966.

Feyerabend, Paul. *Against Method*. London: NLB Press, 1975.

Filkuka, Lambert. *Die metaphysischen Grundlagen der Ethik bei Aristoteles*. Vienna: Carl Konegen, 1895.

Fitts, Sister Mary Pauline. *John Locke's Theory of Meaning: An Exposition and Critique*. Washington: Catholic University of America Press, 1960.

Flew, Antony, ed. *Logic and Language*. Garden City, N.Y.: Doubleday & Co., Doubleday Anchor Books, 1965.

Frege, Gottlob. *The Basic Laws of Arithmetic: Exposition of the System*. Translated and edited by Montgomery Furth. Berkeley and Los Angeles: University of California Press, 1967.

Friedländer, Paul. *Plato*. Vol. 1, *An Introduction*. Translated by Hans Meyerhoff. 2d ed. Princeton: Princeton University Press, Bollingen Paperback, 1973.

Gadamer, Hans-Georg. *Platos dialektische Ethik*. Hamburg: Felix Meiner, 1968.

Gasking, Douglas. "Mathematics and the World." In *Logic and Language*, edited by A. Flew. Garden City, N.Y.: Doubelday & Co., Doubleday Anchor Books, 1965.

Gasking, D., and Jackson, A. "Wittgenstein as a Teacher." In *Ludwig Wittgenstein: The Man and His Philosophy*, edited by K. T. Fann. New York: Dell, 1967.

Gebauer, Gunter. *Wortgebrauch, Sprachbedeutung: Beiträge zu einer Theorie der Bedeutung im Anschluss an die spätere Philosophie Ludwig Wittgensteins*. Munich: Bayerische Schulbuch-Verlag, 1971.

Geymonat, Ludovico. *Galileo Galilei: A Biography and Inquiry into His Philosophy of Science*. Translated by Stillman Drake. New York: McGraw-Hill Book Co., 1965.

Goldsmith, M. M. *Hobbes's Science of Politics*. New York: Columbia University Press, 1966.

Grady, Robert C., Jr. "The Law of Nature in the Christian Commonwealth: Hobbes's Argument for Civil Authority." *Interpretation* 4 (Spring 1975): 217–38.

Green, Thomas Hill. *Hume and Locke*. New York: Thomas Y. Crowell Co., 1968.

Greenleaf, W. H. "Hobbes: The Problem of Interpretation." In *Hobbes and Rousseau*, edited by Maurice Cranston and Richard S. Peters. Garden City, N.Y.: Doubleday & Co., 1972.

Gregory, Raymond. *A Study of Locke's Theory of Knowledge*. Ph.D. diss. Wilmington, Ohio: n.p., 1919.

Grene, Marjorie. *A Portrait of Aristotle*. Chicago: University of Chicago Press, Phoenix Books, 1967.

Griffin, James. *Wittgenstein's Logical Atomism*. Seattle: University of Washington Press, 1969.

Grimm, Laura. *Definition in Plato's Meno: An Inquiry in the Light of Logic and Semantics into the Kind of Definition Intended by Socrates When He Asks, "What is Virtue?"* Historisk, Filosofisk, Klasse, n.s. no. 2, Norske Videnskaps-Academi.

Oslo: Oslo University Press, 1962.

Habermas, Jürgen. *Theory and Practice*. Translated by John Viertel. Boston: Beacon Press, 1973.

Hallett, Garth. *A Companion to Wittgenstein's Philosophical Investigations*. Ithaca, N.Y.: Cornell University Press, 1977.

Hartnack, Justus. *Wittgenstein and Modern Philosophy*. Translated by Maurice Cranston. Garden City, N.Y.: Doubleday & Co., Doubleday Anchor Books, 1965.

Heisenberg, Werner. *Physics and Beyond: Encounters and Conversations*. Translated by Arnold J. Pomerans. New York: Harper & Row, 1972.

Hennis, Wilhelm. *Politik und praktische Philosophie: Eine Studie zur Rekonstruktion der politischen Wissenschaft*. Neuwied am Rhein: Hermann Luchterhand Verlag, 1963.

Höffe, Otfried. *Praktische Philosophie: das Modell des Aristoteles*. Munich: Anton Pustet, 1971.

Husserl, Edmund. *The Crisis of European Sciences and Transcendental Phenomenology*. Translated by David Carr. Evanston: Northwestern University Press, 1970.

Ishiguro, Hidé. "Use and Reference of Names." In *Studies in the Philosophy of Wittgenstein*, edited by Peter Winch. New York: Humanities Press, 1969.

Jackson, Reginald. "Locke's Distinction Between Primary and Secondary Qualities." In *Locke and Berkeley*, edited by D. M. Armstrong and C. B. Martin. Notre Dame, Ind.: University of Notre Dame Press, 1968.

Jaeger, Werner. *Aristotle: Fundamentals of the History of His Development*. Translated by Richard Robinson. Oxford: Oxford University Press, 1962.

Janik, Allan, and Toulmin, Stephen. *Wittgenstein's Vienna*. New York: Simon & Schuster, Touchstone Book, 1973.

Joergensen, Joergen. *The Development of Logical Empiricism*. International Encyclopedia of Unified Science, vol. 2, no. 9. Chicago: University of Chicago Press, 1951.

Kaplan, Abraham. *The Conduct of Inquiry: Methodology for Behavioral Science*. Scranton, Pa.: Chandler Publishing Co., 1964.

Kaplan, Morton A. *On Historical and Political Knowing: An Inquiry into Some Problems of Universal Law and Human Freedom*. Chicago: University of Chicago Press, 1971.

_____. *Macropolitics: Selected Essays on the Philosophy and Science of Politics*. Chicago: Aldine Publishing Co., 1969.

Kenny, Anthony. *Wittgenstein*. London: Penguin Press, 1973.

Klein, Jacob. *A Commentary on Plato's Meno*. Chapel Hill: University of North Carolina Press, 1965.

Kojève, Alexander. *Introduction to the Reading of Hegel*. Translated by James H. Nichols, Jr. Edited by Allan Bloom. New York: Basic Books, 1969.

Kolakowski, Leszek. *Husserl and the Search for Certitude*. New Haven: Yale University Press, 1975.

Koselleck, Reinhart, and Schnur, Roman, eds. *Hobbes-Forschungen*. Berlin: Duncker & Humblot, 1969.

Koyré, Alexandre. *Newtonian Studies*. Chicago: University of Chicago Press, Phoenix Books, 1968.

Krook, Dorothea. "Mr. Brown's Note Annotated." *Political Studies* 1 (1953): 216–27.

_____. "Thomas Hobbes's Doctrine of Meaning and Truth." *Philosophy* 31 (1956): 3–22.

Kuhn, Thomas S. *The Structure of Scientific Revolutions*. 2d ed. International Encyclopedia of Unified Science, vol. 2, no. 2. Chicago: University of Chicago Press, 1970.

Lamprecht, Sterling P. "Hobbes and Hobbism." In *Essays in the History of Political Thought*, edited by Isaac Kramnick. Englewood Cliffs, N.J.: Prentice-Hall, 1969.

Language as a Human Problem. *Daedalus*, Summer 1973, pp. 1–244.

Larkin, Miriam Therese. *Language in the Philosophy of Aristotle*. The Hague: Mouton, 1971.

Louch, A. R. *Explanation and Human Action*. Oxford: Basil Blackwell, 1966.

Malcolm, Norman. *Ludwig Wittgenstein: A Memoir*. New York: Oxford University Press, 1958.

Mintz, Samuel I. *The Hunting of Leviathan*. Cambridge: Cambridge University Press, 1962.

Bibliography

Neurath, Otto. *Foundations of the Social Sciences.* International Encyclopedia of Unified Science, vol. 2, no. 1. Chicago: University of Chicago Press, 1944.

Oakeshott, Michael. Introduction to *Leviathan*, by Thomas Hobbes. Edited by Michael Oakeshott. Oxford: Basil Blackwell, 1946.

Owen, G. E. L., ed. *Aristotle on Dialectic: The "Topics".* Oxford: Clarendon Press, 1968.

Pears, David. *Ludwig Wittgenstein.* New York: Viking Press, 1969.

Peters, Richard S., and Tajfel, Henri. "Hobbes and Hull: Metaphysicians of Behaviour." In *Hobbes and Rousseau*, edited by Maurice Cranston and Richard S. Peters. Garden City, N.Y.: Doubleday & Co., 1972.

Pitcher, George, ed. *Wittgenstein: The "Philosophical Investigations".* Notre Dame, Ind.: University of Notre Dame Press, 1966.

Pitkin, Hanna Fenichel. *Wittgenstein and Justice.* Berkeley and Los Angeles: University of California Press, 1972.

Polin, Raymond. *Politique et philosophie chez Thomas Hobbes.* Paris: Presses universitaires de France, 1953.

Quine, Willard Van Orman. *Elementary Logic.* Rev. ed. New York: Harper & Row, 1965.

_____. "Truth by Convention." In *Philosophical Essays for Alfred North Whitehead.* New York: Longmans, Green & Co., 1936.

_____. *Word and Object.* Cambridge, Mass.: M.I.T. Press, 1960.

Quinton, A. M. "Excerpt from 'Contemporary British Philosophy.'" In *Wittgenstein*, edited by G. Pitcher. Notre Dame, Ind.: University of Notre Dame Press, 1966.

Randall, John Herman, Jr. *Aristotle.* New York: Columbia University Press, 1960.

Riedel, Manfred. "Zum Verhältnis von Ontologie und politischer Theorie bei Hobbes." In *Hobbes-Forschungen*, edited by Reinhart Koselleck and Roman Schnur. Berlin: Duncker & Humblot, 1969.

Riezler, Kurt. *Physics and Reality: Lectures of Aristotle on Modern Physics at an International Congress of Science, 679 Olympiad, Cambridge, 1940 A.D.* New Haven: Yale University Press, 1940.

Rousseau, Jean-Jacques. *Discourse on the Origins of Inequality.*

In *The First and Second Discourses*, edited and translated by Roger D. Masters. New York: St. Martin's Press, 1964.

Rudner, Richard S. *Philosophy of Social Science*. Englewood Cliffs, N.J.: Prentice-Hall, 1966.

Ryle, Gilbert. "Dialectic in the Academy." In *Aristotle on Dialectic*, edited by G. E. L. Owen. Oxford: Oxford University Press, 1968.

————. "John Locke on the Human Understanding." In *Locke and Berkeley*, edited by D. M. Armstrong and C. B. Martin. Notre Dame, Ind.: University of Notre Dame Press, 1968.

————. "Teaching and Training." In *Plato's Meno with Essays*, edited by Malcolm Brown. Indianapolis: Bobbs-Merrill Co., 1971.

Santillana, Giorgio de, and Zilsel, Edgar. *The Development of Rationalism and Empiricism*. International Encyclopedia of Unified Science, vol. 2, no. 8. Chicago: University of Chicago Press, 1941.

Schmitt, Richard George. "Plato's Theory of Knowledge in the Meno: a Commentary." Master's thesis, University of Chicago, 1952.

Seliger, Martin. *The Liberal Politics of John Locke*. London: Allen & Unwin, 1968.

Shorey, Paul. *What Plato Said*. Abridged ed. Chicago: University of Chicago Press, Phoenix Books, 1965.

Shwayder, D. S. "Wittgenstein on Mathematics." In *Studies in the Philosophy of Wittgenstein*, edited by Peter Winch. New York: Humanities Press, 1969.

Simon, Herbert. *The Sciences of the Artificial*. Cambridge, Mass.: M.I.T. Press, 1969.

Solmsen, Friedrich. "Dialectic without the Forms." In *Aristotle on Dialectic*, edited by G. E. L. Owen. Oxford: Oxford University Press, 1968.

Stahl, H. -P. "Beginnings of Propositional Logic in Plato." In *Plato's Meno with Essays*, edited by Malcolm Brown. Indianapolis: Bobbs-Merrill Co., 1971.

Stephen, Sir Leslie. *Hobbes*. Ann Arbor: University of Michigan Press, Ann Arbor Paperbacks, 1961.

Strauss, Leo. *Natural Right and History*. Chicago: University of Chicago Press, Phoenix Books, 1965.

_____. *The Political Philosophy of Hobbes*. Translated by Elsa M. Sinclair. Chicago: University of Chicago Press, Phoenix Books, 1963.

_____. "On the Basis of Hobbes's Political Philosophy." In *What is Political Philosophy?* Glencoe, Ill.: The Free Press, 1959.

Strawson, P. F. "Review of Wittgenstein's Philosophical Investigations." In *Wittgenstein*, edited by G. Pitcher. Notre Dame, Ind.: University of Notre Dame Press, 1966.

Taylor, A. E. "The Ethical Doctrine of Hobbes." *Philosophy* 13 (1938): 406–24.

Thompson, Wayne N. *Aristotle's Deduction and Induction: Introductory Analysis and Synthesis*. Amsterdam: Rodopi, 1975.

Thornton, M. T. "Locke's Criticism of Wittgenstein." *Philosophical Quarterly* 19 (1969): 266–71.

Tönnies, Ferdinand. *Thomas Hobbes: Der Mann und der Denker*. Leipzig: Zickfeldt, 1912.

Van Peursen, C. A. *Ludwig Wittgenstein: An Introduction to His Philosophy*. New York: Dutton, 1970.

Voegelin, Eric. *The New Science of Politics: An Introduction*. Chicago: University of Chicago Press, 1952.

von Leyden, W. "John Locke and Natural Law." *Philosophy* 31 (1956): 23–55.

_____. *Seventeenth Century Metaphysics: An Examination of Some Main Concepts and Theories*. London: George Duckworth, 1968.

_____. "What is a Nominal Essence the Essence of?" In *John Locke: Problems and Perspectives*, edited by John W. Yolton. Cambridge: Cambridge University Press, 1969.

von Mises, Richard. *Positivism: A Study in Human Understanding*. New York: Dover Publications, 1968.

Vygotsky, L. S. *Thought and Language*. Translated and edited by Eugenia Hanfmann and Gertrude Vakar. Cambridge, Mass.: M.I.T. Press, 1962.

Watkins, J. W. N. *Hobbes's System of Ideas: A Study in the Political Significance of Philosophical Theories*. New York: Barnes & Noble, 1965.

Weinberger, J. "Hobbes's Doctrine of Method." *American Political Science Review* 69 (1975): 1336–53.

Wertheimer, Alan. "Is Ordinary Language Analysis Conservative?" *Political Theory* 4 (1976): 405–22.

Whorf, Benjamin Lee. *Language, Thought, and Reality: Selected Writings of Benjamin Lee Whorf*. Edited by John B. Carroll. Cambridge, Mass.: M.I.T. Press, 1956.

Wilson, Bryan R., ed. *Rationality: Key Concepts in the Social Sciences*. Oxford: Basil Blackwell, 1970.

Wilson, John. *Language & The Pursuit of Truth*. Cambridge: Cambridge University Press, 1969.

Winch, Peter. *The Idea of a Social Science and Its Relation to Philosophy*. London: Routledge & Kegan Paul, 1958.

_____, ed. *Studies in the Philosophy of Wittgenstein*. New York: Humanities Press, 1969.

_____. "Understanding a Primitive Society." In *Rationality: Key Concepts of the Social Sciences*, edited by Bryan R. Wilson. Oxford: Basil Blackwell, 1970.

Wolin, Sheldon S. *Politics and Vision: Continuity and Innovation in Western Political Thought*. Boston: Little, Brown & Co., 1960.

Woodbridge, Frederick J. E. *Aristotle's Vision of Nature*. Edited by John Herman Randall, Jr. New York: Columbia University Press, 1965.

Wuchterl, Kurt. *Struktur und Sprachspiel bei Wittgenstein*. Frankfurt am Main: Suhrkamp Verlag, 1969.

Yolton, John W. "Locke's Concept of Experience." In *Locke and Berkeley*, edited by D. M. Armstrong and C. B. Martin. Notre Dame, Ind.: University of Notre Dame Press, 1968.

_____, ed. *John Locke: Problems and Perspectives*. Cambridge: Cambridge University Press, 1969.

Ziff, Paul. *Semantic Analysis*. Ithaca, N.Y.: Cornell University Press, Cornell Paperbacks, 1967.

Index

Abstraction, 119, 163; in geometry, 38–39, 166; Locke's account of, 54–57

Activities: and grammar, 111–12; language in, 77; and language learning, 108

Activity: language as, 82, 84; as irreducible, 119–20

Adeimantus, 215

Analysis: and language games, 92–93; in political science, 32; and simple ideas, 53. *See also* Resolutive-compositive method

Animals, and language, 86

Anytus, 180, 184, 186, 187

Applied science, 123. *See also* Practical wisdom; Prudence

Archimedean point, 178, 237

Archimedes, 213

Aretē, 188–89. *See also* Excellence; Virtue

Aristides, 66, 184, 187

Aristotle, 11–12, 14, 19, 122–54, 203, caution of, 183; and definitions, 58, 149–50; failure of, 27; and grammar, 151–52; and Hobbes, 124, 146; and language, 71–72; and Plato, 191–94; political science of, 124–54; and Wittgenstein, 154, 191–94

Art, 130, 132; neutrality of, 133–34; and

prudence, 133
Articulation, and knowledge, 126
Astronomy, 16–17
Athens, 156
Audience, for Aristotle's *Ethics*,
126–27, 143–44, 193, 230
Augustine, Saint, 74, 76, 89, 90; mistake of, 94
Axioms, in Euclidean geometry, 31

Bacon, Sir Francis, 9, 206, 218, 241
Bees, 158, 159–61
Behaviorism, and Wittgenstein,
224–25
Bible, 68
Blue and Brown Books, 83, 86, 111
Boredom, 228
Boundaries: of concepts, 99–103; and
definition by example, 104
Boyle, Robert, 220
Builder's language, 76–80, 82

Calculative faculty, 128, 129
Carnap, Rudolph, 5
Carpenter, precision of, 126
Cave, in *Republic*, 187, 198, 202
Cephalus, 232
Certainty, 148, 193; absence of, in
prudence, 21; in geometry, 31; and
philosophy, 200–202; in political
science, 40; and theoretical science,
123
Chaos, natural world as, 39
Charmides, 236, 237
Children, and language learning,
77–78, 107–10
Chomsky, Noam, 224–25
Circularity, 147; in inquiry, 173,
176–77, 182, 204; of recollection
myth, 237
Civil philosophy, 16–17, 34. *See also*
Political science
Citizen: excellence of, 162; perspective of, 144–45
Classical political science, failure of,
10, 12–13

Classical thought, 39; and language,
196; and Wittgenstein, 194–98
Cleverness, 142
Color, 150, 188; definition of, 103;
and geometry, 39; grammar of,
112; and language, 22–23; in the
Meno, 164–67
Common elements, 160; and definitions, 102
Common sense, and science, 4
Common speech, 42, 48–49, 167,
192–93; as classical starting point,
71, 178–80, 182; confusion in, 64–
65; and dialectic, 147, 150; and
Locke, 66; in *Meno*, 158; and
political science, 126; and prudence, 133
Communications code, language as,
44–46, 50, 54, 80, 82, 86
Competition: in politics, 35, 36; in
games, 98
Complex ideas, 52–53, 57–60
Component parts, in political concepts, 32. *See also* Parts
"Composites." *See* "Simples"
Conceptions: defined, 33; Hobbes's
account of, 25; words as symbols
for, 47, 49–51
Concepts: boundaries of, 100–101;
naturalness of, 115–16
Conditioning, 11, 22
Confessions of Saint Augustine, 74–
75, 109
Construction: of complex ideas,
57–58; geometric knowledge as, 31;
and knowledge, 146–47; of mixed
modes, 61–63; of political terms,
41
Contemplation, 128
Contradiction, in common speech,
195
Controversy: in classical philosophy,
27–30; language as cause of, 59; in
philosophy, 18–19
Convenience, and invention of
names, 67

Convention: and definitions, 28–29;
and goals, 120; and nature, 70,
115–18
Conventionality: and grammar, 115–
18; of mixed modes, 60–65; of
names, 48–49
Copernicus, Nicolaus, 17
Courage, 138, 179; grammar of, 151;
Hobbes's resolution of, 36; and
moderation, 144
Cratylus, 196, 222, 239
Crisis of European Sciences, 3–7
Cultural relativism. *See* Relativism
Curiosity, 201

De Cive, 16, 18, 20; and resolutive-
compositive method, 34
Deductive method, 10–11. *See also*
Syllogism
Definitions, 29–30, 33, 38, 106–7,
159, 165; in Aristotle, 58, 149; and
common elements, 102–3; and
complex ideas, 57–60; and dialectic, 192; and ends, 160–61; in
Euclidean geometry, 31; by
example, 100–101, 104; and forms,
196; as goal of *Meno*, 159, 160–61;
Hobbes's understanding of, 28–29,
30–34; Locke's account of, 58, 65;
and meanings, 71; and inarticulate
knowledge, 104–5; and Socrates,
164–68
De Homine, 29, 49, 87
Deliberation: and prudence, 133; and
science, 128–29
Demonstration, 232, 233; and dialectic, 147–49; of first principles,
38; in moral science, 65–66; in
political science, 125; and science,
146–47; and syllogism, 130–31
Descartes, 9, 206, 241
Description: and names, 226; as task
of philosophy, 83
Dialectic, 146–49, 150–53, 165, 191–
92; and first principles, 147; as
friendly, 165, 168; limits of, 148;

and Wittgenstein, 197–98
Disputes, language as cause of, 47,
49–50
Distinctions, importance of, 169,
204–5
Duhem, Pierre Maurice, 4–5

Eidos. See Form
Einstein, Albert, 209
Elements of Law, 18–20; account of
knowledge in, 21–27
Empedocles, 166, 167
Empirical science, 37; geometry as,
31–32; social science as, 1–2
Empiricism, 7, 8
Epistemology, 4; preeminence of,
199, 200. *See also* Knowledge
*Essay concerning Human Under-
standing*, 13, 44, 190
Essence, as goal of inquiry, 158,
159–61
Ethics: and political science, 125; in
Tractatus, 105
Ethics. See Nicomachean Ethics
Euclid, 29, 30–31, 36, 212, 213; and
irrationals, 175
Eudoxus, 213
Euthydemus, 236
Evidence: and knowledge, 24–26, 50;
for Hobbes's model, 37
Exactness, of concepts, 100–101, 102
Examples, and definition, 100–101
Excellence, 155, 156, 157–64; gram-
mar of, 188–89; and knowledge,
168–69, 181–85. *See also* Virtue
Experience: and ideas, 51–52; and
prudence, 21; and science, 37, 137
Explanation, 14, 204–5; as goal of
social science, 1

Family resemblances, 97–98
Figure (*schēma*), 164–67, 188
First principles: definitions as, 33; and
dialectic, 147; in *Ethics*, 136–38; in
geometry, 31; lacking in science,
135; of political science, 124–28

Form, 180, 188, 235; and definition, 196; doctrine of, 159
Forms of life, 117–21; and human goals, 120
Fraser, Alexander Campbell, 53
Frege, Gottlob, 101, 226

Galileo, 9, 17, 213, 218–19
Games, 77, 97–99, 103–4; and grammar, 110–11
Generality, 204–5; craving for, 83, 94
General names, and abstraction, 54–56
Genus-differentia definitions, 149
Geometry, 8, 19, 153, 181; Euclidean, and propositions, 30–31; and Hobbes's political science, 10–11, 212; in *Meno*, 163–64, 165, 166; as only classical science, 28; and physics, 41; and political reality, 187–88; precision of, 126–27; and prudence, 134; and recollection, 174–75; as theoretical science, 38–39; and utility, 123
Glaucon, 215
Goals, 119–20; competing conceptions of, 199–200; conventional and natural, 120; Hobbes's treatment of, 35–36; and meaning of justice, 94; and political science, 2–3, 190
Gorgias, 155–56, 163, 166, 185
Grammar, 81, 88, 110–14, 227; and conventionality, 115–18; of courage, 151; and definitions, 149–50; *Ethics* as inquiry into, 127–28; and forms of life, 117–18; of knowledge, 111; mistakes in learning, 112; openness of, 114; in Platonic inquiry, 161–62, 195; and recollection, 176–77, 178–80, 189
Green, T. H., 221

Habituation, and fundamental principles, 127
Happiness, and rational faculties, 140

Harvey, Dr. William, 17, 213
Hegel, 191, 240
Heidegger, Martin, 240
Hempel, Carl, 208
Historicism, and political science, 41–42
History, and Hobbes's science, 37–38
Hitler, Adolf, 3
Hobbes, Thomas, 9, 12, 14, 60, 115, 121, 130, 132, 190, 192, 197, 199, 200, 202–3, 206; and Aristotle, 126–27, 145, 146, 149; and classical philosophy, 16–18, 27, 72; and cleverness, 142; and definitions, 28–29; and dialectic, 147; as founder of political science, 10–11, 65; and inarticulate knowledge, 105; and language, 22–23, 26–27; and Locke, 67–68, 192–93; and man's place, 205; and Meno, 157–58; and reckoning, 128, 129; and reduction, 154; and skepticism, 171; view of science of, 123; and Wittgenstein, 87, 200–201
Homer, 187
Human nature: and historicism, 41–42; and language, 67, 68
Hume, David, 240
Husserl, Edmund, 3, 4, 12, 131, 149, 206, 240; life work of, 6–7; and truth, 5
Hypothesis: argument by, 181–85, 188; in empirical science, 11, 213
Hypothetical knowledge, science as, 131, 146–47

Ideas: Locke's account of, 50–54; of mixed modes, 58–60; real and nominal essence of, 60–61; simple and complex, 52–53; of substances, 58–60
Ignorance, Socratic, 156, 172
Intelligence, 130, 136, 142
Intersubjective agreement, 208–9
Invention, and language, 40

Jargon, and definitions, 167
Justice, 162, 163, 171; analysis of, 93–94; Hobbes's definition of, 36; and political science, 29, 121; in *Republic*, 195; subjectivity of, 70

Kant, Immanuel, 240
Knowledge, 20–21, 70, 138–39, 194; ambiguity in, 125–26; articulation of, 103–7, 126; boundaries of, 61; of causes, 30–31; classical understanding of, 71; conditional, 229; of goals, 2–3; Hobbes's account of, 21–27; and language, 40, 178–80; Meno's conception of, 170; objectivity, 4; and opinion, 158, 175–78, 185–89; and prudence, 184–85; and Socrates, 111; and virtue, 168–69, 170, 181–85
Kolakowski, Leszek, 7, 8

Labels: and language learning, 109; words as, 46–47, 49–50, 87
Language, 80–82, 94–95; and abstraction, 55–57; and animals, 86; and Aristotle, 71–72, 150, 153–54; and classical thought, 196; common sense view of, 43–44; flexibility of, 104, 109–10; and Hobbes, 12, 44–49; invention of, 44, 217; and knowledge, 40, 178–80; and natural science, 69; and Plato, 71–72; and reason, 22–23; reform of, 38; in science, 11; and thought, 55–57; and truth, 25–26; in Wittgenstein's *Tractatus*, 73–74
Language games, 78, 82–87, 89; and convention, 115; essence of, 94–95; and goals, 120–21; and language learning, 107–9; and "simples," 91
Language learning, 107–10; and abstraction, 55–56; Augustine's account of, 74–75; complexity of, 89; and confusion, 63–64; as training, 77

Larisa, 186
Law, grammar of, 113, 114
Laws, in science, 4–5, 10
Learning: of excellence, 183–84; as recollection, 173–75
Leibniz, 9
Leviathan, 12, 20–21, 207; and historicism, 41–42
Liberal democracy, and social science, 2
Liberalism, 2
"Life-world," 3; described, 6–7; and science, 131
Linguistic cave, 198, 202
Linking definition, 164–65, 188; and recollection, 174–75
Locke, John, 13, 26, 44, 115, 119, 190, 192; and Hobbes, 67; and language, 49–65, 110; mistake of, 94; and natural law, 63; and Wittgenstein, 84, 91
Logos, 128, 130, 135; and dialectic, 147
Lucien, 17

Mach, Ernst, 5, 208
Machiavelli, 199
Marks (signs), 26, 44–45. *See also* Symbols
Marx, Karl, 191
Mathematics: and definitions, 166; and knowledge, 238–39; and moral science, 65; and natural science, 40. *See also* Geometry
Meaning, 25, 50, 102, 106–7; agreement on, 48–49; in Aristotle, 150–51; and definitions, 71; and grammar, 111–14; and ideas, 51; as mental process, 81; as object "stood for," 75; origin of, 47–49; as use, 79, 82, 103; and valuing activity, 85–86; Wittgenstein's account of, 96–121
Meno, 155–89, 234; character of, 156, 168–72, 235

Meno, 14, 93, 112, 155–89, 194, 195, 197; theme of, 155

Mental processes: in Hobbes, 25; and ideas, 51–53; and meaning, 76, 81; as misleading, 86

Method: and Aristotle, 124–28, 145–50; and Hobbes, 10–11, 35, 122–23; in philosophy, 30–34; and Plato, 155; two types of, 165, 168

Mistakes, in language learning, 108–9

Mixed modes, 58–60; conventionality of, 60–65; defect of, 64–65; and Wittgenstein, 91

Models, 3, 205–6

Moderation, 134, 162; and courage, 144

Moral science, 18, 70; failure of, 69; and Locke, 65–69; and political science, 34

Moral words, as mixed modes, 63–64

Moses, 106, 226

Multiplicity, in Meno, 157–58

Myth: of recollection, 172–75; scientific theories as, 5

Names: and abstraction, 54–57; in Cratylus, 196; defined, 46; and description, 226; and ideas, 53–54; in science, 22–23

Naming, 87–90

"Natural conventions," 117

Natural language, 110, 226

Natural law, 66–67, 68; and Locke's understanding, 63–64

Natural science: and common sense, 43–44; and Hobbes, 22; and language, 43–44; and social world, 69; and Tractatus, 85

Natural world, inaccessible, 61, 205

Nature: and convention, 70, 115–18; and forms of life, 116–19; man's place in, 205–6; as standard for ideas, 61

Necessity: and language, 40; and scientific knowledge, 130–31

Newton, Sir Isaac, 9

Nicomachean Ethics, 13, 14, 124; audience for, 193; purpose of, 127, 128, 135, 138, 143–44

Nietzsche, Friedrich, 197, 232, 240

Nihilism, and modern science, 5

"Nominal essence," of ideas, 60

Nominalism, 214, 218

Normative questions, 2, 3, 203

Nouns, 75

Number, concept of, 98–99

Objectivity, 4. See also Knowledge

Observation: in geometry, 31–32; of political world, 35; and science, 11

Operationalization, of definitions, 40

Operational truths, and skepticism, 171

Opinion: ancient philosophy as, 18; and dialectic, 191–92; and knowledge, 4, 158, 175–78, 185–89; and political science, 126–27

Ordinary language, 105. See also Common speech

Ostensive definitions, 87–90

Ostensive teaching, 77

Parts: of excellence, 171; knowledge of, 30; and wholes, 160–61, 173–74, 182

Passivity, of mind, in receiving ideas, 52–53

Peace, as Hobbes's aim, 35

Pericles, 132, 187

Philosophical Investigations, 74, 96–97

Philosophy, 111, 137; of ancients, 17–18; and certainty, 201–2; and common speech, 179; as descriptive, 83; and excellence, 189; Hobbes's definition of, 20; limits of, for Locke, 61; and public spirit, 199–201; reasons for, 200–201; and scientific method, 83; task of, 196; and transcendental phenomenology, 6–7; utility of, 18; Wittgenstein's conception of, 201–2. See

also Political philosophy
Philosophy of Science, 3, 14
Phronēsis. See Prudence
Physics, 214; and geometry, 41; in Hobbes's thought, 33, 34
Picture-theory, of language, 73–74, 84–85, 97
Pitkin, Hanna, 108–9, 110, 117
Plato, 14, 155–89; and Aristotle, 151, 191–94; and doctrine of Forms, 159; and inquiry, 172–73; and language, 71–72; and public spiritedness, 200; skepticism of, 197; and Wittgenstein, 189, 194–98
Polemarchus, 93, 195, 225, 232
Political philosophy: and justice, 121; place of, 193, 198–202; as subversive, 17–18
Political science, 1–3, 35, 122; and action, 153; as *a priori*, 29; of Aristotle, 124–44, 145–50; and certainty, 40; enrichment of, 203–5; *Ethics* as, 139–40; and Euclidean geometry, 32; and goals, 2, 190; Hobbes as founder of, 9–11; and natural science, 40, 131, 215; and normative questions, 2; place of, 138–45; possibility for Locke, 65–69; and prudence, 139, 140; and theoretical wisdom, 136–45; and virtue, 141–42, 143
Politics: and bees, 160–61; and self-preservation, 120
Posterior Analytics, 130–31, 147
Postulates, in Euclidean geometry, 31
Power, as neutral means, 35–36, 37
Practical science, political science as, 38–39, 122–23
Practical wisdom, 130, 132–36. *See also* Prudence
Precision, in political science, 125
Pride, as obstacle to science, 68
Primitive language, 76, 77
Prior Analytics, 146
Private languages, 227–28

Prodicus, 165
Proper names, 46
Proper nouns, Locke's account of, 53–54
Propositions: general form of, 95; Hobbes's view of, 20; and truth, 24; in Wittgenstein's *Tractatus*, 73–74
Protagoras, 237
Prudence, 132–36, 137–38, 139–40, 182, 183–84, 186–87; and happiness, 141; Hobbes's account of, 21–23; and political science, 10–11, 132; two senses of, 231
Psychology: in Hobbes, 32–33, 34; in Locke, 67, 68; and political science, 215
Public spiritedness, 199–202
Pythagoras, 17, 236

Qualities, 220, 221

Randall, John H., Jr., 191–92
Rational faculties, 128–36
Rationalism, and modern science, 14
Real essence, 60, 221
Reasoning, and deliberation, 128–29
Reckoning, as rational faculty, 28, 128, 129
Recollection, 236, 237; in *Meno*, 172–75, 186
Reduction: and definitions, 160–61; in Socratic inquiry, 166
Reductionism, 78–79, 80–83, 94; and forms of life, 118–21; in political science, 203–4
Reference, and definitions, 106
Relativism, 228–29; in Hobbes, 35–36, 66–67; linguistic, 49; in Locke, 62–63, 66–67
Religion, 68–69; and language, 38
Republic, 93, 187, 195, 215, 225, 232; cave metaphor in, 198
Resolution, and scientific method, 10–11
Resolutive-compositive method, 32–

33, 34, 37–38, 67, 91–92, 127, 129, 214
Rhetoric, 233
Rousseau, Jean-Jacques, 3, 69, 216, 240
Rules: and language games, 99; and natural language, 110
Ruling, and excellence, 163, 183–84
Russell, Bertrand, 106, 226

Saint Alban's, man from, 22–23, 25, 103
Schēma, 164–67, 188
Scholastic philosophy, 48
Science, 1, 3–8, 124, 130; and common sense, 4; as creative myth, 5; as *epistēmē*, 130–31; and goals, 2, 190; Hobbes's account of, 23, 26, 210; as human construction, 29; and language, 22–23, 153–54; limitation of, 131; of morality, 65; and starting points, 27–30; and theoretical wisdom, 136–37; and transcendental phenomenology, 6–7; utility of, 20
Scientific knowledge, and political science, 203
Scientific method: Hobbes's account of, 32–33; of Meno, 162, 164–68; in political science, 122–23; preoccupation with, 83; in seventeenth century, 8
Scientific theories, 209, 214
Second Treatise of Government, 66
Self-preservation, 36, 37, 68; as goal of politics, 120
Sensation: distinct from knowledge, 23; and ideas, 51–52; and simple ideas, 53
Sentences, kinds of, 84
Signification, 44–46, 79; and language, 26, 43–65
Signs, words as, 26, 44–45. *See also* Symbols
Similarities (family resemblances), 97–98

Simonides, 225
Simple ideas, 52–53, 121; and agreement, 119
"Simples," 31, 83, 90–93, 204; in definition, 166; and geometry, 20; in Hobbes's political science, 36; in science, 11
Skepticism: of Meno, 170–72; of Plato, 197; and political philosophy, 193; and sloth, 178
Slave boy, and recollection, 172–75
Social science, goal of, 1, 2
Socrates, 93, 111, 112, 142–43, 155–89, 195, 196, 225; and Aristotle, 183; and citizen's perspective, 145; and ignorance, 156, 172; irony of, 159; and physics, 235; and public spirit, 200; and Wittgenstein, 90, 176, 194–95, 240
Socratic ignorance, 156, 172
Solmsen, Friedrich, 191–92, 233
Sophists, and excellence, 185
Soul, and recollection thesis, 173–75
Speech: Hobbes's definition of, 46; and thinking, 224. *See also* Language
Spinoza, 9
"Standing for," 26, 34, 75–76, 85; Locke's account of, 56–57; in *Tractatus*, 74
Starting point: opinion as, 179, 182; in science, 27–30; and undefined terms, 164–65, 172–75
State of nature, 36, 66, 67; Rousseau's version of, 69
Subjectivism, 70, 232–33
Subjectivity, and science, 4
Substances, 58–60, 221; natural standard for, 61; as unknowable, 60
Subversiveness, of classical philosophy, 17–18, 199
Syllogism, and demonstration, 130–31
Symbols, words as, 46, 74. *See also* Signs
Symbol system, language as, 219

Teaching: of excellence, 156; and language learning, 77; and science, 130

Technē, and excellence, 182. *See also* Art

Teiresias, 187

Teleology, of language, 85

Theaetetus, 90, 194, 222, 236

Themistocles, 184, 187

Theoretical knowledge, *Ethics* as, 127

Theoretical wisdom, 130, 136–37; and happiness, 141

Theories: as creative myths, 5; in social science, 1

Theory and practice, 38–42, 122–23, 214

Thinking: and language, 56; and talking, 224

Thrasymachus, 215

Thucydides, 184

Tocqueville, Alexis de, 240

Tool, words as, 44, 79–80

Topics, 147–50

Tractatus Logico-Philosophicus, 73–74, 97; and ethics, 105; and natural science, 85; and "objects," 90; picture-theory of, 84–85

Transcendental phenomenology, 6–7, 8

Translation, 63, 117, 228–29

Truth: and forms of life, 119; as goal of science, 4–5; and knowledge, 24–25; and politics, 199

Uncertainty: in philosophy, 18, 201–2; of prudence, 21

Understanding: and equivocal names, 47; as goal of science, 151; and language learning, 108; and truth, 25; Wittgenstein's view of, 77

Universal goals, 120

Universal names, 46–48

Universals: in psychology, 32–33; as simple elements, 31

Use: and meaning, 79, 103; and ostensive definition, 89

Utility: of geometry, 19; of philosophy, 199; of political science, 123, 193; of science, 20, 39; and virtue, 140, 144

Virtue, 127, 135, 143, 188–89; and cleverness, 142; conceptions of, 199–200; foundations of, 145; and knowledge, 138–39, 168–69, 181–85; and political science, 138–45; as subject of *Meno*, 155. *See also* Excellence

Value judgments, in science, 2, 3, 12, 203

Values: knowledge of, 170; and nihilism, 5; and political science, 2–3. *See also* Goals

Value terms, 42, 70

Vulgar discourse, 35; as classical starting point, 27–30; and dialectic, 147. *See also* Common speech

Whitehead, Alfred North, 240

Wholes and parts, knowledge of, 30–31, 160–61, 173–74, 182

Wisdom. *See* Theoretical wisdom

Wittgenstein, Ludwig, 11, 12, 72, 73–121, 149, 191, 206; and Aristotle, 127, 151–52, 154, 233; and behaviorism, 224–25; and classics, 194–98; as conservative, 226–27; and Hobbes, 103, 200–201; and *Meno*, 157; and mental processes, 25; and political philosophy, 198–202; and recollection thesis, 173, 177, 189; and skepticism, 178; and Socrates, 176, 240

Words: and ideas, 54; intentional misuse of, 64; as signs, 26–27, 45–46; in *Tractatus*, 74

Ziff, Paul, 107